# THE AMERICAN DREAM?

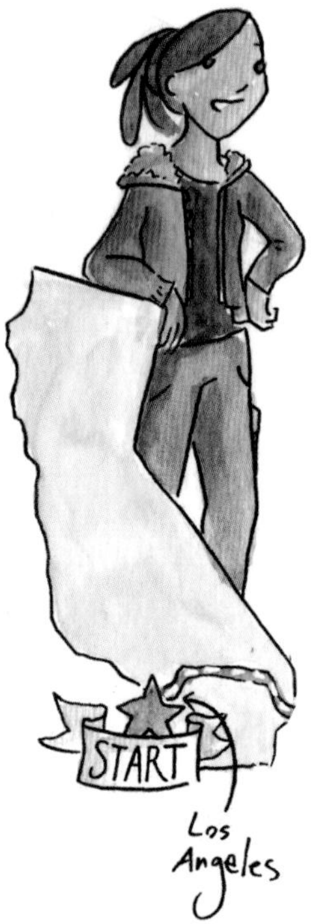
START
Los Angeles

**Shing Yin Khor** is an Ignatz-winning cartoonist and installation artist who is exploring personal narrative, new human rituals, and collaborative worldbuilding through graphic memoir, science fiction, and large-scale art structures. As a cartoonist, their work has been published in *The Toast*, *The Nib*, *Catapult*, *Huffington Post*, and *Bitch* magazine. They make the road-trip adventure comic Tiny Adventure Journal and the tender queer science fiction comic Center for Otherworld Science. Shing lives in Los Angeles.



Zest Books™
An imprint of Lerner Publishing Group, Inc.
241 First Avenue North
Minneapolis, MN 55401 USA

For reading levels and more information, look up this title at www.lernerbooks.com. Visit us at zestbooks.net.

Main body text set in Dirty Mermaid.

**Library of Congress Cataloging-in-Publication Data**

Names: Khor, Shing Yin, author.
Title: The American dream? : a journey on Route 66 discovering dinosaur statues, muffler men, and the perfect breakfast burrito / by Shing Yin Khor.
Description: Minneapolis : Zest Books, [2019] | Audience: Ages: 11–18. | Audience: Grades: 9–12. |
Identifiers: LCCN 2018060700 (print) | LCCN 2019003990 (ebook) | ISBN 9781541578531 (eb pdf) | ISBN 9781541578524 (lb : alk. paper) | ISBN 9781942186373 (pb : alk. paper)
Subjects: LCSH: Khor, Shing Yin—Travel—Comic books, strips, etc.—Juvenile literature. | United States Highway 66—Description and travel—Comic books, strips, etc.—Juvenile literature. | Asian American women—Travel—Comic books, strips, etc.—Juvenile literature. | Immigrants—United States—Biography—Comic books, strips, etc.—Juvenile literature. | Asian American women artists—Biography—Comic books, strips, etc.—Juvenile literature.
Classification: LCC F595.3 (ebook) | LCC F595.3 .K46 2019 (print) | DDC 917.804/34—dc23

LC record available at https://lccn.loc.gov/2018060700

Manufactured in the United States of America
1-46974-47843-1/9/2019

# THE AMERICAN DREAM?

## A JOURNEY ON ROUTE 66

### Discovering DINOSAUR STATUES, MUFFLER MEN, and the PERFECT BREAKFAST BURRITO

A Graphic Memoir by **SHING YIN KHOR**

 **ZEST BOOKS**
MINNEAPOLIS

For Jason

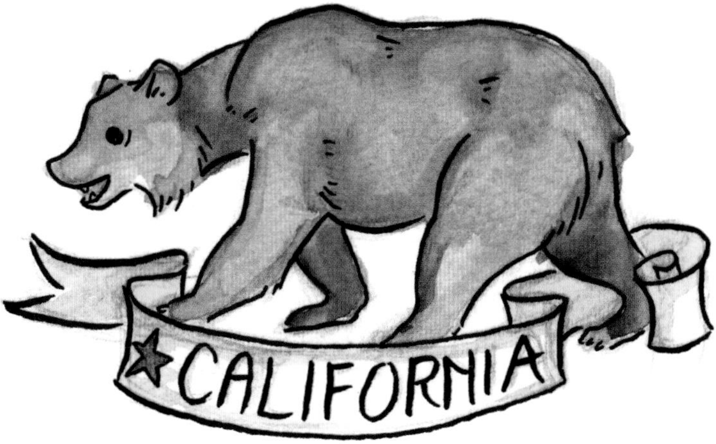
CALIFORNIA

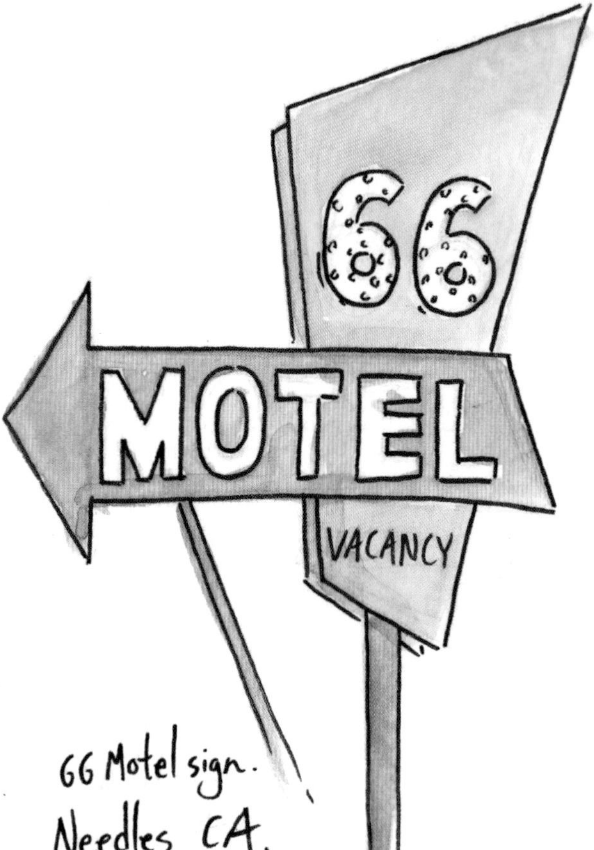
66
MOTEL
VACANCY

66 Motel sign.
Needles, CA.

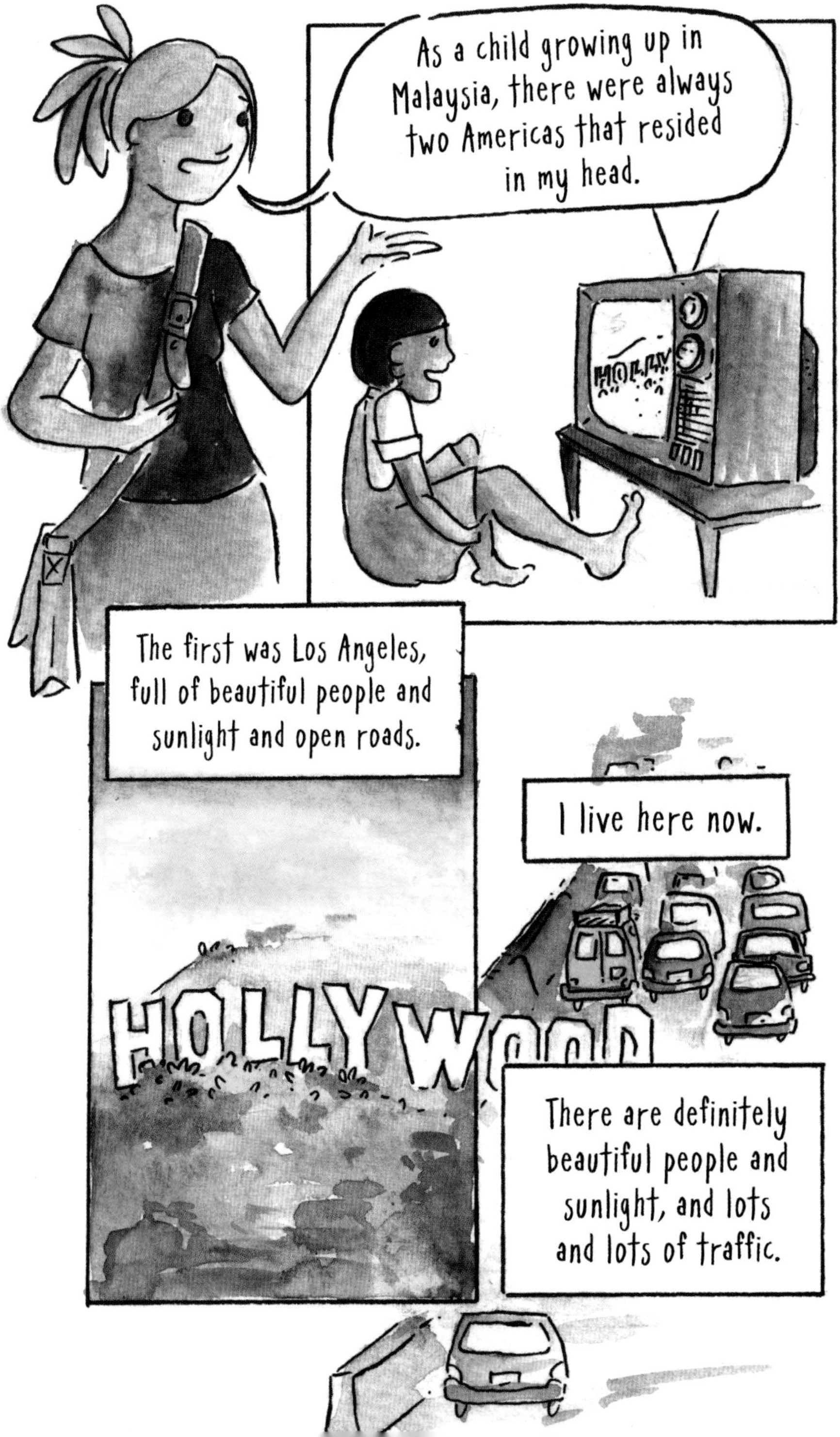
As a child growing up in Malaysia, there were always two Americas that resided in my head.
HOLLY
The first was Los Angeles, full of beautiful people and sunlight and open roads.
HOLLYWOOD
I live here now.
There are definitely beautiful people and sunlight, and lots and lots of traffic.

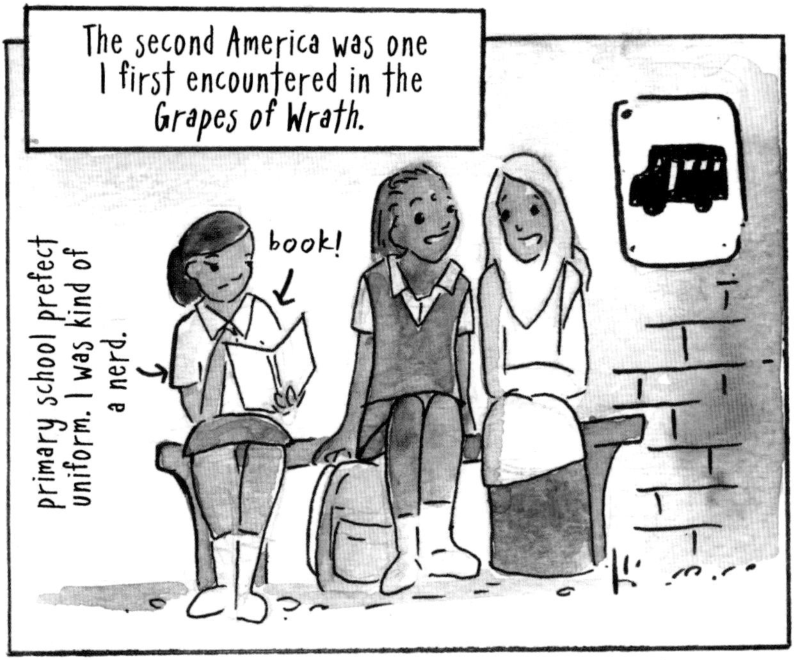
The second America was one I first encountered in the *Grapes of Wrath*.
book!
primary school prefect uniform. I was kind of a nerd.

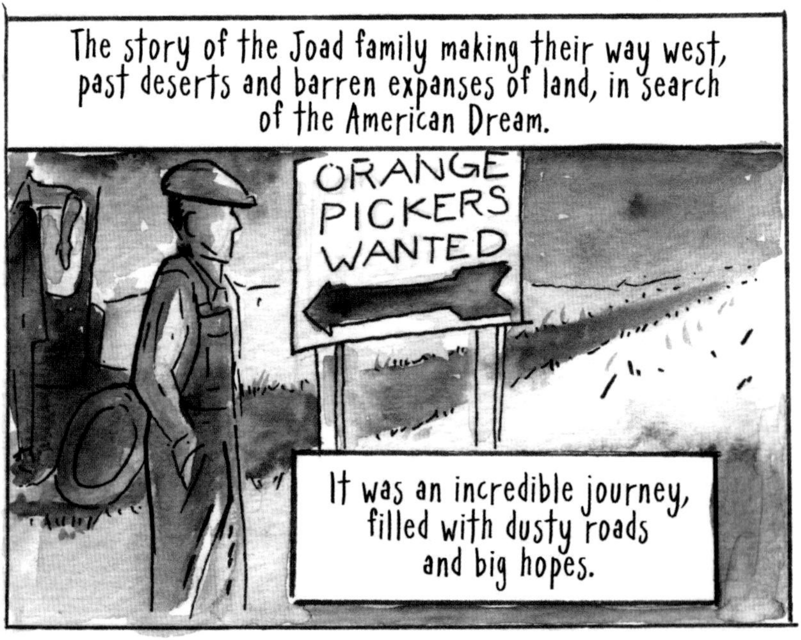
The story of the Joad family making their way west, past deserts and barren expanses of land, in search of the American Dream.
ORANGE PICKERS WANTED
It was an incredible journey, filled with dusty roads and big hopes.

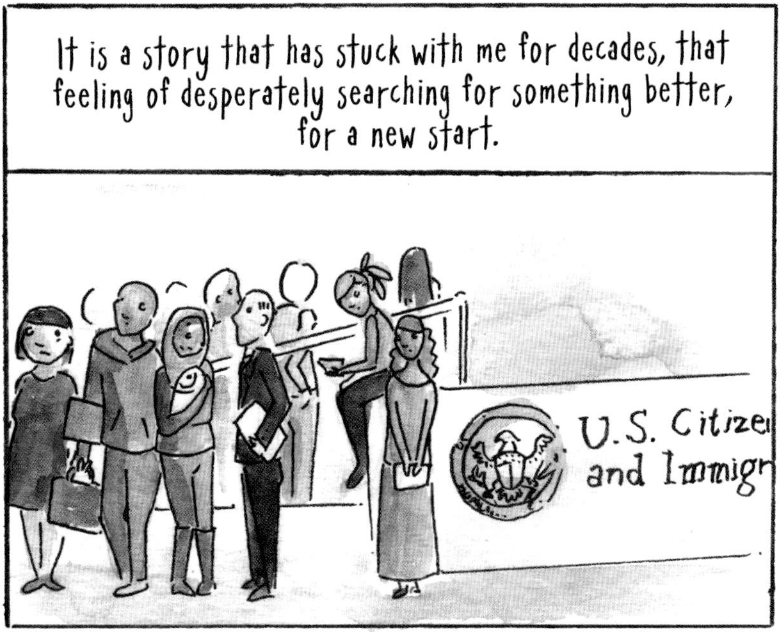
It is a story that has stuck with me for decades, that feeling of desperately searching for something better, for a new start.
U.S. Citize
and Immigr

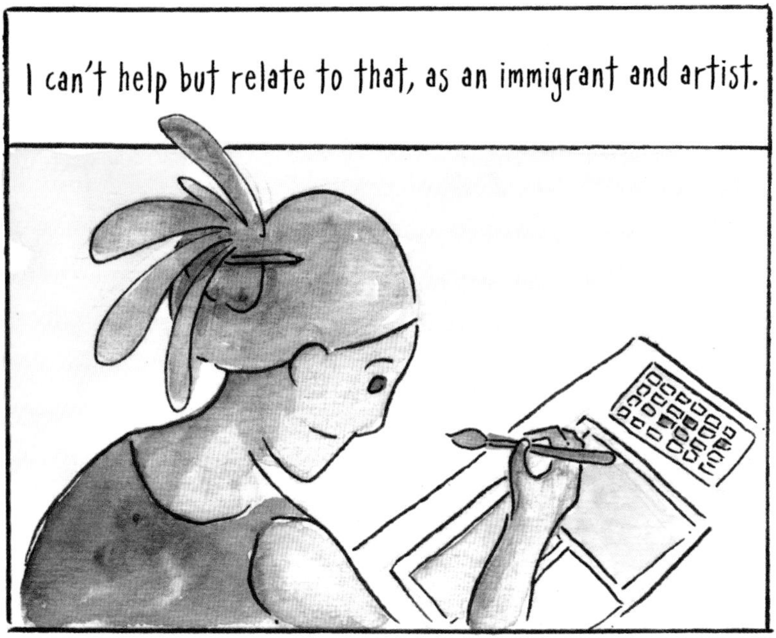
I can't help but relate to that, as an immigrant and artist.

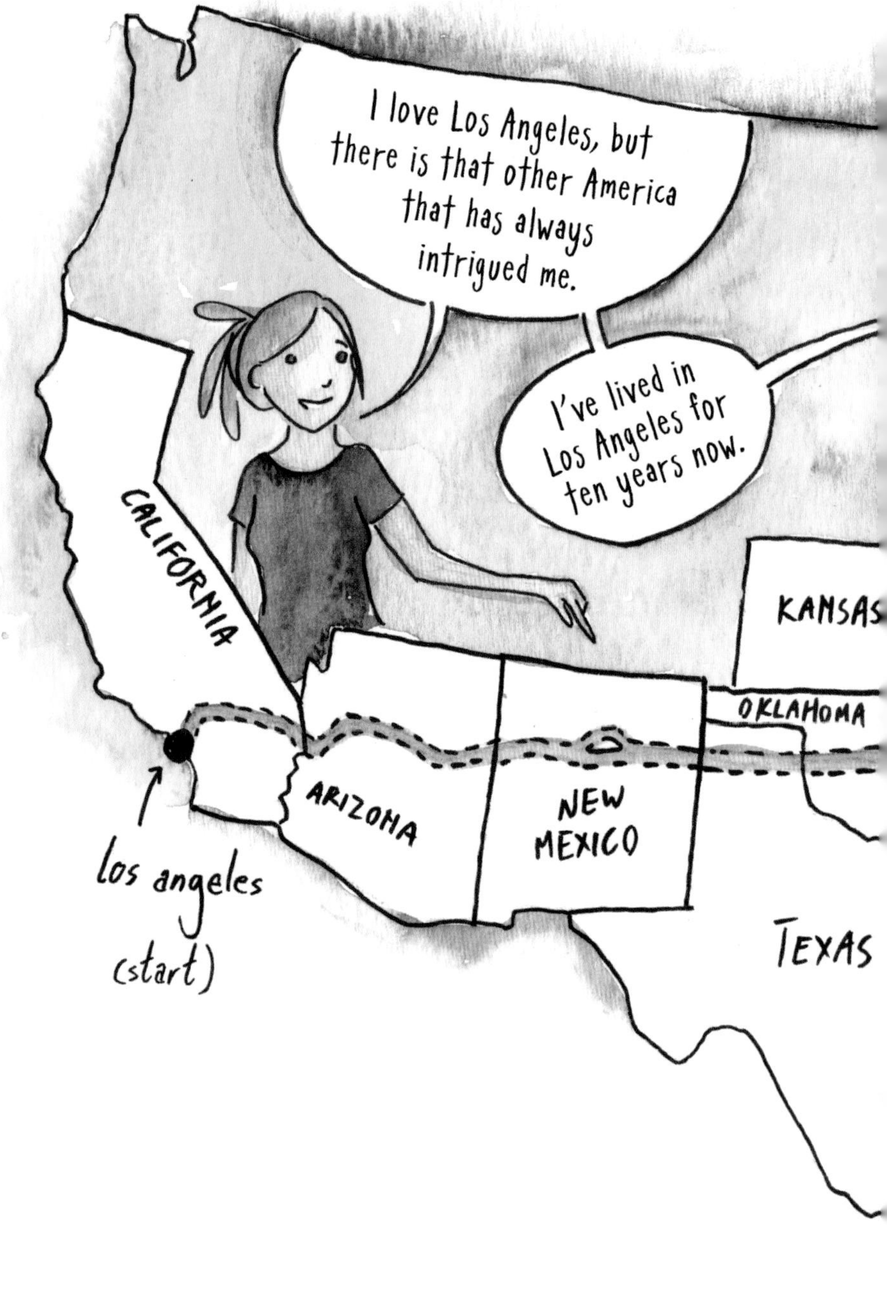
I love Los Angeles, but there is that other America that has always intrigued me.
I've lived in Los Angeles for ten years now.
CALIFORNIA
KANSAS
OKLAHOMA
ARIZONA
NEW MEXICO
TEXAS
los angeles (start)

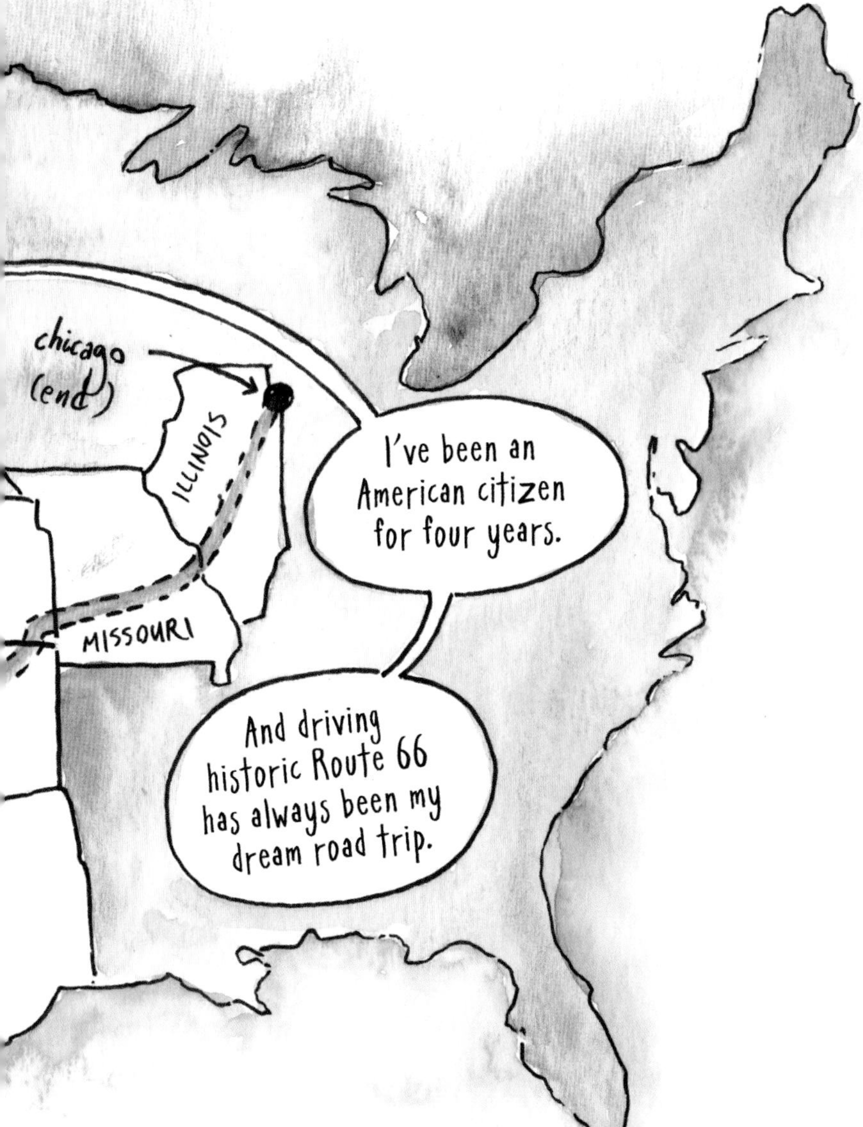
chicago
(end)
ILLINOIS
MISSOURI
I've been an American citizen for four years.
And driving historic Route 66 has always been my dream road trip.

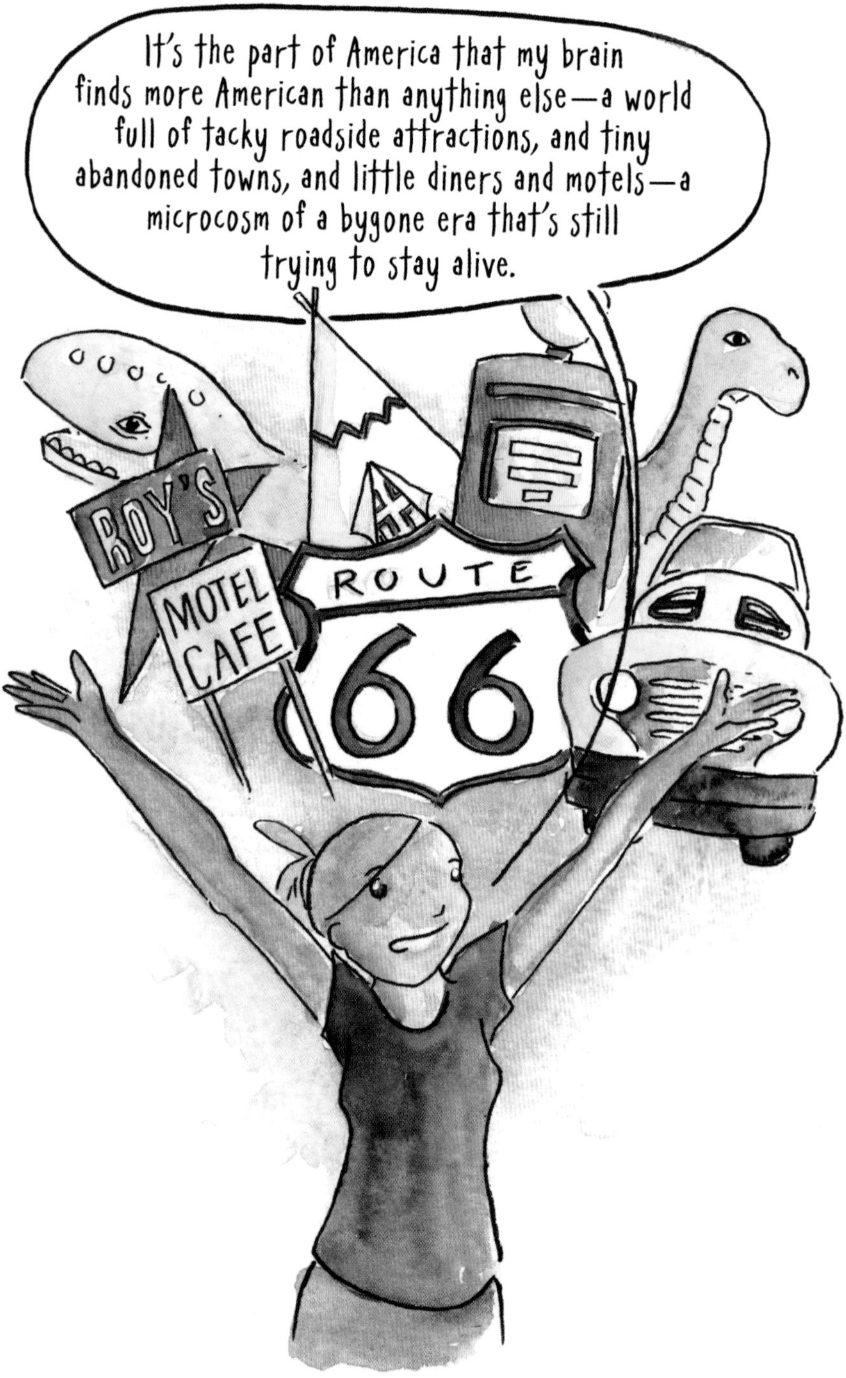
It's the part of America that my brain finds more American than anything else—a world full of tacky roadside attractions, and tiny abandoned towns, and little diners and motels—a microcosm of a bygone era that's still trying to stay alive.
ROY'S
MOTEL
CAFE
ROUTE
66

For me, this is a pilgrimage.

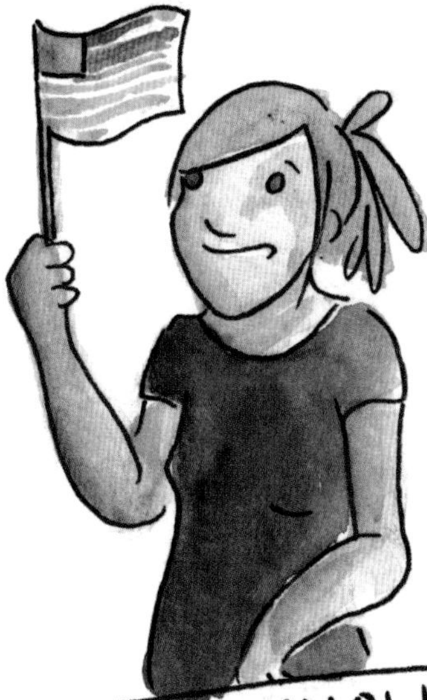

The concept of the American Dream is something that I've long struggled with.

I understand the modern immigrant interpretation, the one where we work hard, get the right visas, and eventually get to stand in a large room as newly minted American citizens watching terrible patriotic videos.

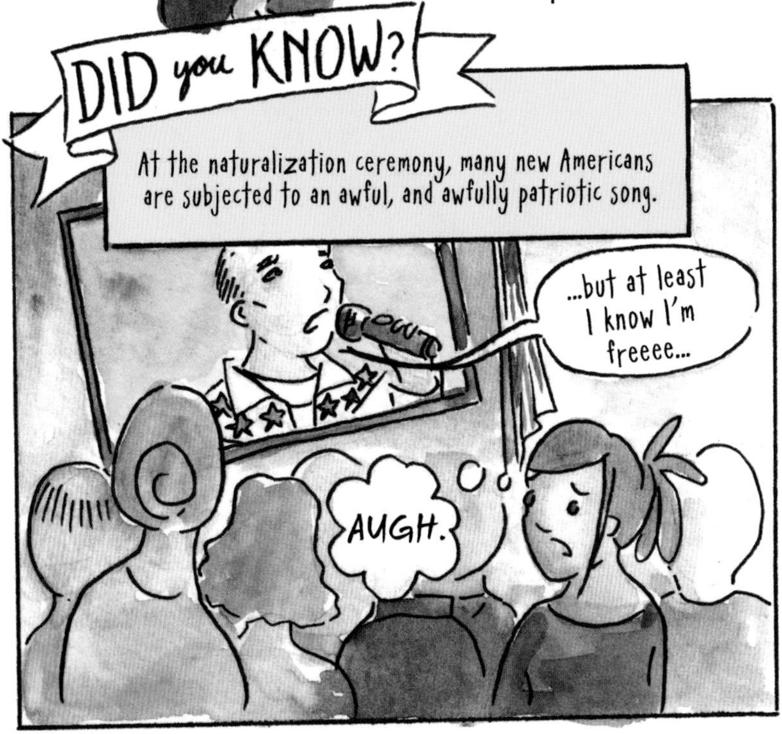
DID you KNOW?
At the naturalization ceremony, many new Americans are subjected to an awful, and awfully patriotic song.
...but at least I know I'm freeee...
AUGH.

But this westward trail is still more foreign to me. I've lived in my Los Angeles bubble for over a decade, but I'm not sure I'll feel really American until I see more of America.

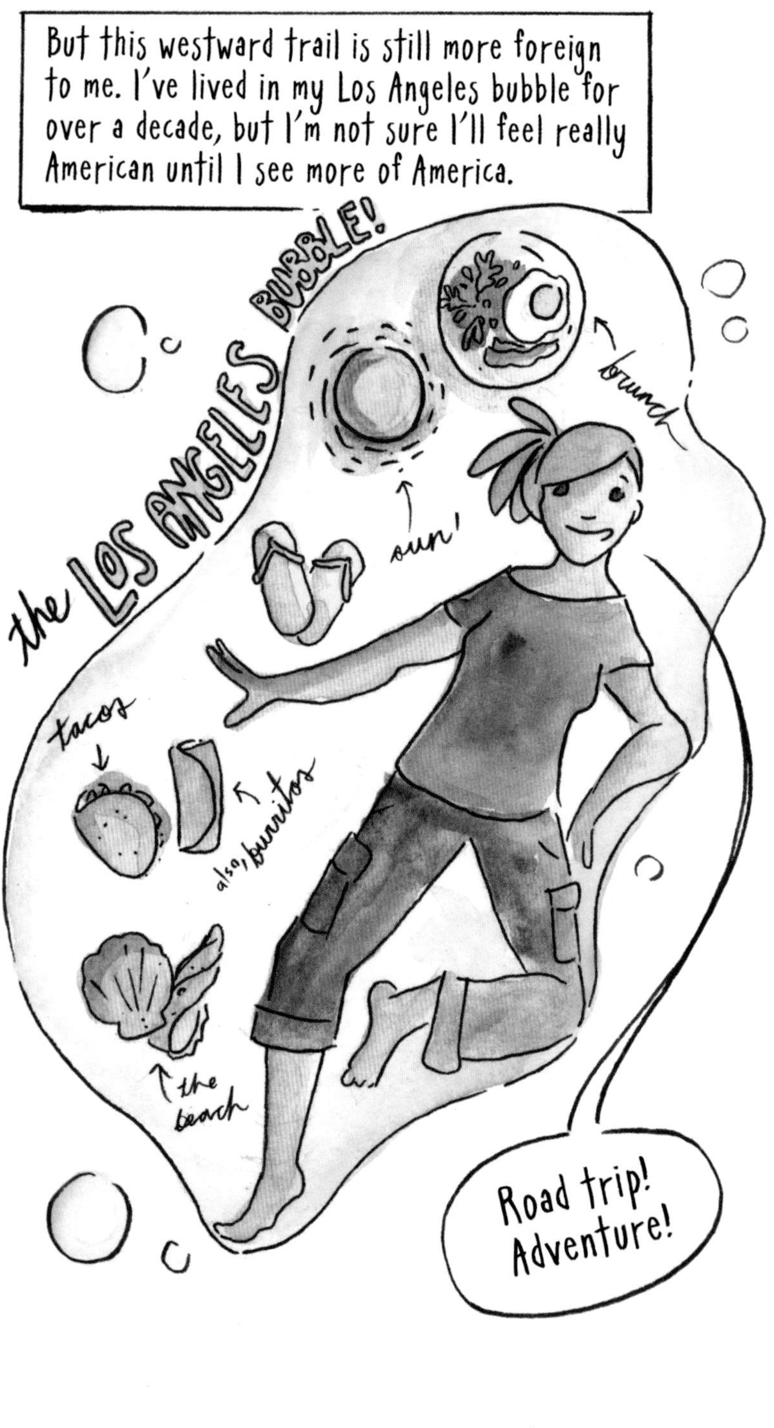
the LOS ANGELES BUBBLE!
brunch
sun!
tacos
also, burritos
the beach
Road trip! Adventure!

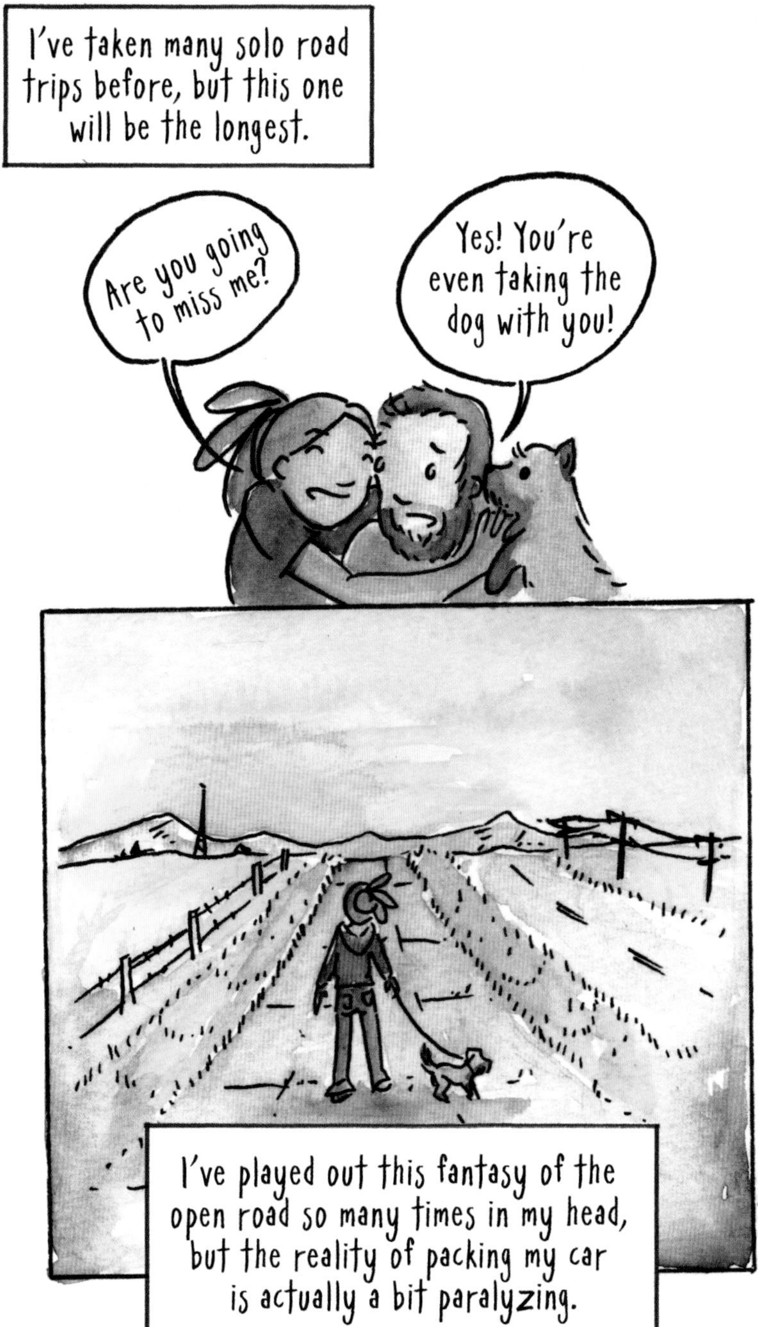
I've taken many solo road trips before, but this one will be the longest.
Are you going to miss me?
Yes! You're even taking the dog with you!
I've played out this fantasy of the open road so many times in my head, but the reality of packing my car is actually a bit paralyzing.

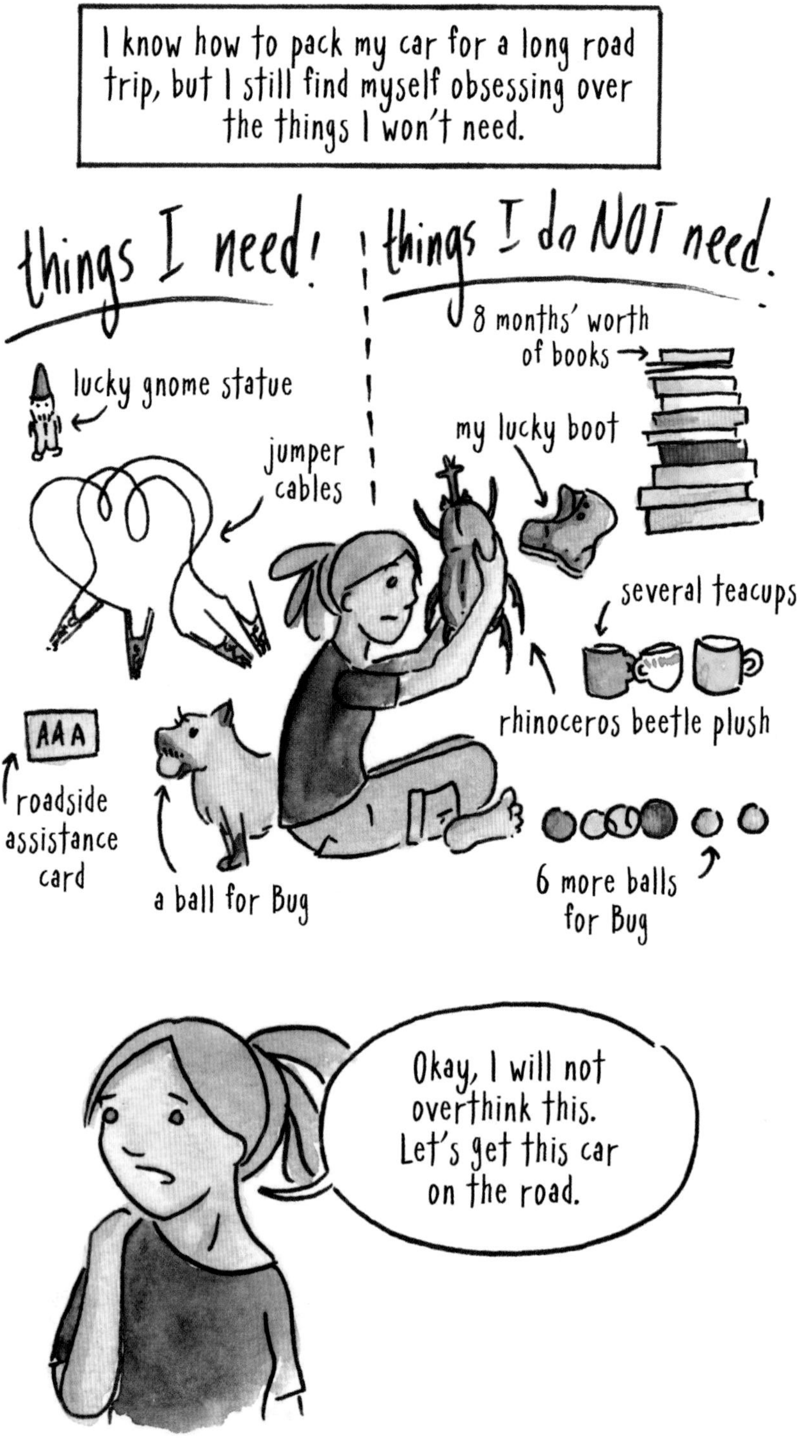
I know how to pack my car for a long road trip, but I still find myself obsessing over the things I won't need.
things I need!
things I do NOT need.
8 months' worth of books
lucky gnome statue
my lucky boot
jumper cables
several teacups
rhinoceros beetle plush
AAA
roadside assistance card
a ball for Bug
6 more balls for Bug
Okay, I will not overthink this. Let's get this car on the road.

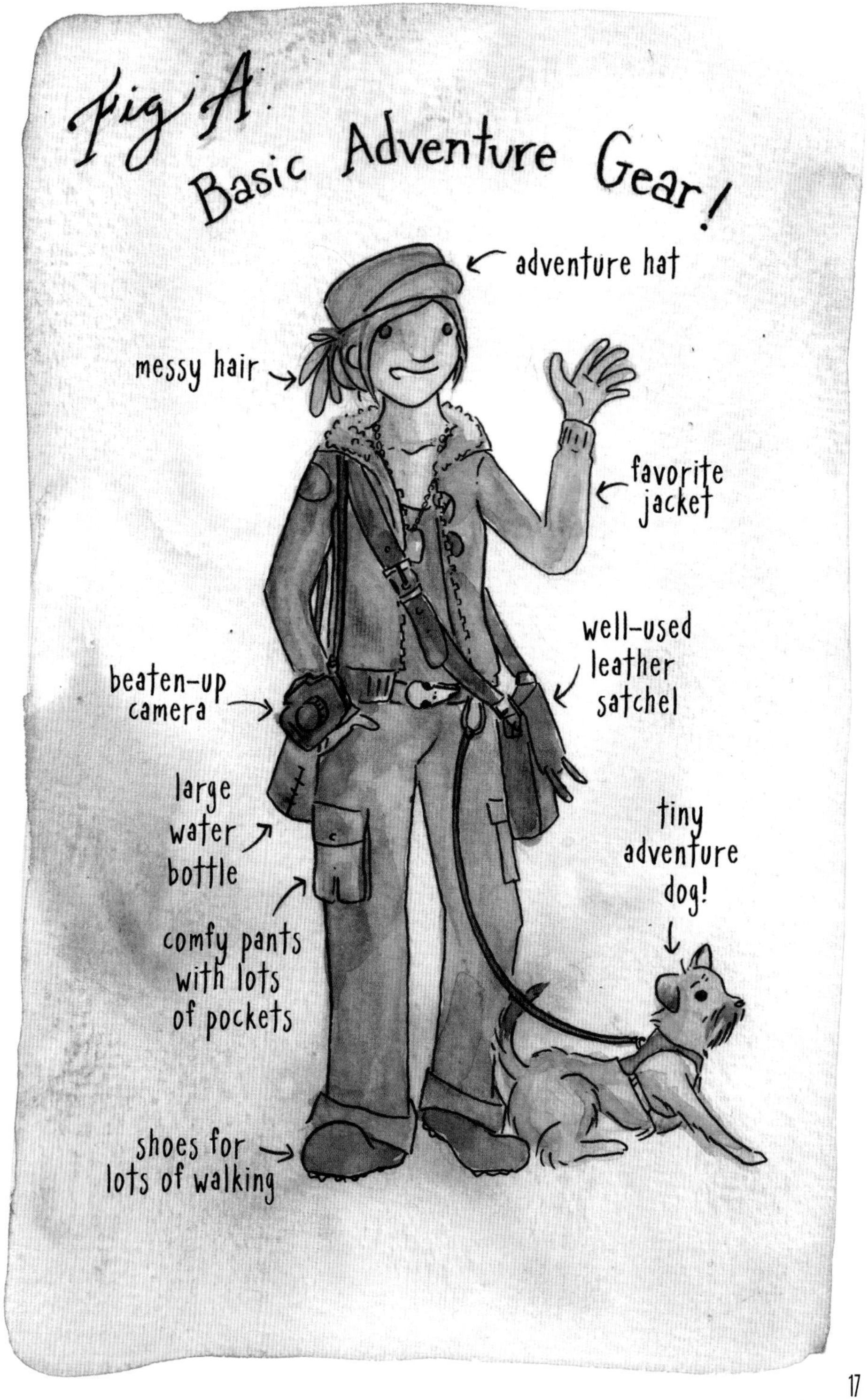
Fig A.
Basic Adventure Gear!
adventure hat
messy hair
favorite jacket
well-used leather satchel
beaten-up camera
large water bottle
tiny adventure dog!
comfy pants with lots of pockets
shoes for lots of walking

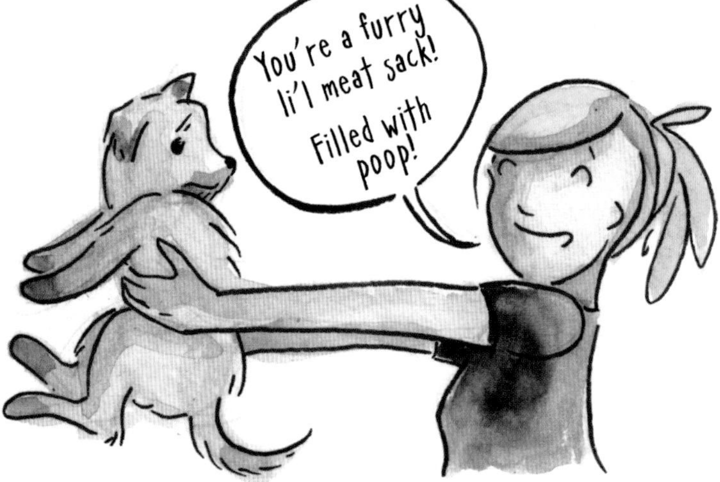
You're a furry li'l meat sack!
Filled with poop!

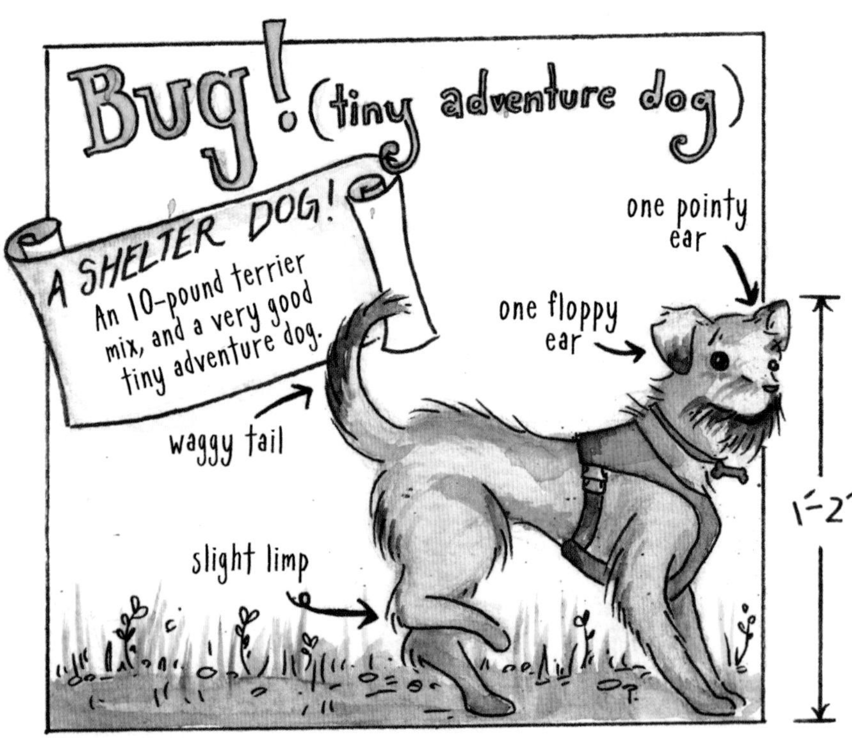
Bug! (tiny adventure dog)
A SHELTER DOG!
An 10-pound terrier mix, and a very good tiny adventure dog.
one pointy ear
one floppy ear
waggy tail
slight limp
1'-2"

# MY CAMPING ESSENTIALS...

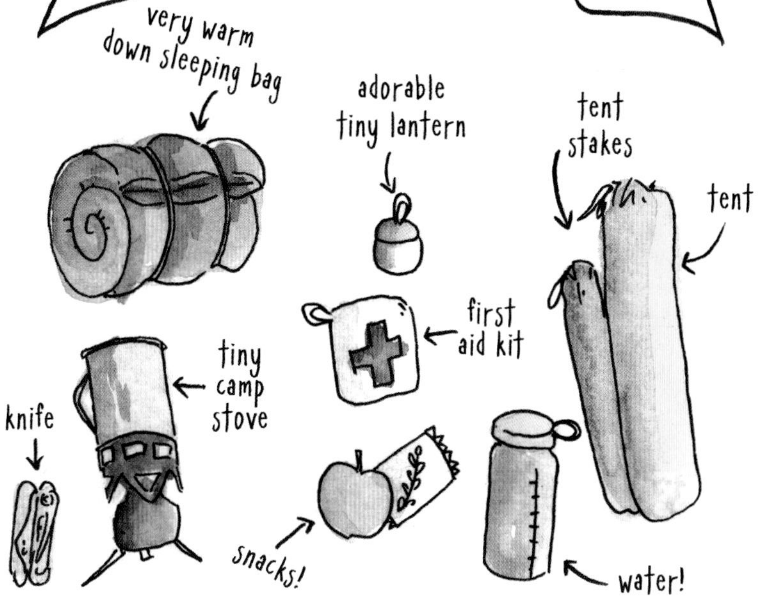
very warm down sleeping bag
adorable tiny lantern
tent stakes
tent
first aid kit
tiny camp stove
knife
snacks!
water!

Our budget is small, so we'll be spending a lot of time camping, but I'm not exactly roughing it.

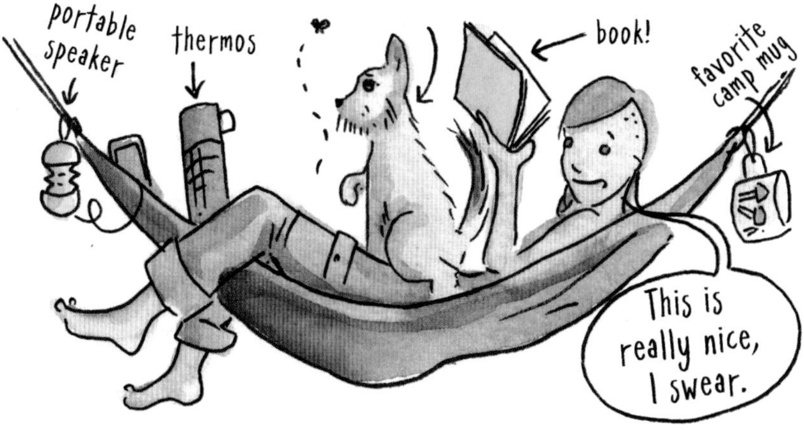
portable speaker
thermos
book!
favorite camp mug
This is really nice, I swear.

The actual historical start (or end) of Route 66 in California is the intersection of Lincoln and Olympic. There is a sign at the Santa Monica Pier, which is prettier. Here, there is just a dentist's office.

Lincoln   Olympic

TO REQUEST GREEN WALL

Weste̶ Dental & Orthodontic

Bug, isn't this exciting?

IT'S WHERE YOU GO FOR A ROOT 66 CANAL!

(a bad pun interlude, from my friend Scott)

The original Route 66 never extended to this sign at the Santa Monica Pier, but it is still a nice view.

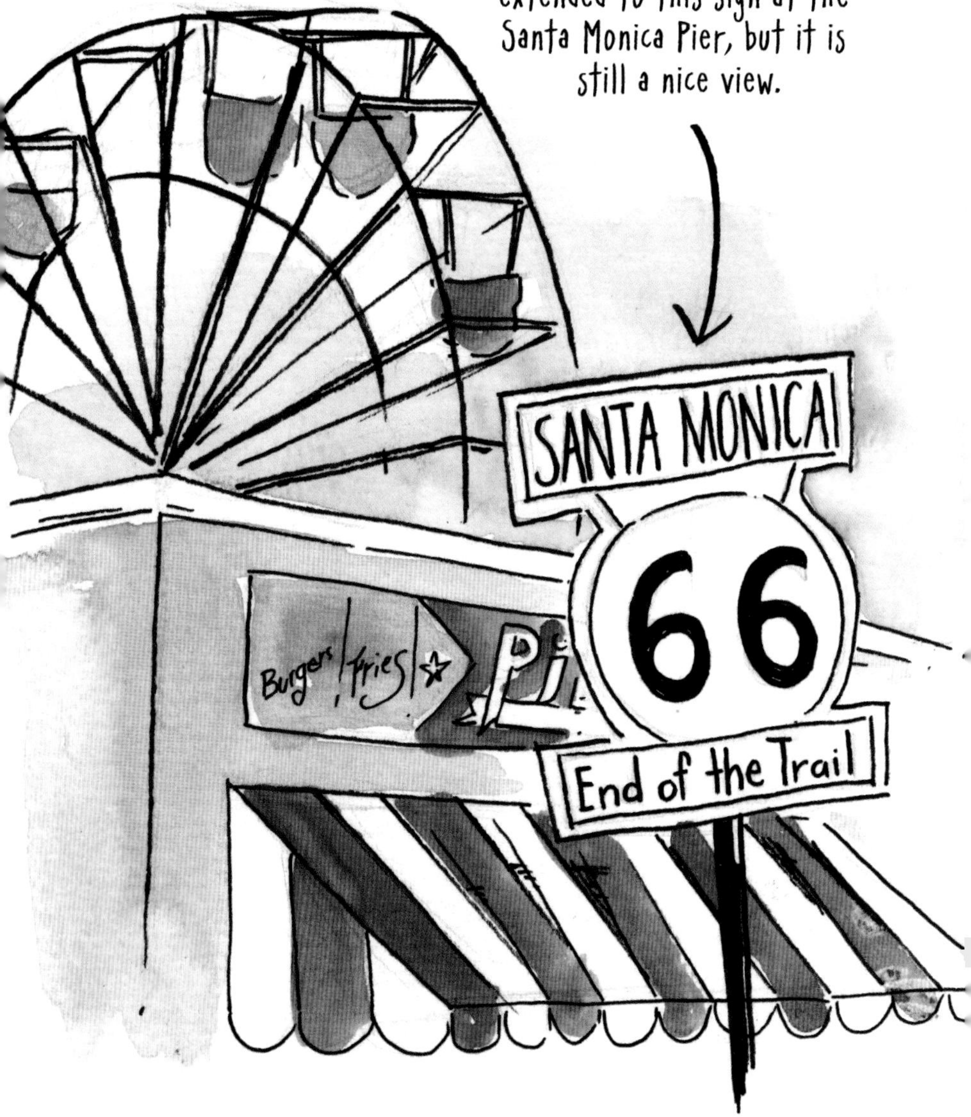

Burgers
Fries
SANTA MONICA
66
End of the Trail

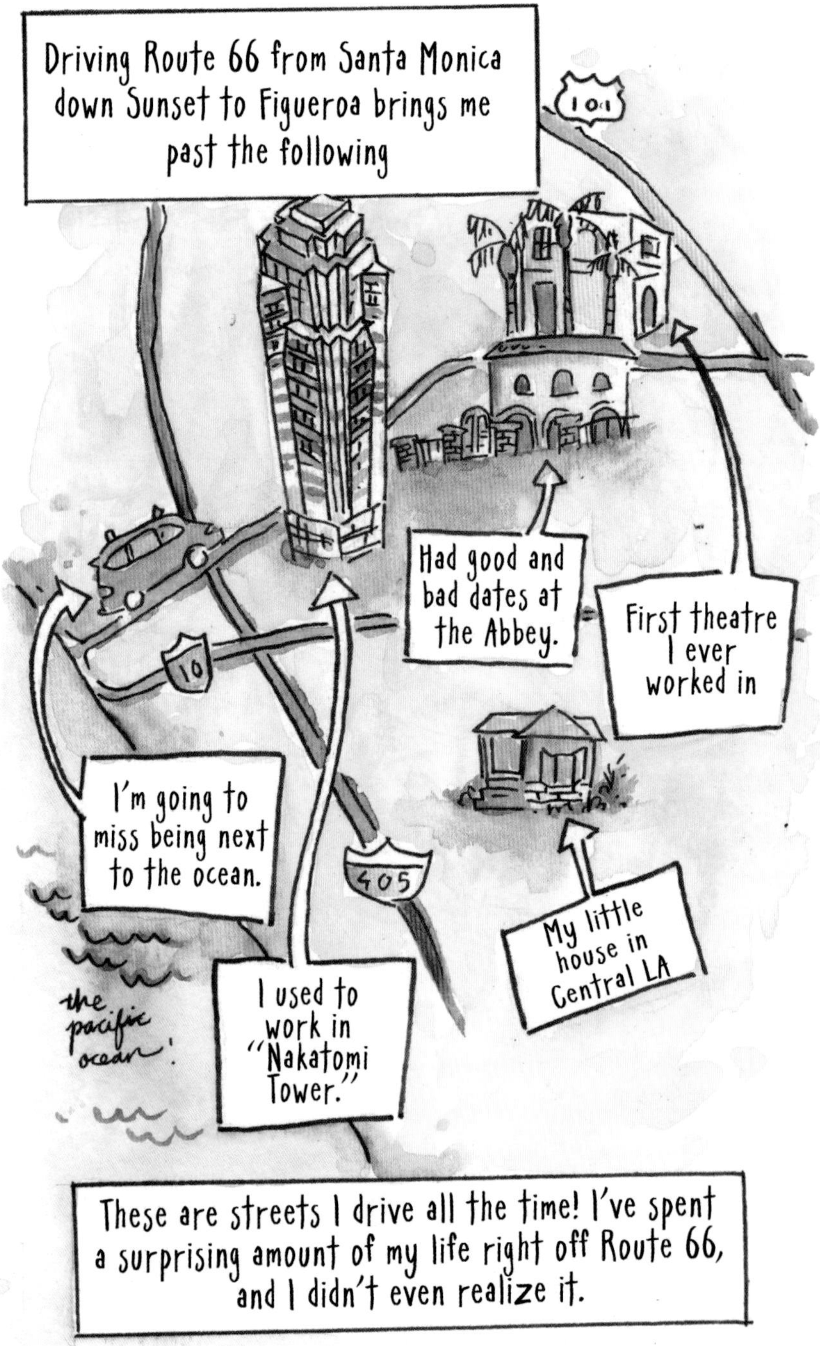
Driving Route 66 from Santa Monica down Sunset to Figueroa brings me past the following
101
I'm going to miss being next to the ocean.
10
I used to work in "Nakatomi Tower."
405
Had good and bad dates at the Abbey.
First theatre I ever worked in
My little house in Central LA
the pacific ocean!
These are streets I drive all the time! I've spent a surprising amount of my life right off Route 66, and I didn't even realize it.

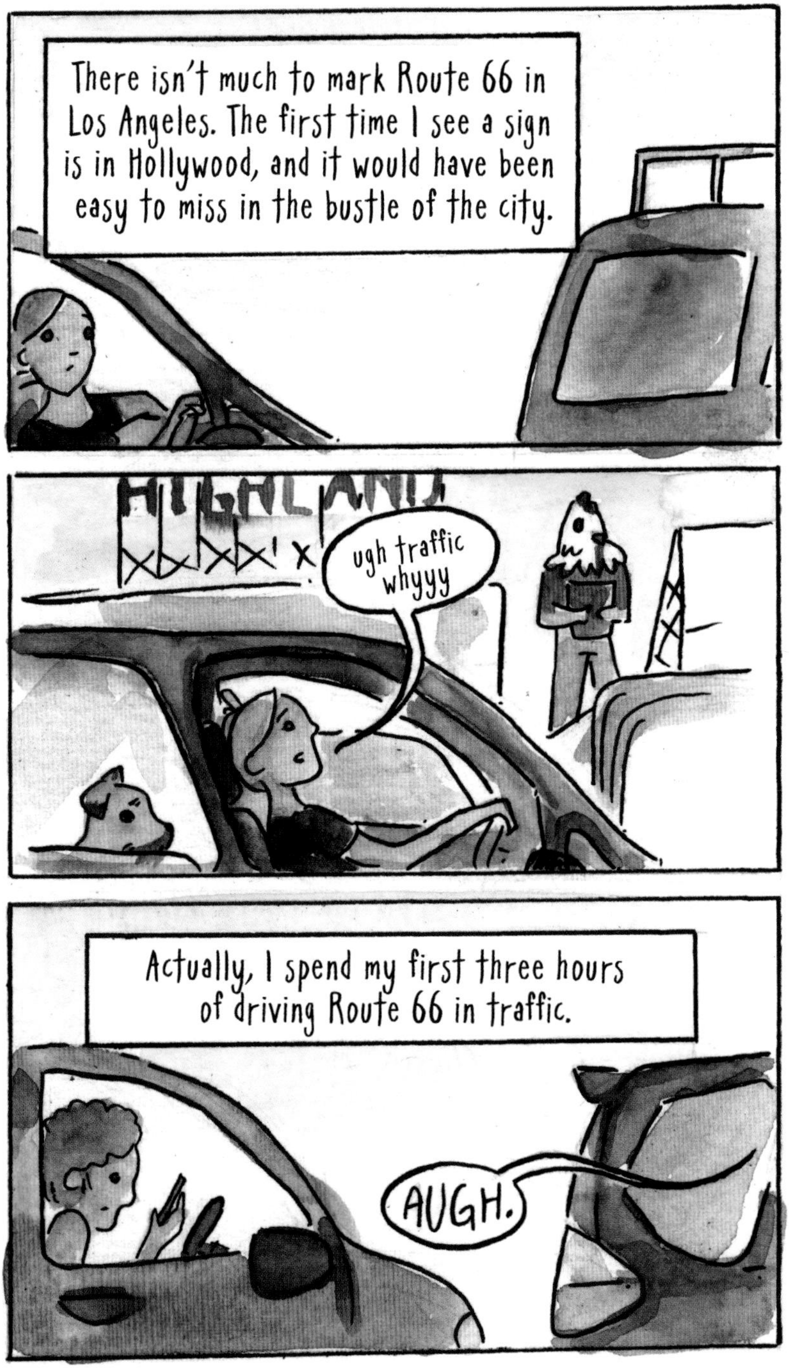
There isn't much to mark Route 66 in Los Angeles. The first time I see a sign is in Hollywood, and it would have been easy to miss in the bustle of the city.
ugh traffic whyyy
Actually, I spend my first three hours of driving Route 66 in traffic.
AUGH.

I decide to stop for the night near Barstow. I'm traveling on a tiny budget, so I consider the two closest campgrounds.

One is named Sawtooth Canyon.
The other is named Owl Canyon.

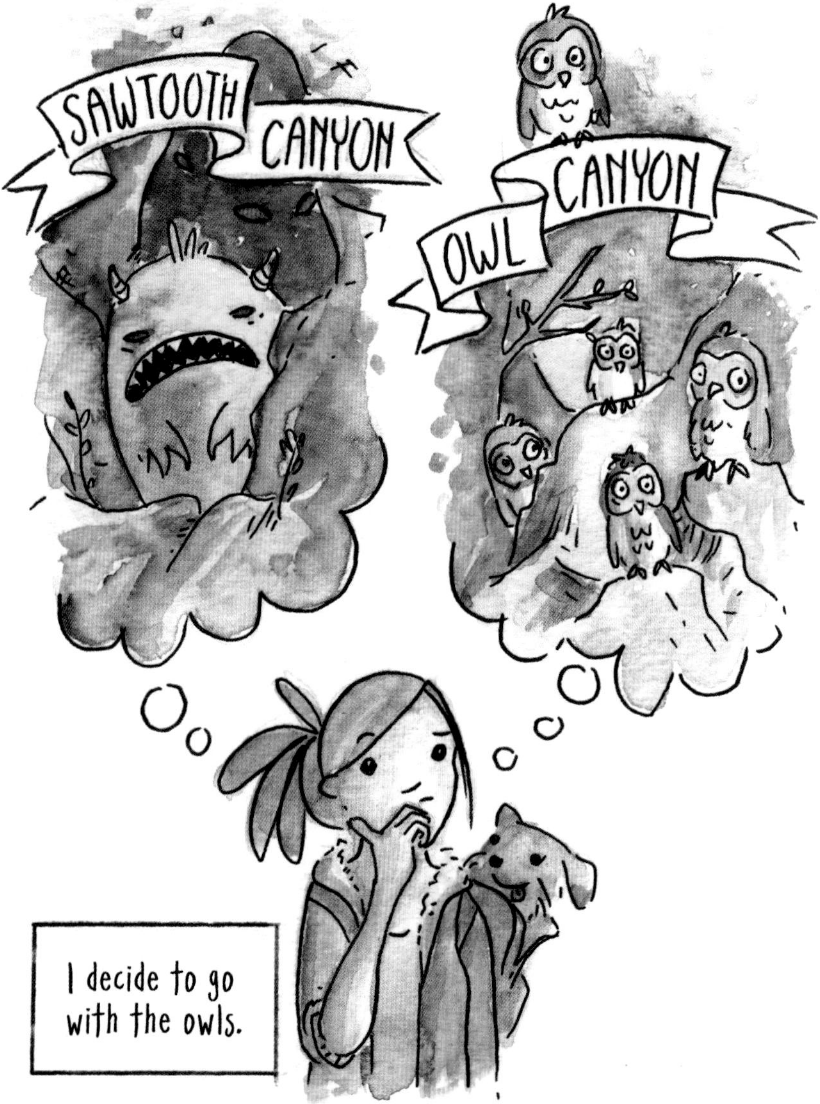
SAWTOOTH CANYON
OWL CANYON
I decide to go with the owls.

I'm trying out my car camping setup for the first time. Which is to say, I'm just trying to sleep in my car.

My car is a 2010 Honda Fit, with the back seats folded down.

easily accessible backpack

Bug's food and water

A comfy pillow is important.

sleeping pad and blankets

Bug's crate and pillows

Most things I have are stored in plastic bins.

It's working out well, although I wouldn't recommend it for anyone taller than 4'6", and I am 5'0".

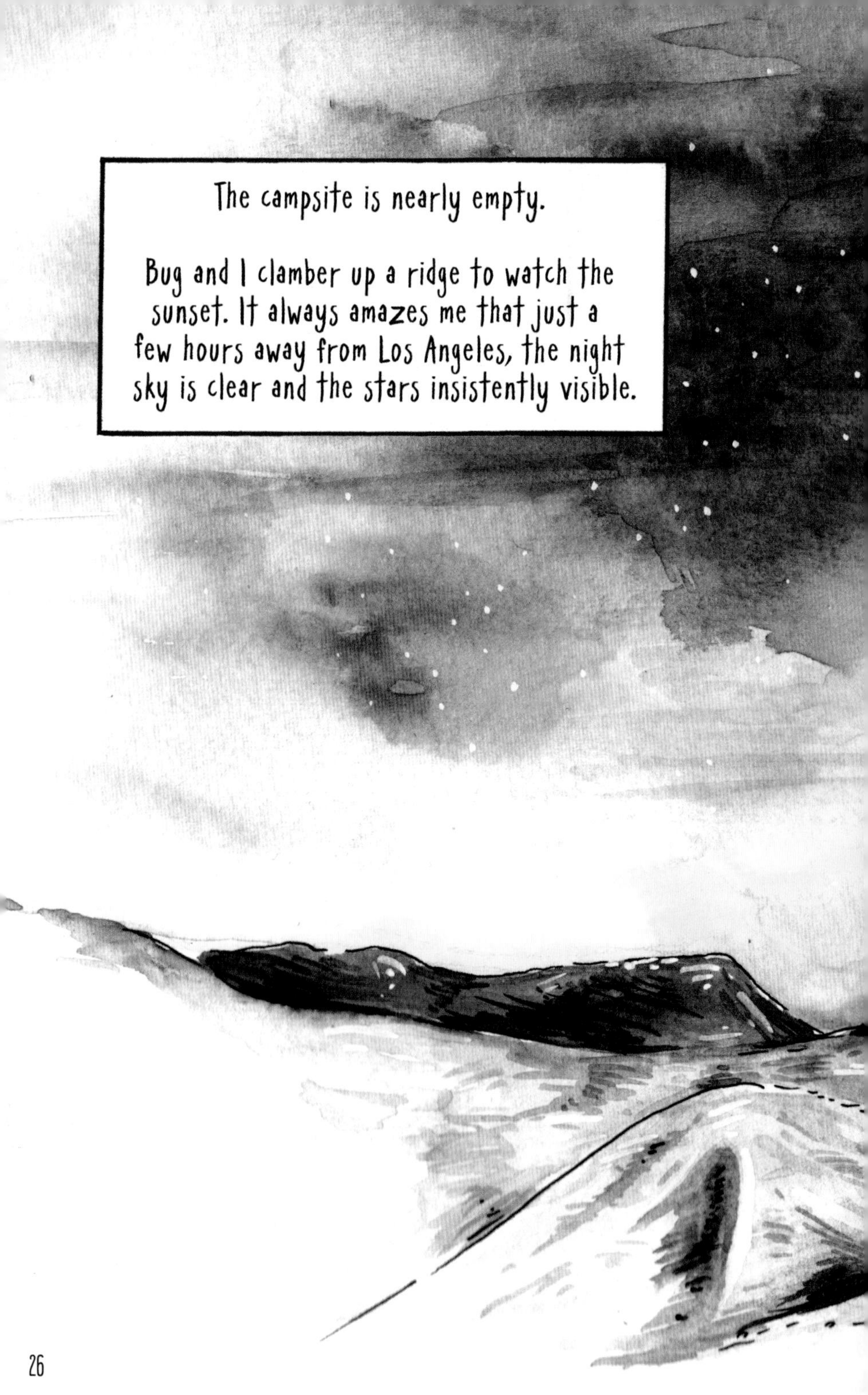
The campsite is nearly empty.
Bug and I clamber up a ridge to watch the sunset. It always amazes me that just a few hours away from Los Angeles, the night sky is clear and the stars insistently visible.

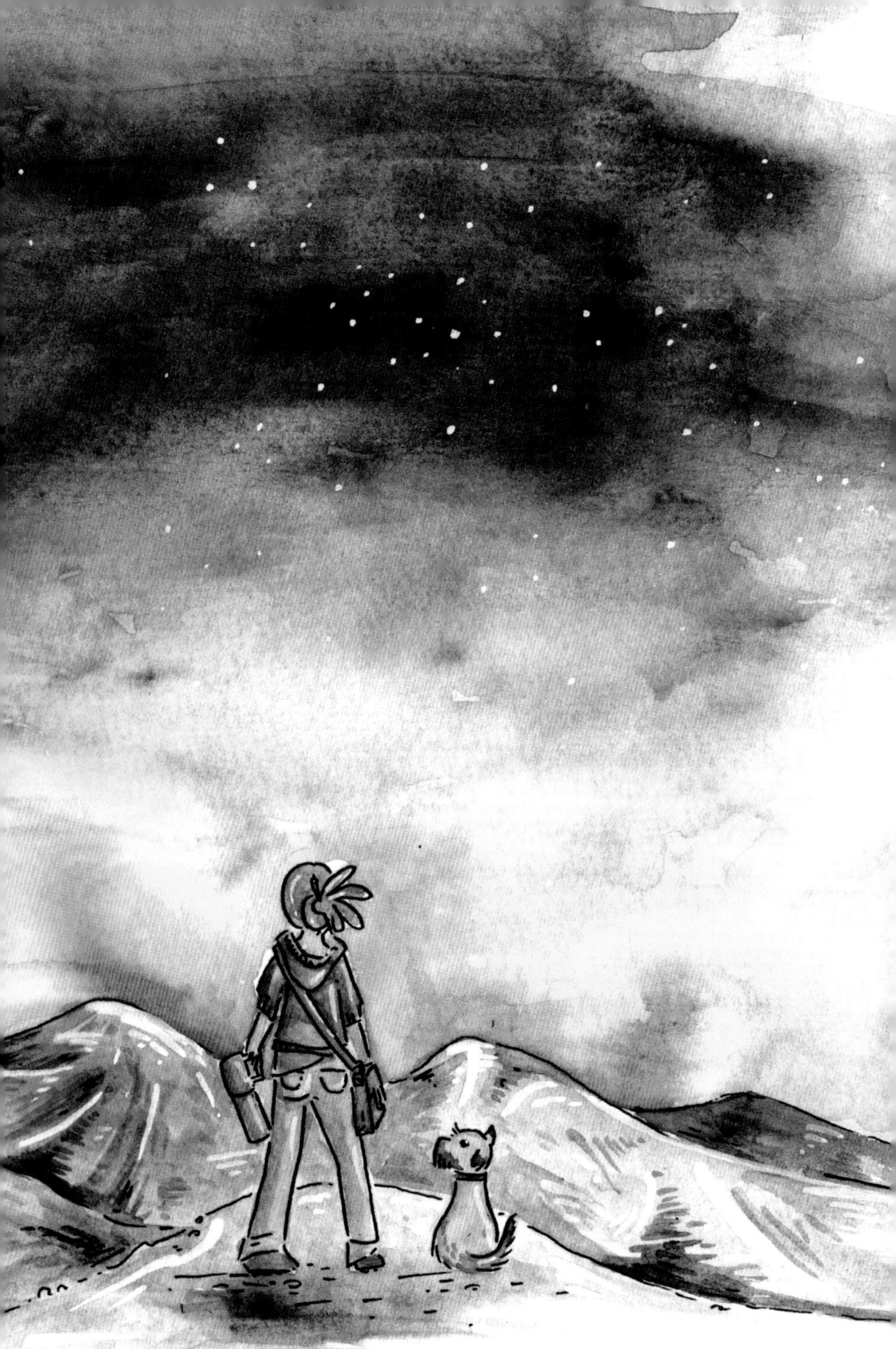

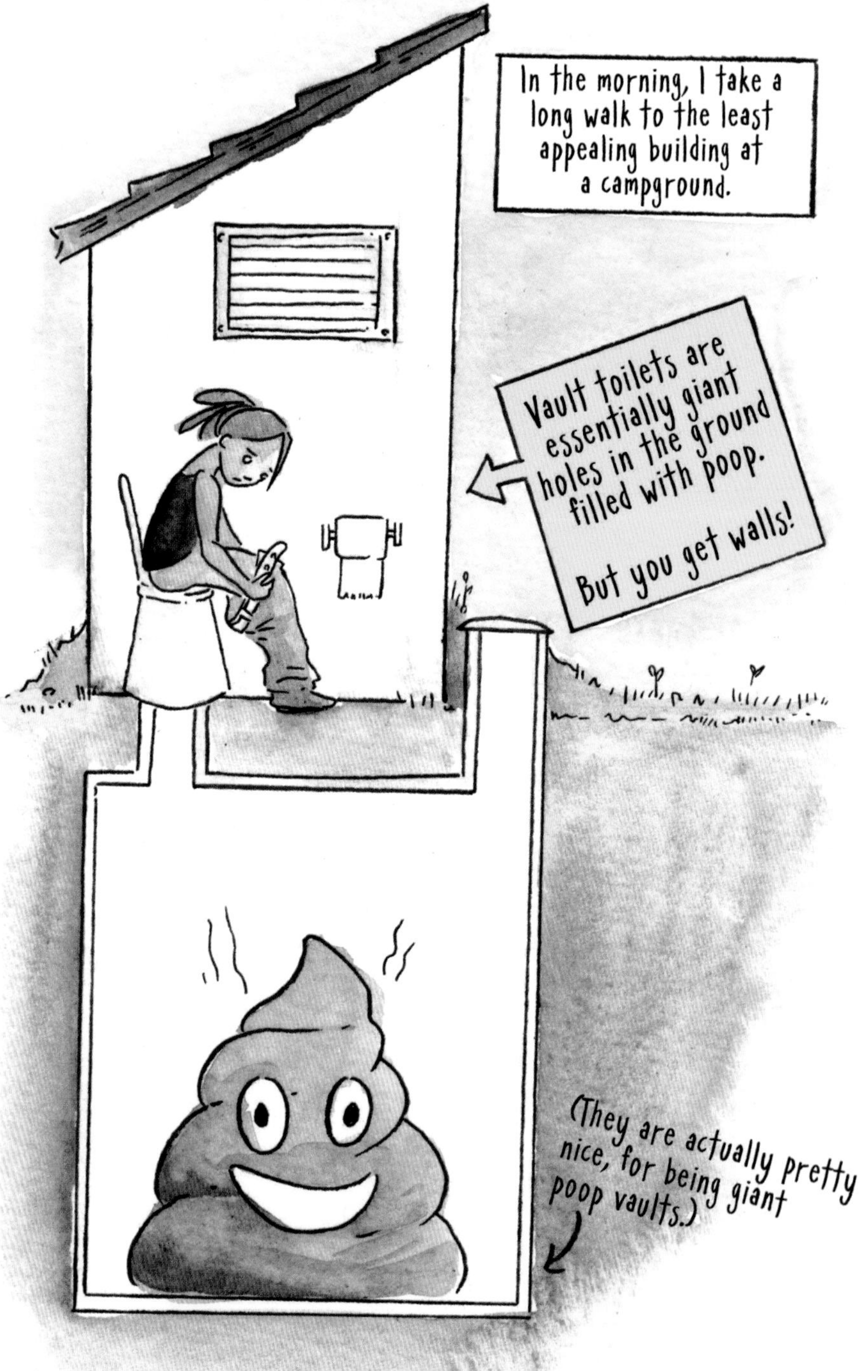
In the morning, I take a long walk to the least appealing building at a campground.
Vault toilets are essentially giant holes in the ground filled with poop.
But you get walls!
(They are actually pretty nice, for being giant poop vaults.)

On the way back, I run into two friendly rangers, Arthur and Miguel. Arthur grew up in East Los Angeles, but he loves the desert.

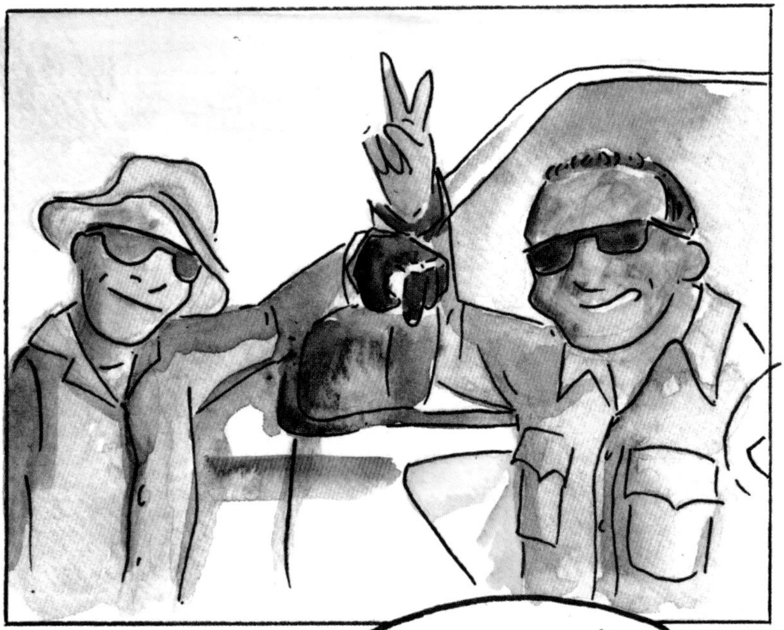

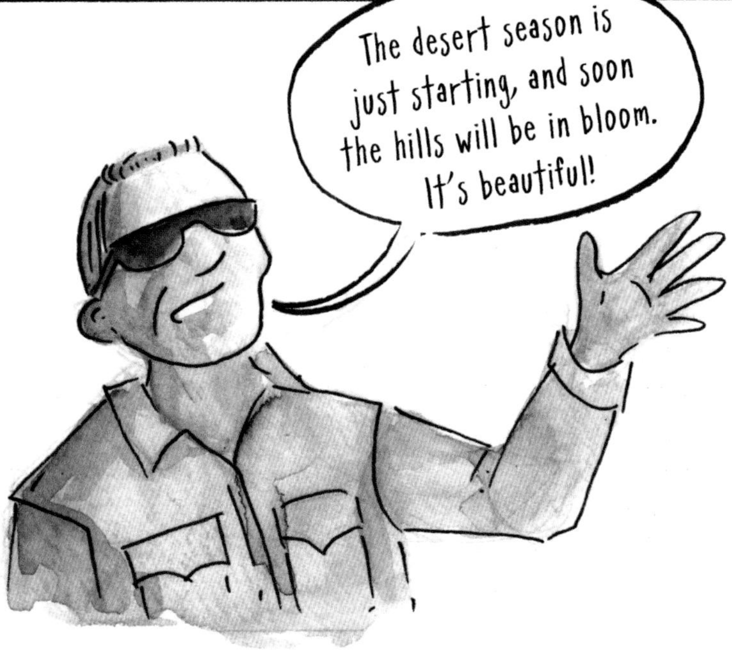
The desert season is just starting, and soon the hills will be in bloom. It's beautiful!

They send me off to the Bureau of Land Management field office in Barstow, where they tell me I can learn a lot about their Route 66 restoration work.

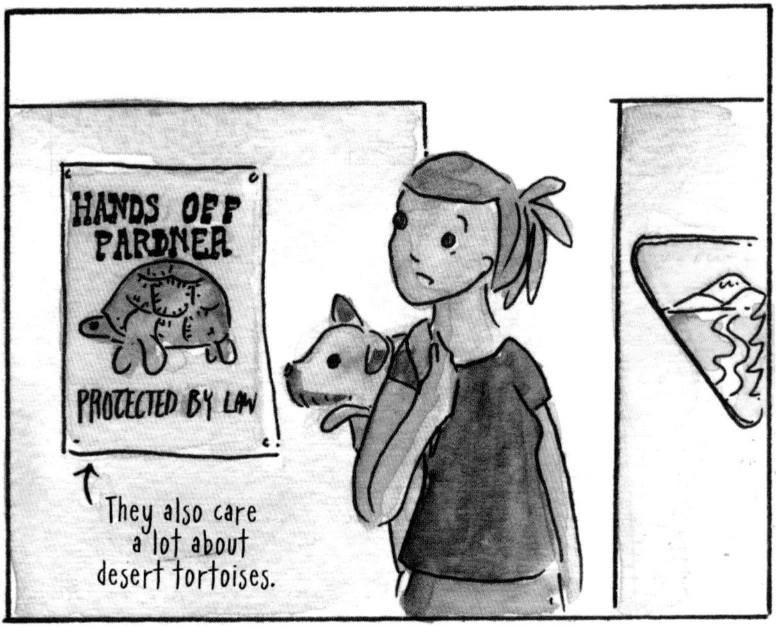
HANDS OFF PARDNER
PROTECTED BY LAW
They also care a lot about desert tortoises.

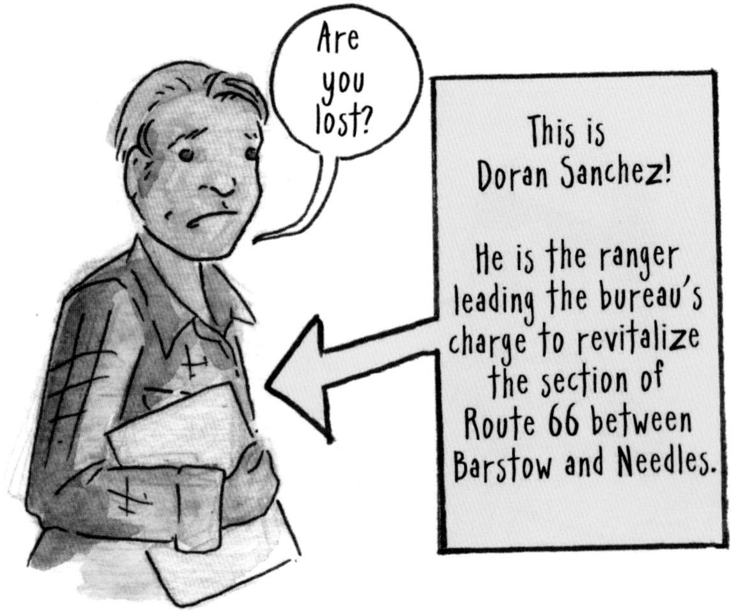
Are you lost?
This is Doran Sanchez!
He is the ranger leading the bureau's charge to revitalize the section of Route 66 between Barstow and Needles.

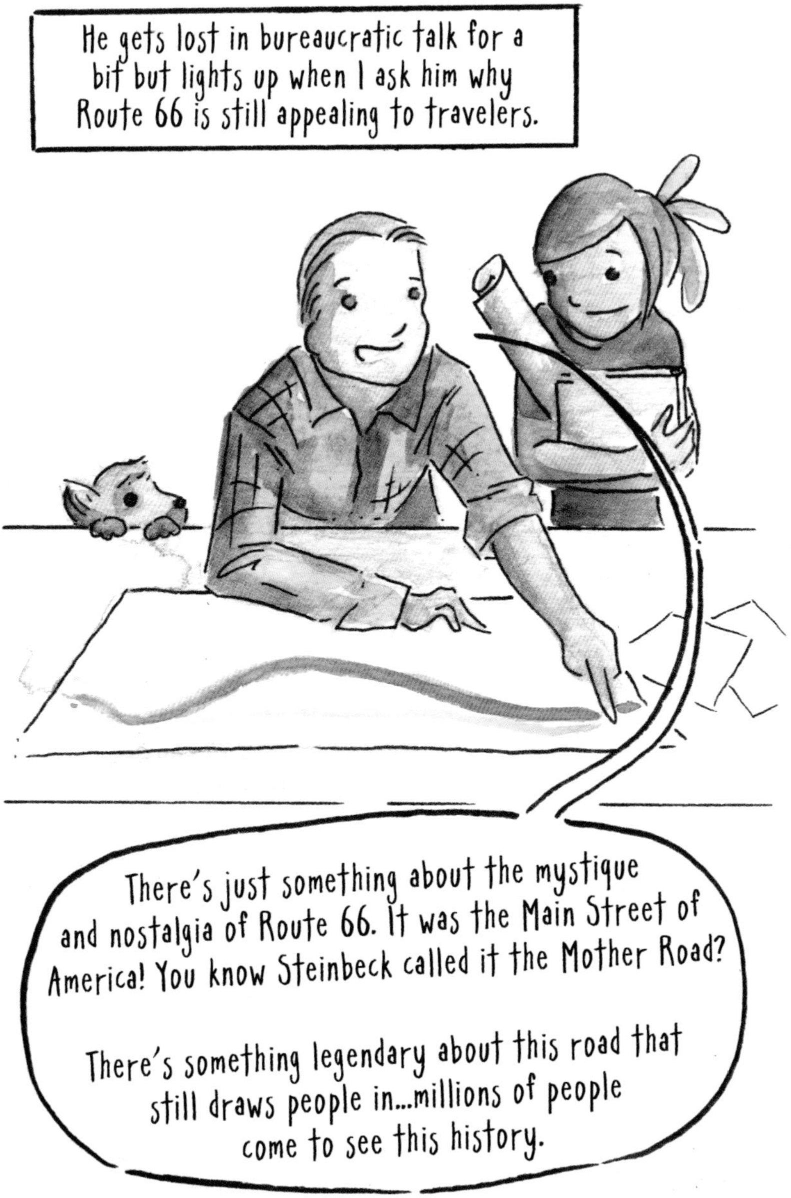
He gets lost in bureaucratic talk for a bit but lights up when I ask him why Route 66 is still appealing to travelers.
There's just something about the mystique and nostalgia of Route 66. It was the Main Street of America! You know Steinbeck called it the Mother Road?
There's something legendary about this road that still draws people in...millions of people come to see this history.

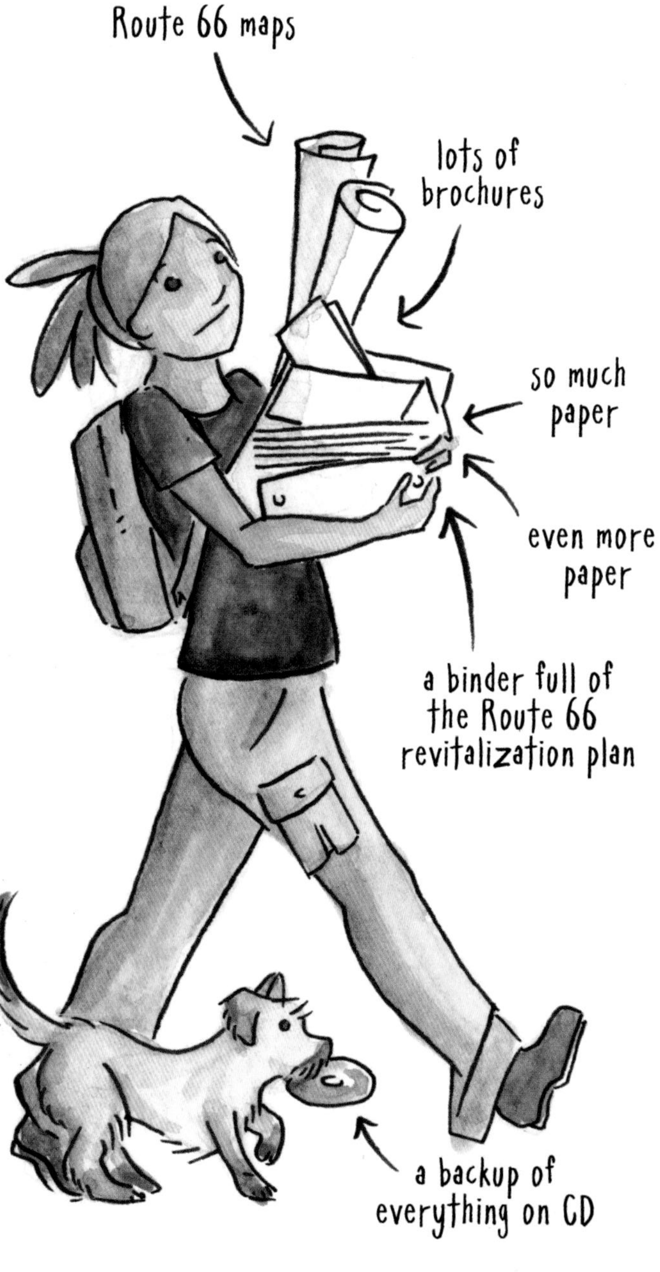
Route 66 maps
lots of brochures
so much paper
even more paper
a binder full of the Route 66 revitalization plan
a backup of everything on CD

There is a stretch of road between Newberry Springs and Ludlow that is a teeth-chattering combination of potholes and patches.

It runs entirely parallel to I-40, where smooth asphalt mocks me as I wonder if this road is going to rattle my tiny car apart.

It would be much easier to take the highway.

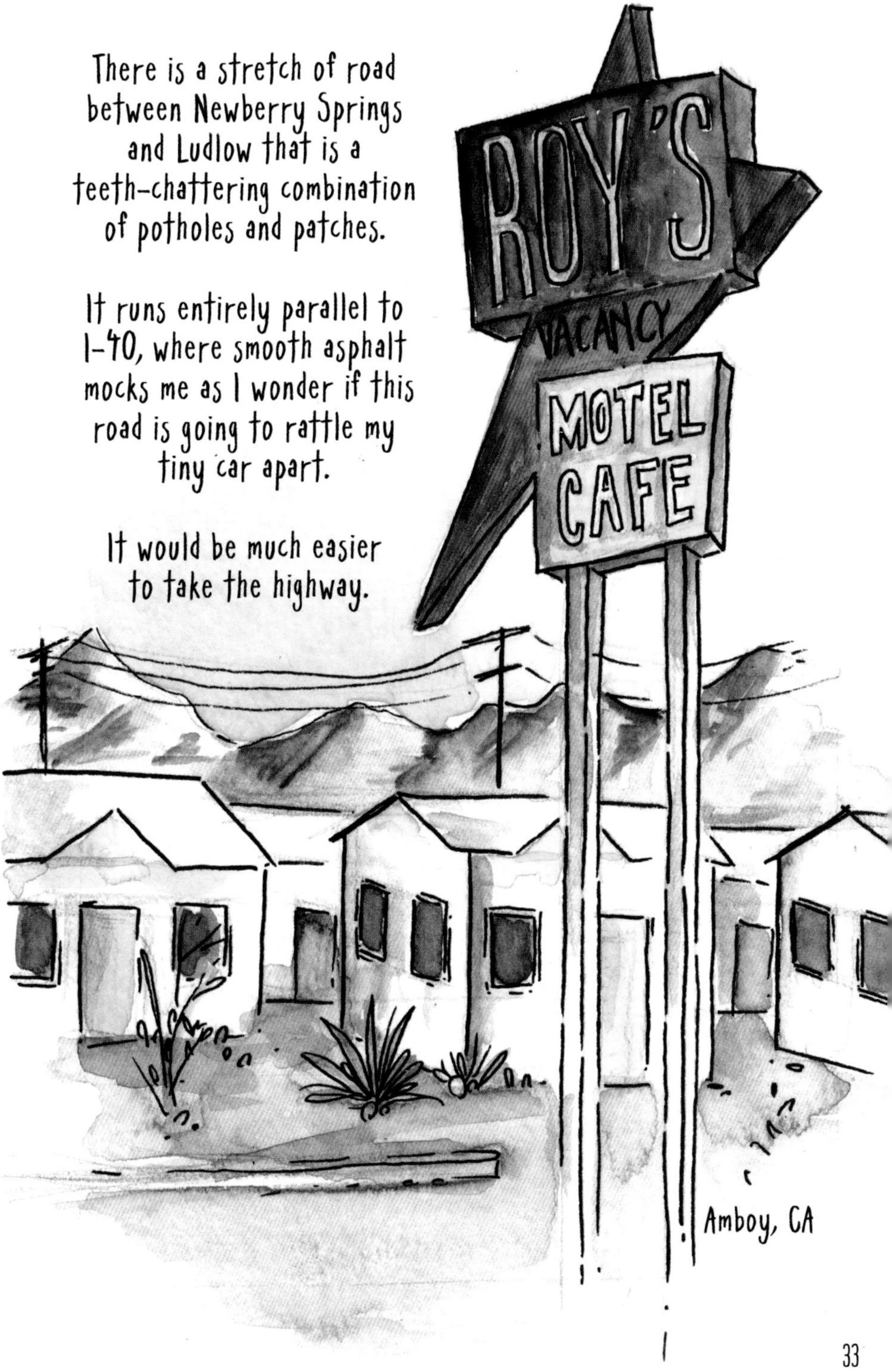
ROY'S
VACANCY
MOTEL
CAFE

Amboy, CA

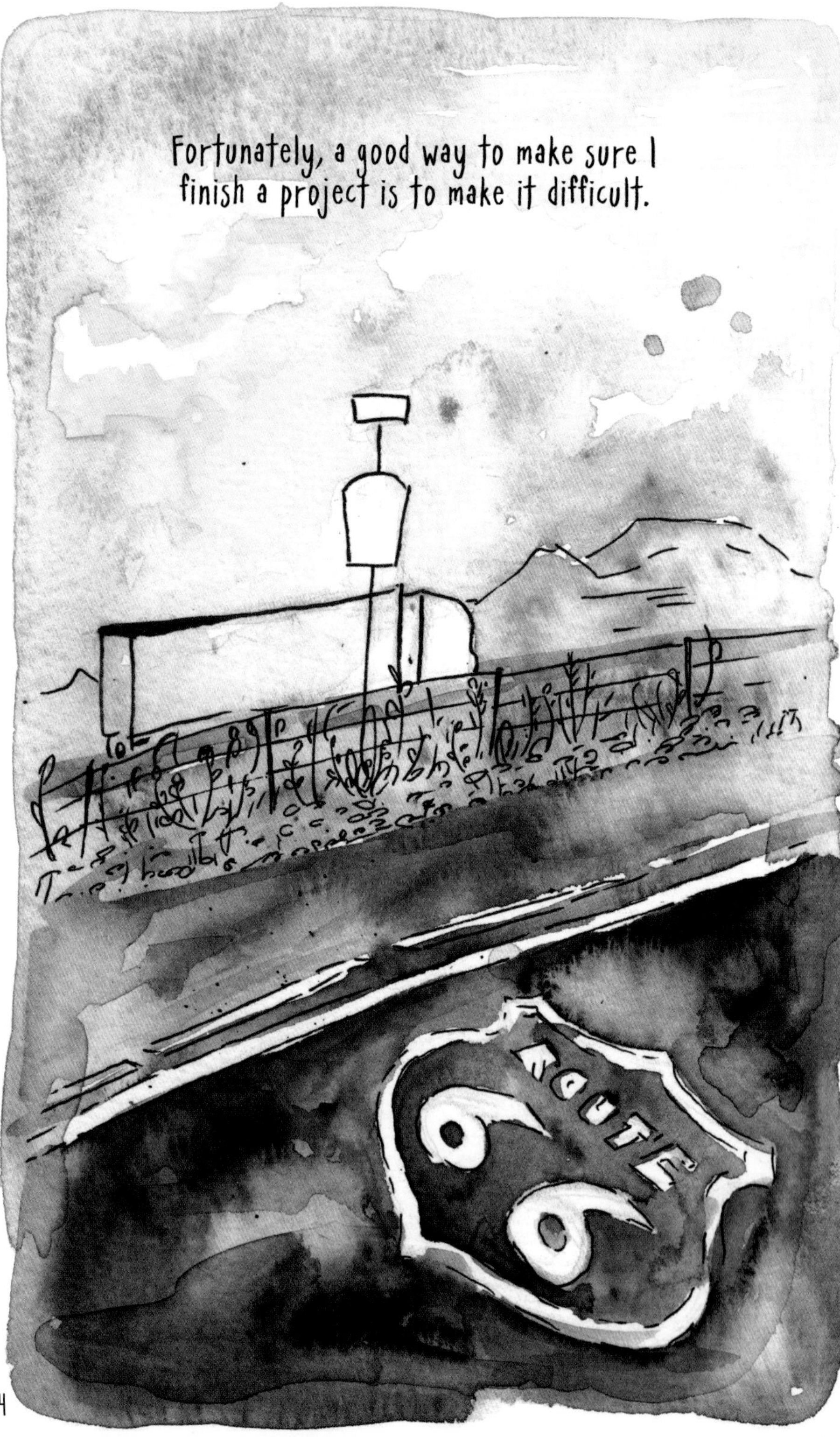
Fortunately, a good way to make sure I finish a project is to make it difficult.
ROUTE
66

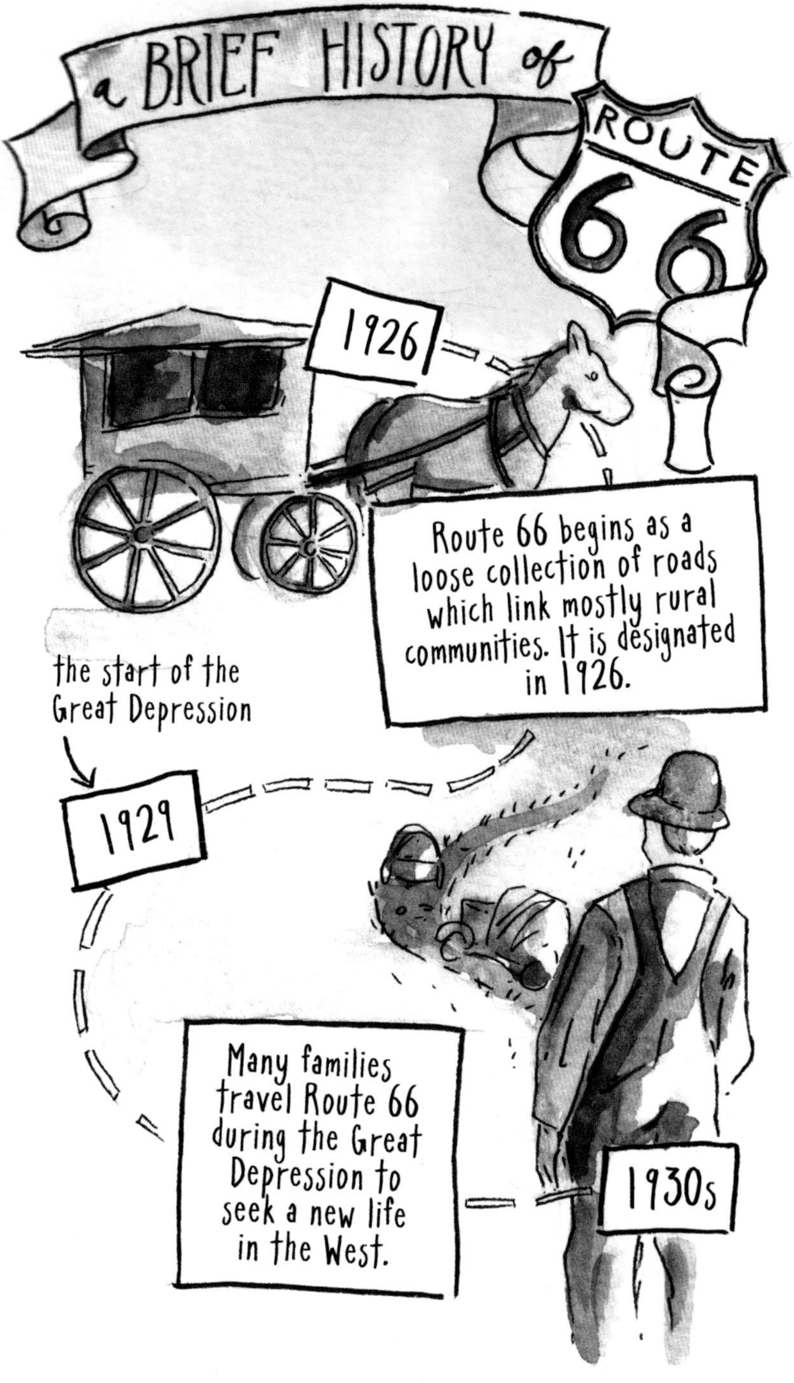
a BRIEF HISTORY of
ROUTE 66
1926
Route 66 begins as a loose collection of roads which link mostly rural communities. It is designated in 1926.
the start of the Great Depression
1929
Many families travel Route 66 during the Great Depression to seek a new life in the West.
1930s

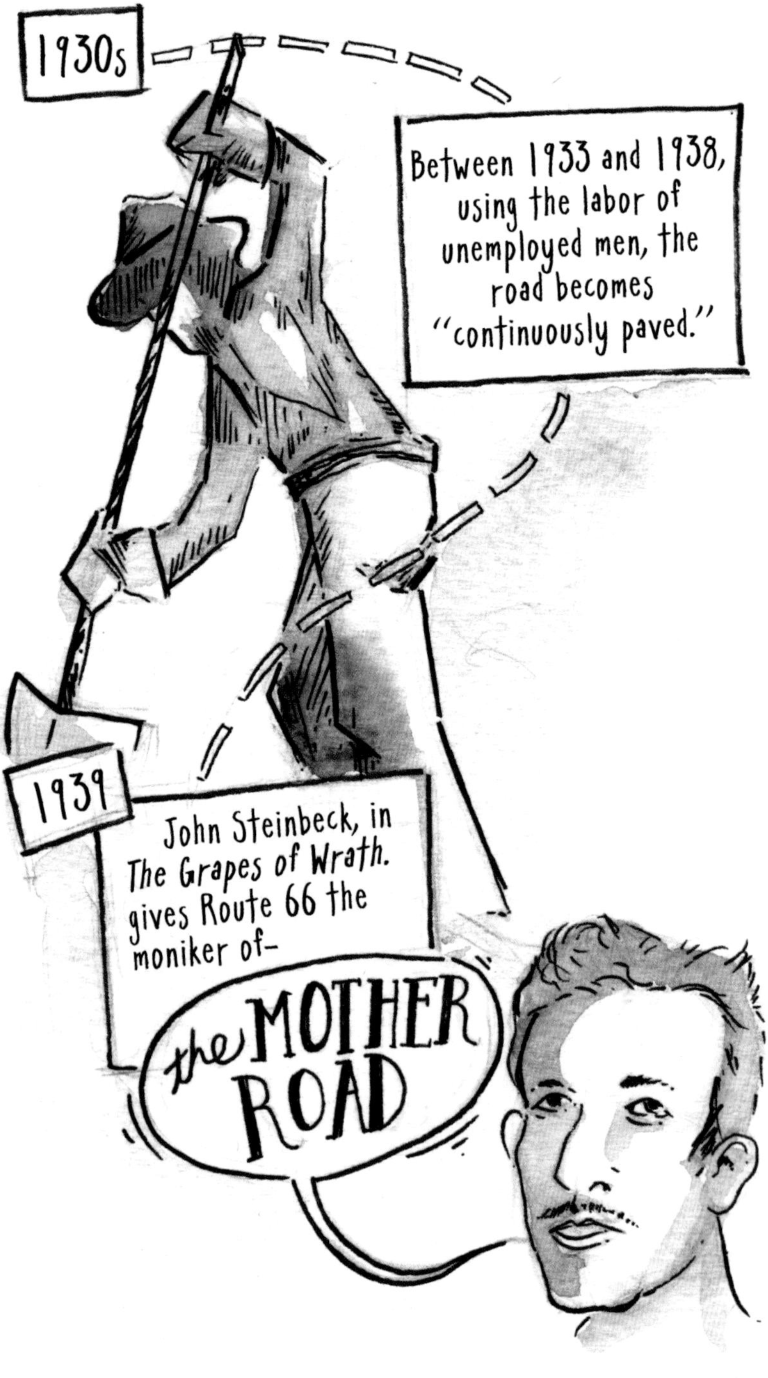
1930s
Between 1933 and 1938, using the labor of unemployed men, the road becomes "continuously paved."
1939
John Steinbeck, in *The Grapes of Wrath.* gives Route 66 the moniker of–
the MOTHER ROAD

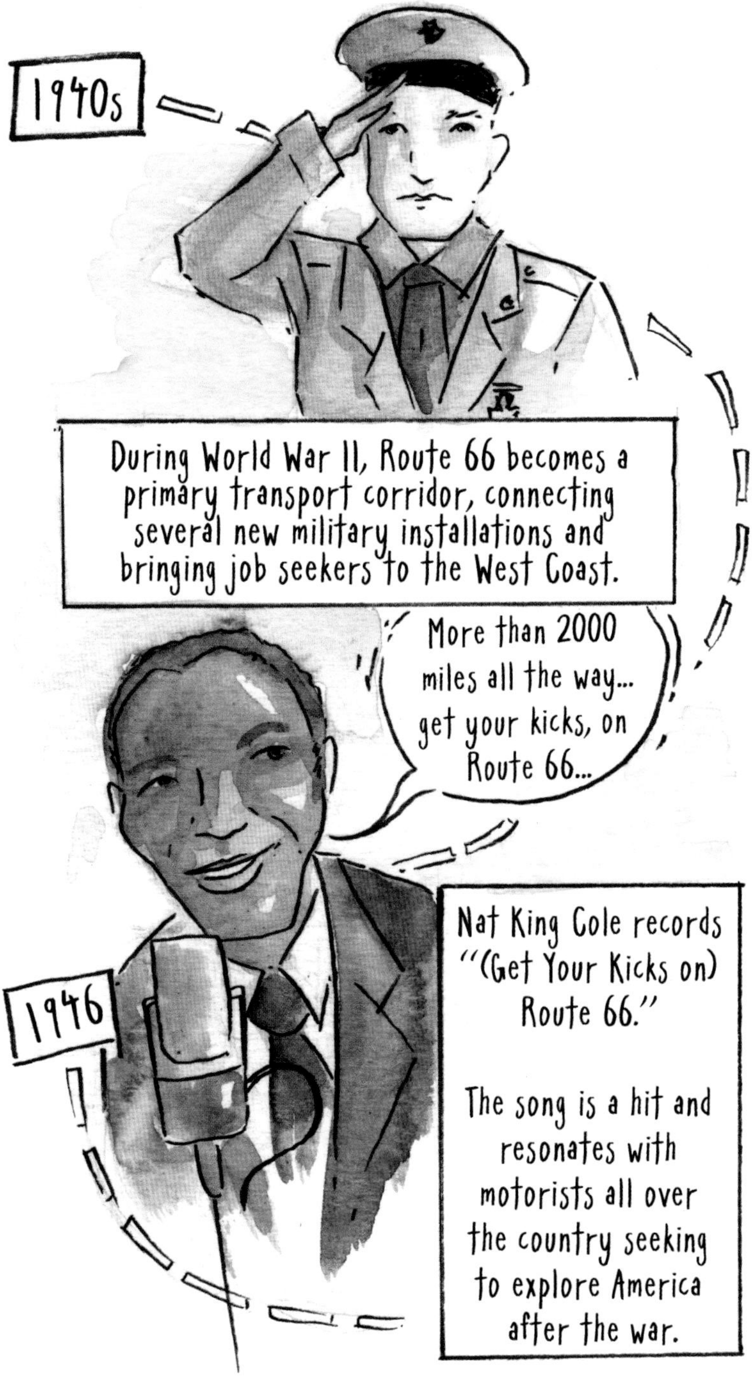
1940s
During World War II, Route 66 becomes a primary transport corridor, connecting several new military installations and bringing job seekers to the West Coast.
More than 2000 miles all the way... get your kicks, on Route 66...
1946
Nat King Cole records "(Get Your Kicks on) Route 66."
The song is a hit and resonates with motorists all over the country seeking to explore America after the war.

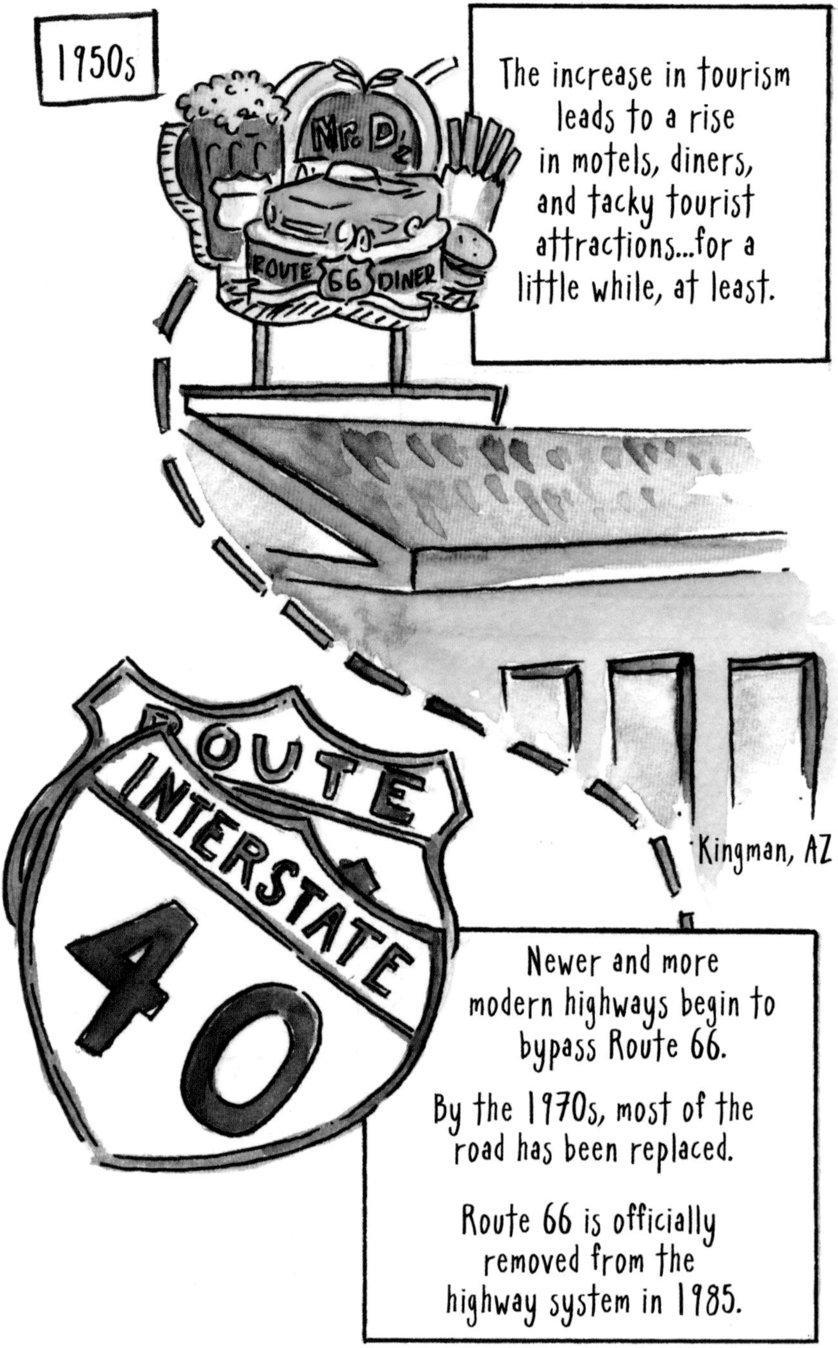
1950s
The increase in tourism leads to a rise in motels, diners, and tacky tourist attractions...for a little while, at least.
Mr. D'z
ROUTE 66 DINER
Kingman, AZ
ROUTE
INTERSTATE
40
Newer and more modern highways begin to bypass Route 66.
By the 1970s, most of the road has been replaced.
Route 66 is officially removed from the highway system in 1985.

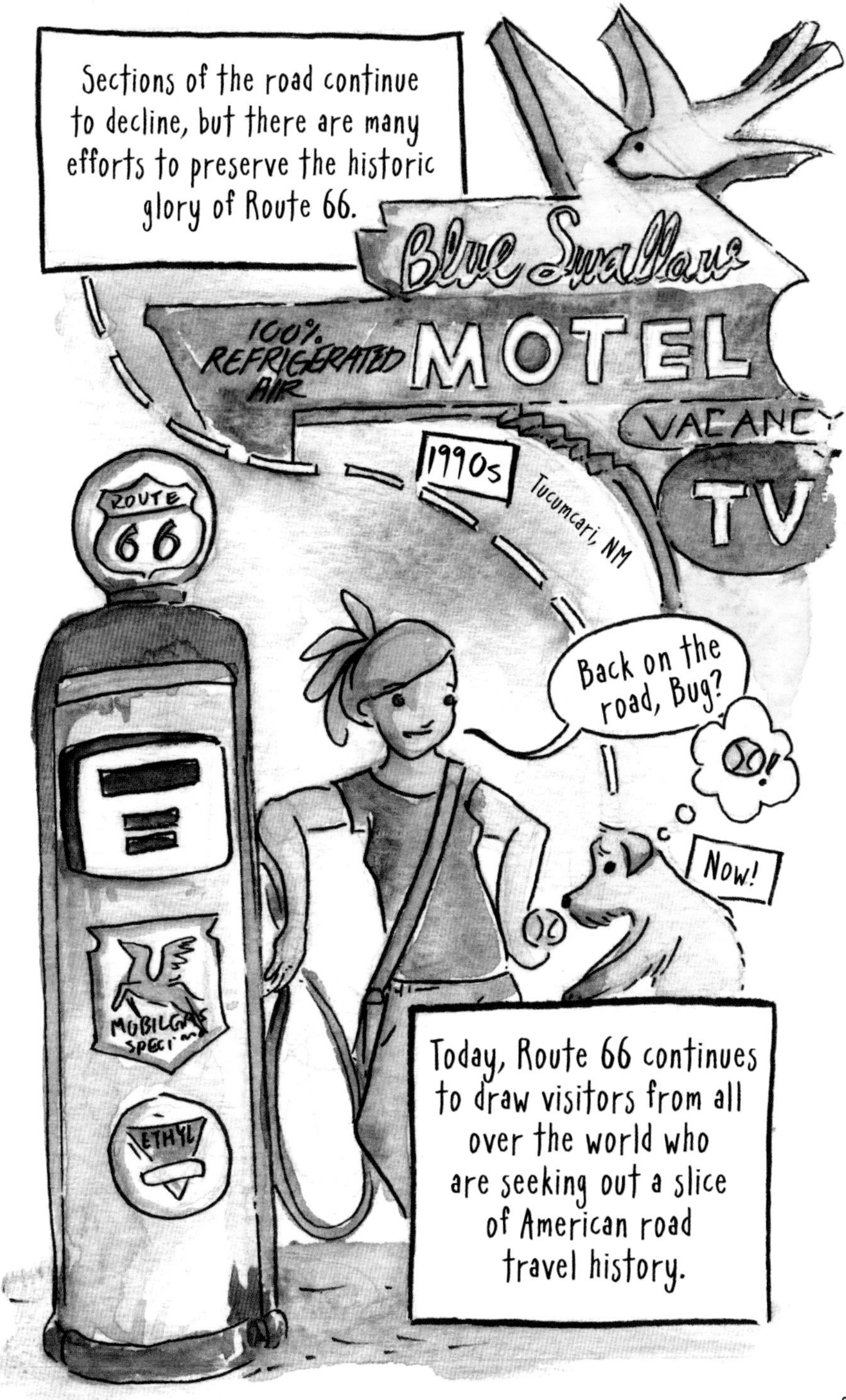
Sections of the road continue to decline, but there are many efforts to preserve the historic glory of Route 66.
Blue Swallow
100% REFRIGERATED AIR
MOTEL
VACANC
TV
1990s
Tucumcari, NM
ROUTE 66
Back on the road, Bug?
Now!
ETHYL
Today, Route 66 continues to draw visitors from all over the world who are seeking out a slice of American road travel history.

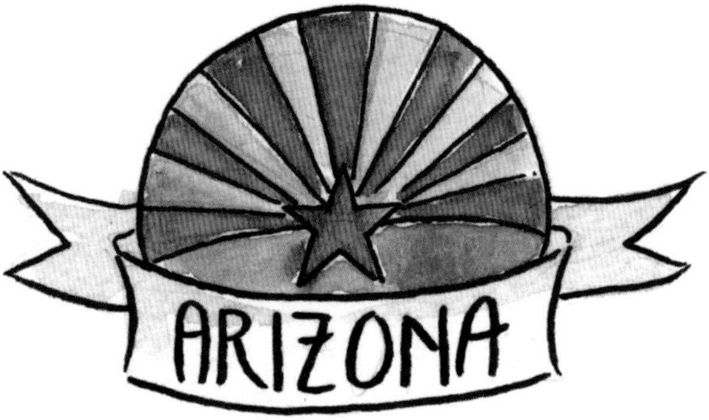
ARIZONA

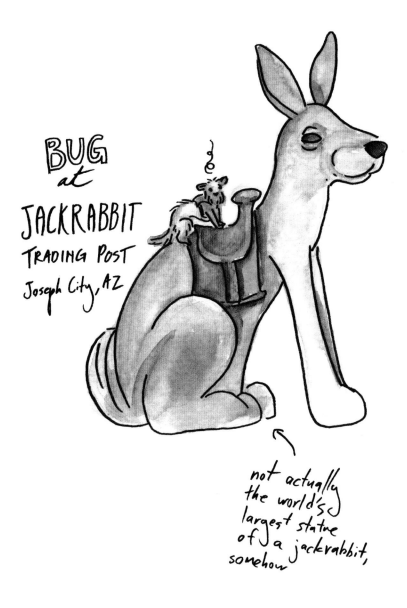

BUG *at* JACKRABBIT TRADING POST
Joseph City, AZ

not actually the world's largest statue of a jackrabbit, somehow

Arizona greets me with the most charming mountain pass landscapes and wild donkeys.

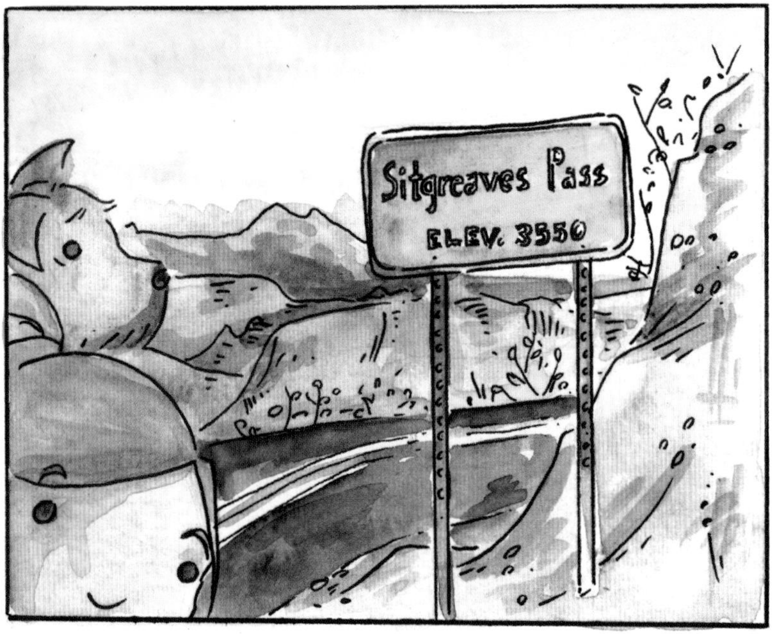
Sitgreaves Pass
ELEV. 3550

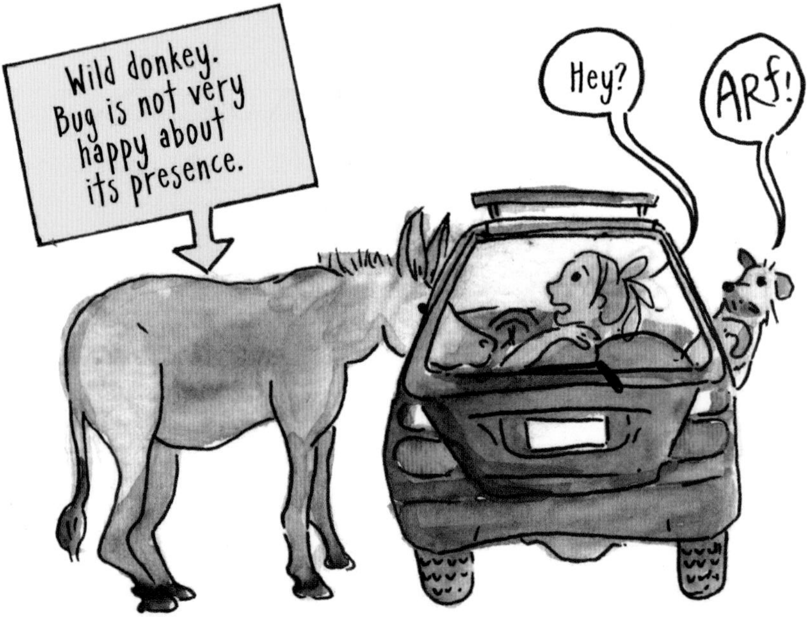
Wild donkey. Bug is not very happy about its presence.
Hey?
ARf!

# OATMAN, AZ

Oatman is an old mining town that has reinvented itself many times and now is entirely a cheesy but charming Route 66 tourist attraction.

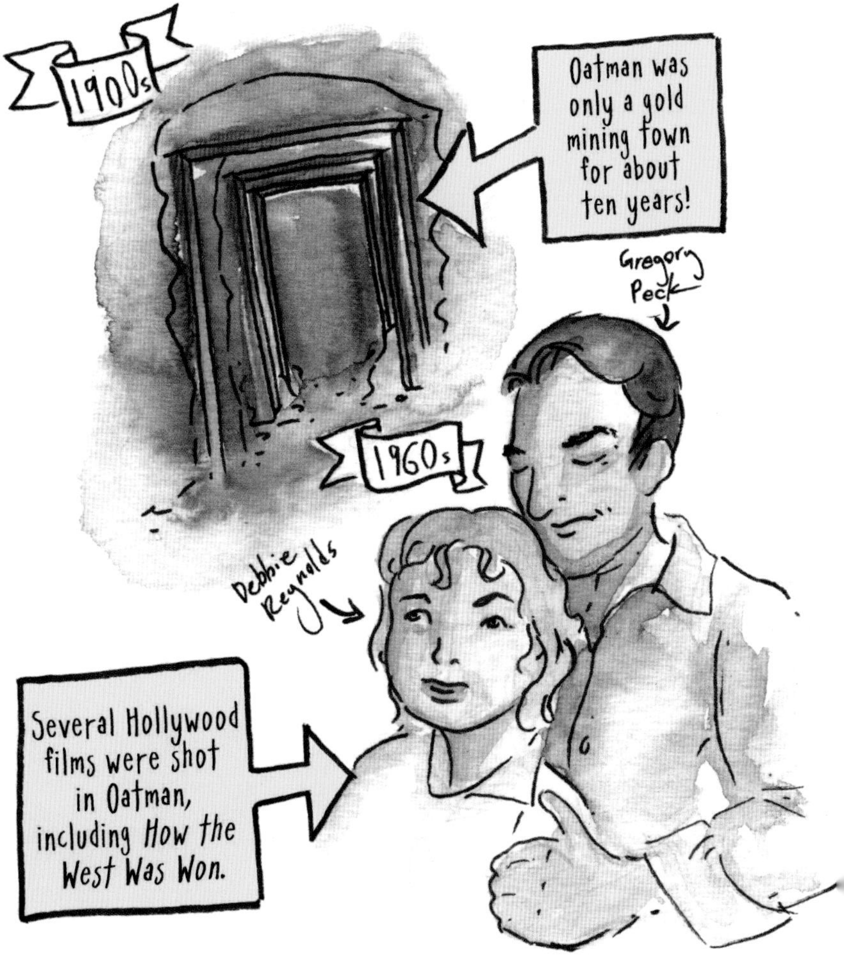

1900s
Oatman was only a gold mining town for about ten years!
Gregory Peck
1960s
Debbie Reynolds
Several Hollywood films were shot in Oatman, including *How the West Was Won.*

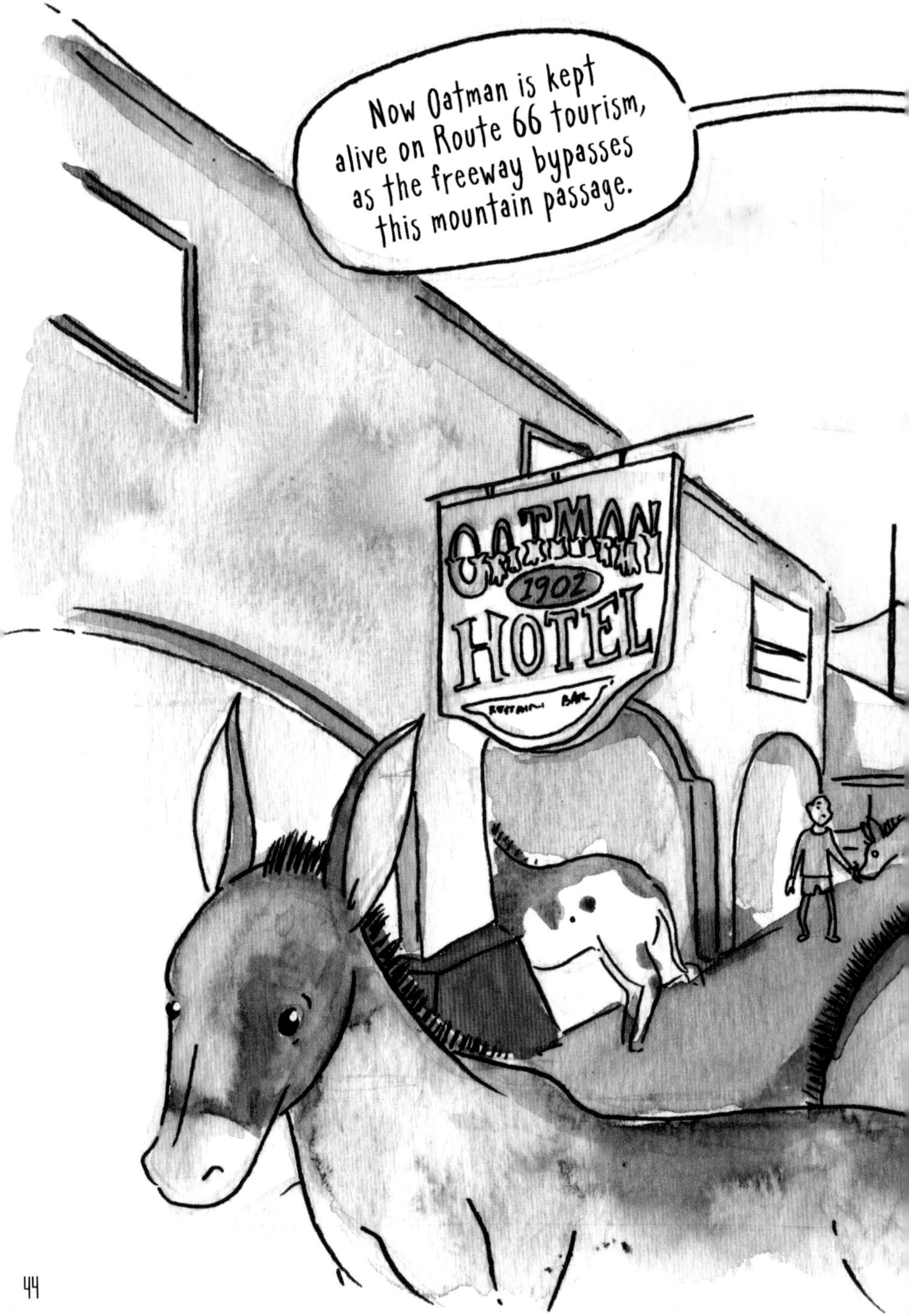
Now Oatman is kept alive on Route 66 tourism, as the freeway bypasses this mountain passage.
OATMAN
1902
HOTEL

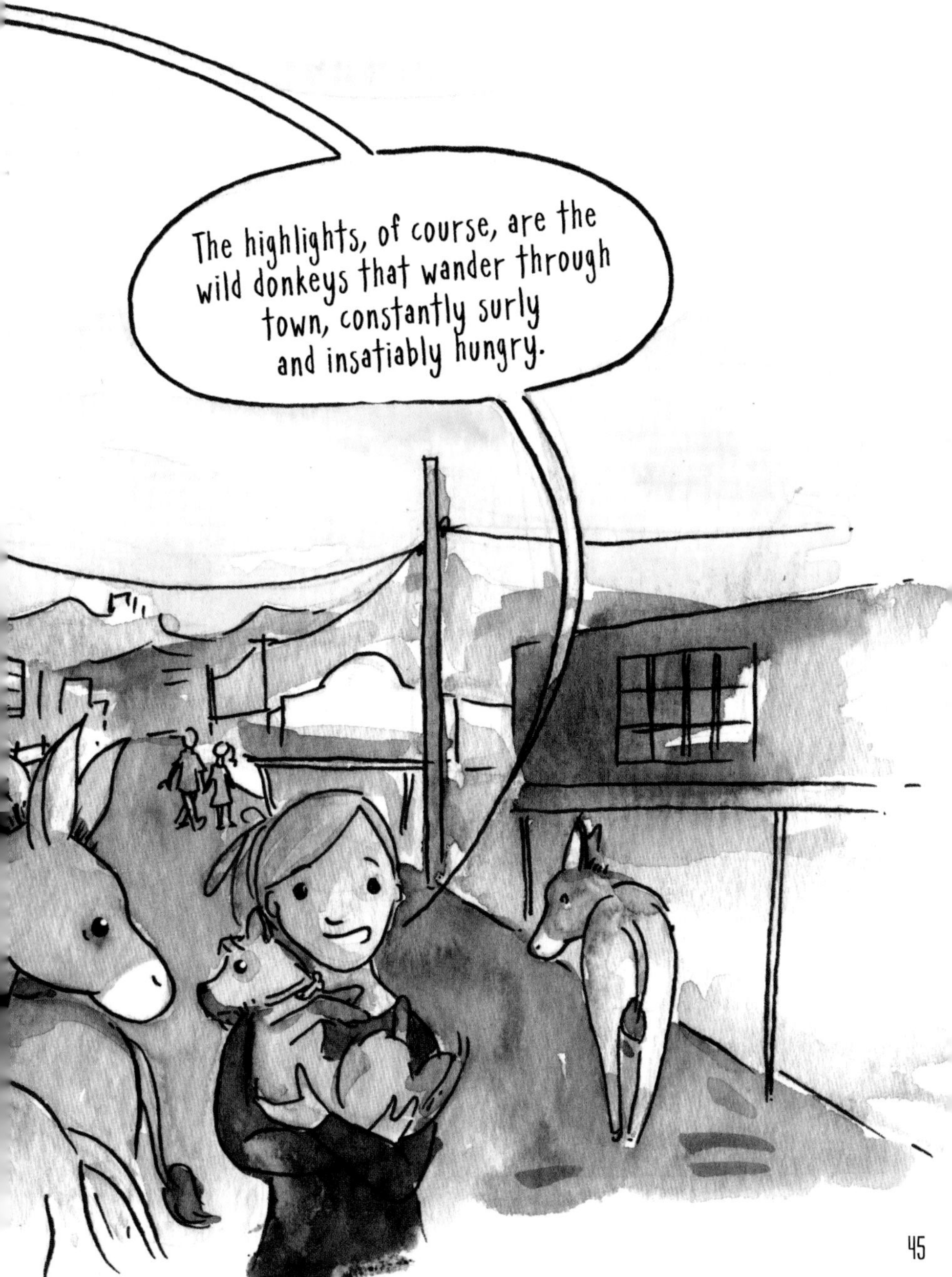
The highlights, of course, are the wild donkeys that wander through town, constantly surly and insatiably hungry.

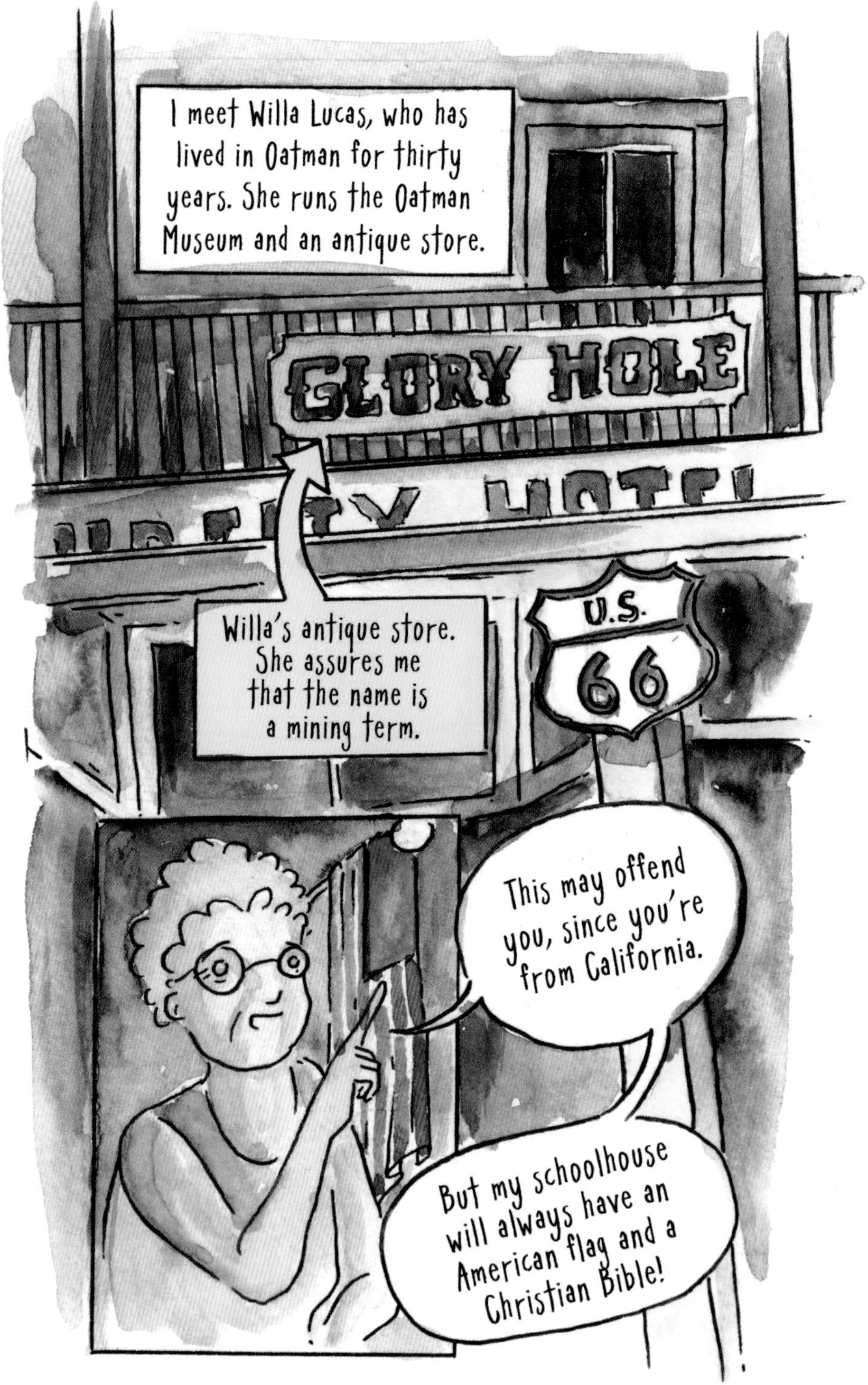
I meet Willa Lucas, who has lived in Oatman for thirty years. She runs the Oatman Museum and an antique store.
GLORY HOLE
Willa's antique store. She assures me that the name is a mining term.
U.S. 66
This may offend you, since you're from California.
But my schoolhouse will always have an American flag and a Christian Bible!

After we drive through the mountain pass, Kingman delivers on its promise of vintage American kitsch. It is a perfectly curated blend of intentionally placed trains and diners, and, if you wander, abandoned motels and garages that used to serve Route 66 traffic.

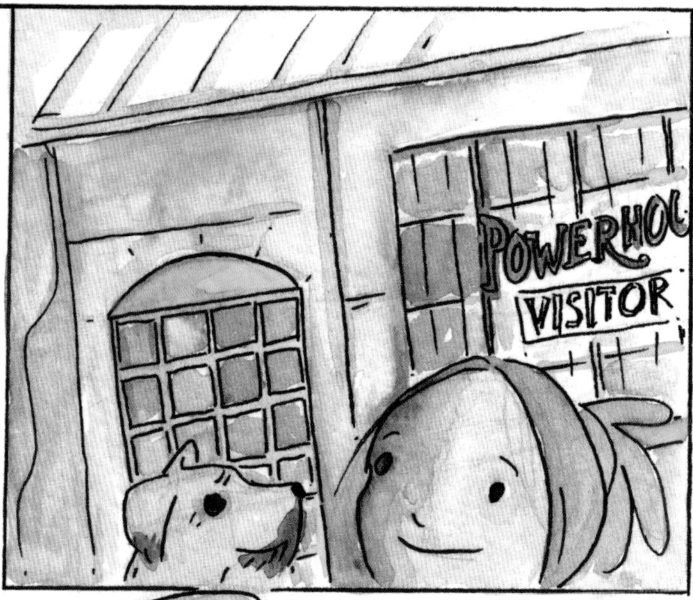
POWERHOU
VISITOR

The Powerhouse Visitor Center used to be an electrical substation. It is a Route 66 museum now.

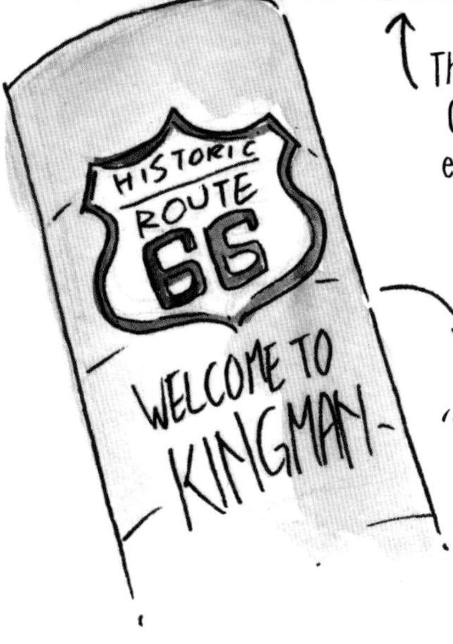
HISTORIC
ROUTE
66
WELCOME TO
KINGMAN

Kingman's motto is "The Heart of Historic Route 66."

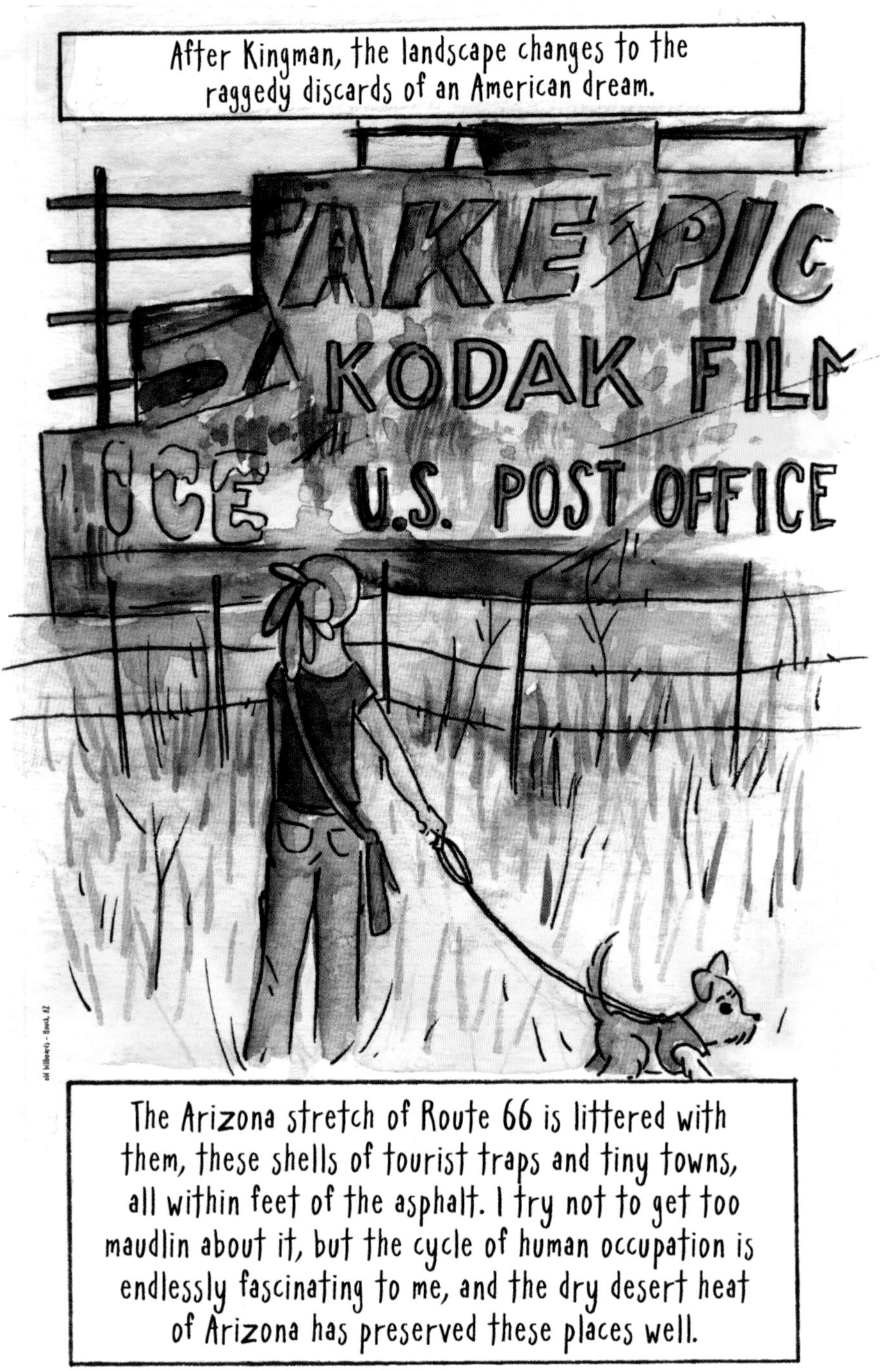
After Kingman, the landscape changes to the raggedy discards of an American dream.
AKE PIC
KODAK FIL
CE
U.S. POST OFFICE
old billboards – Houck, AZ
The Arizona stretch of Route 66 is littered with them, these shells of tourist traps and tiny towns, all within feet of the asphalt. I try not to get too maudlin about it, but the cycle of human occupation is endlessly fascinating to me, and the dry desert heat of Arizona has preserved these places well.

At Two Guns, an abandoned former campground and tourist attraction, I run into a biker, Bruce, and we explore the town together.

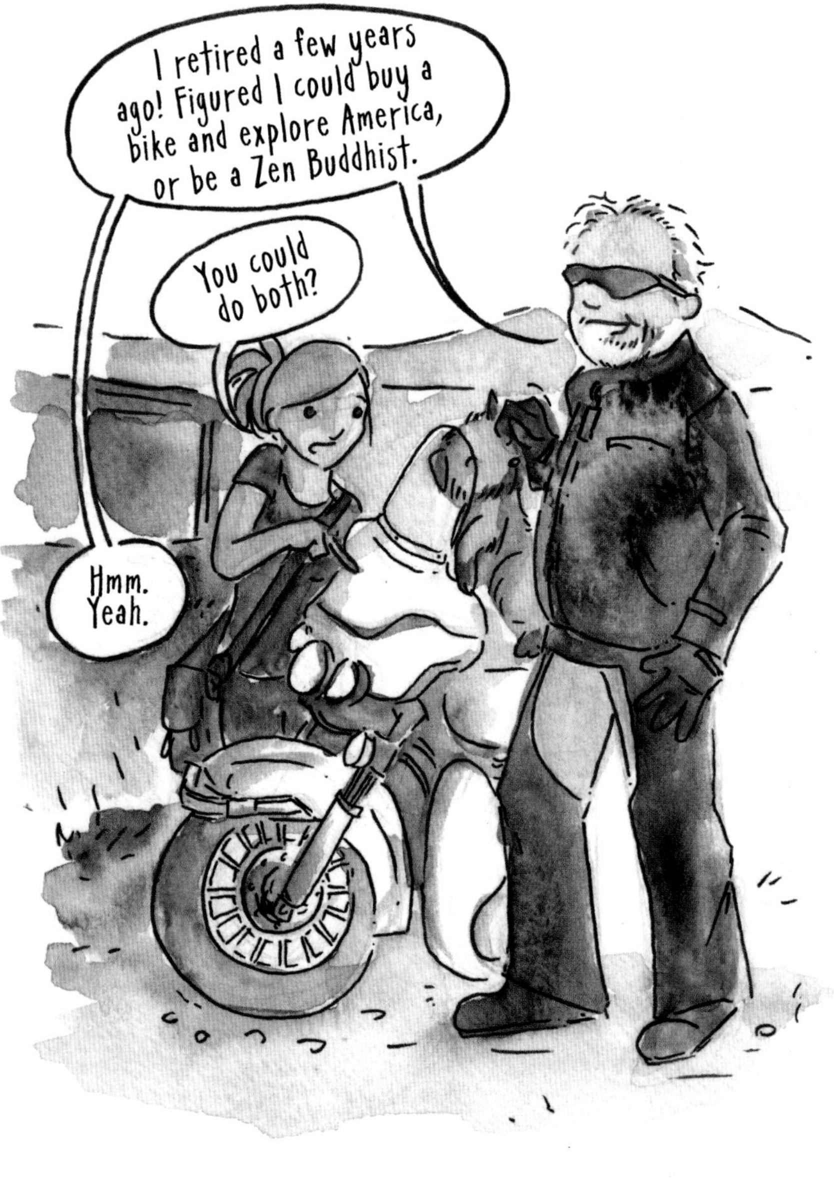
I retired a few years ago! Figured I could buy a bike and explore America, or be a Zen Buddhist.
You could do both?
Hmm. Yeah.

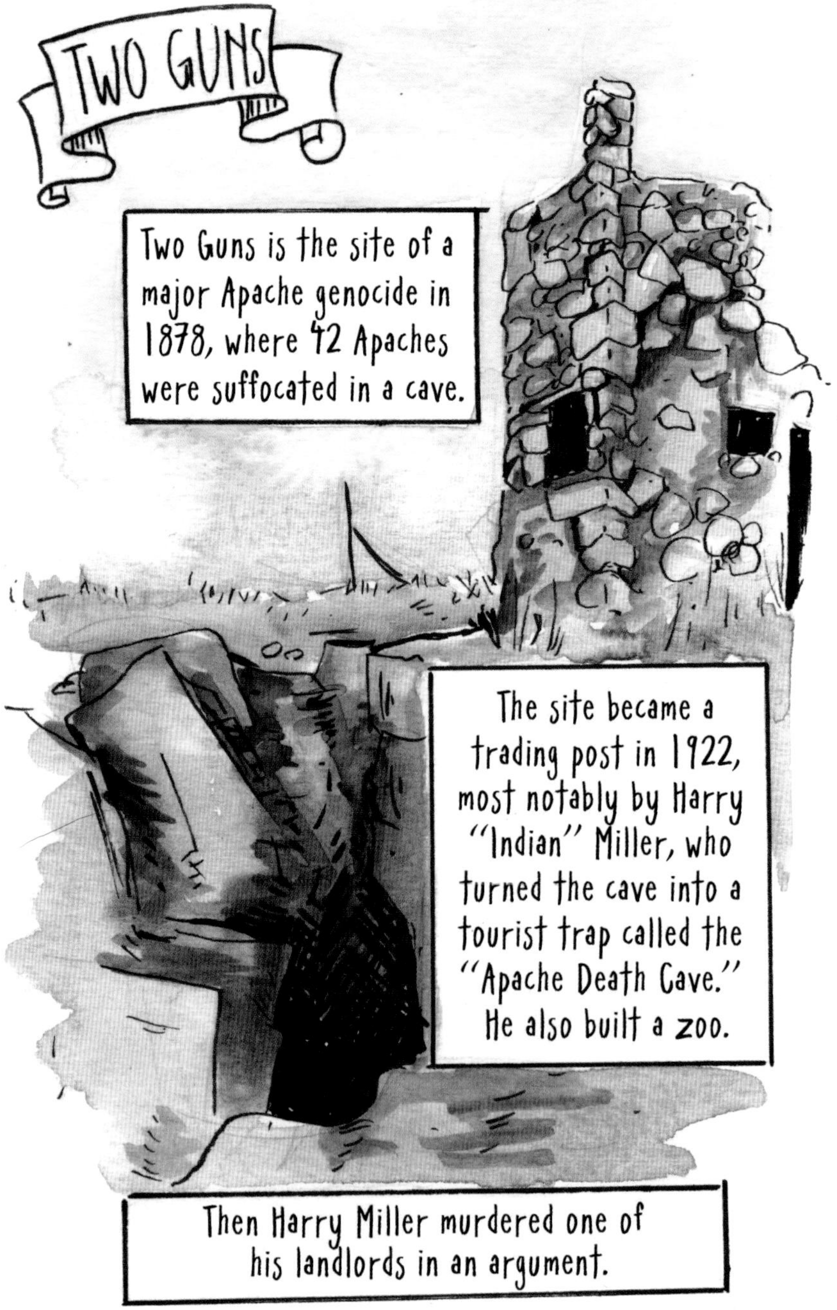
TWO GUNS
Two Guns is the site of a major Apache genocide in 1878, where 42 Apaches were suffocated in a cave.
The site became a trading post in 1922, most notably by Harry "Indian" Miller, who turned the cave into a tourist trap called the "Apache Death Cave." He also built a zoo.
Then Harry Miller murdered one of his landlords in an argument.

He was then attacked by his mountain lion, lynx, and Gila monster, and also had a slew of legal troubles.

Eventually, taking the hint, he left Two Guns in 1930.

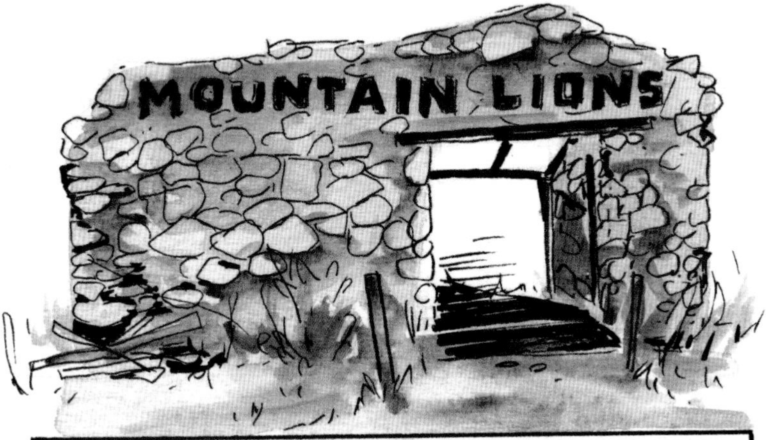
MOUNTAIN LIONS

Two Guns went on to live a varied life as a campground and rest stop, although the entire town caught fire in 1971. The last caretaker of the place died in 2000; the place is now abandoned.

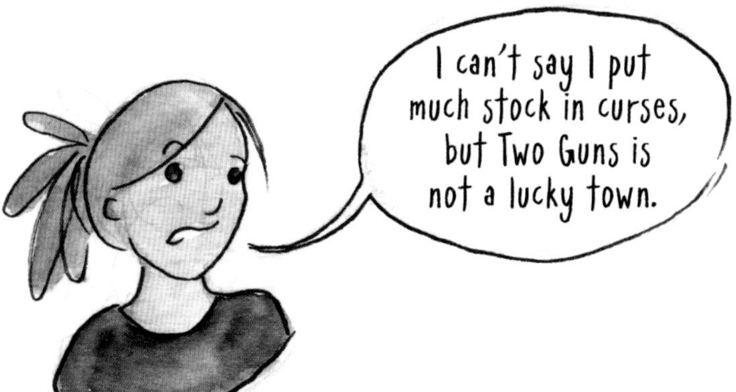
I can't say I put much stock in curses, but Two Guns is not a lucky town.

Indistinct shapes dance in my periphery and are never there when I look. I'm glad Bruce is here, because if there is a vengeful prowling beast of cursed souls past hanging around, he might get eaten first.

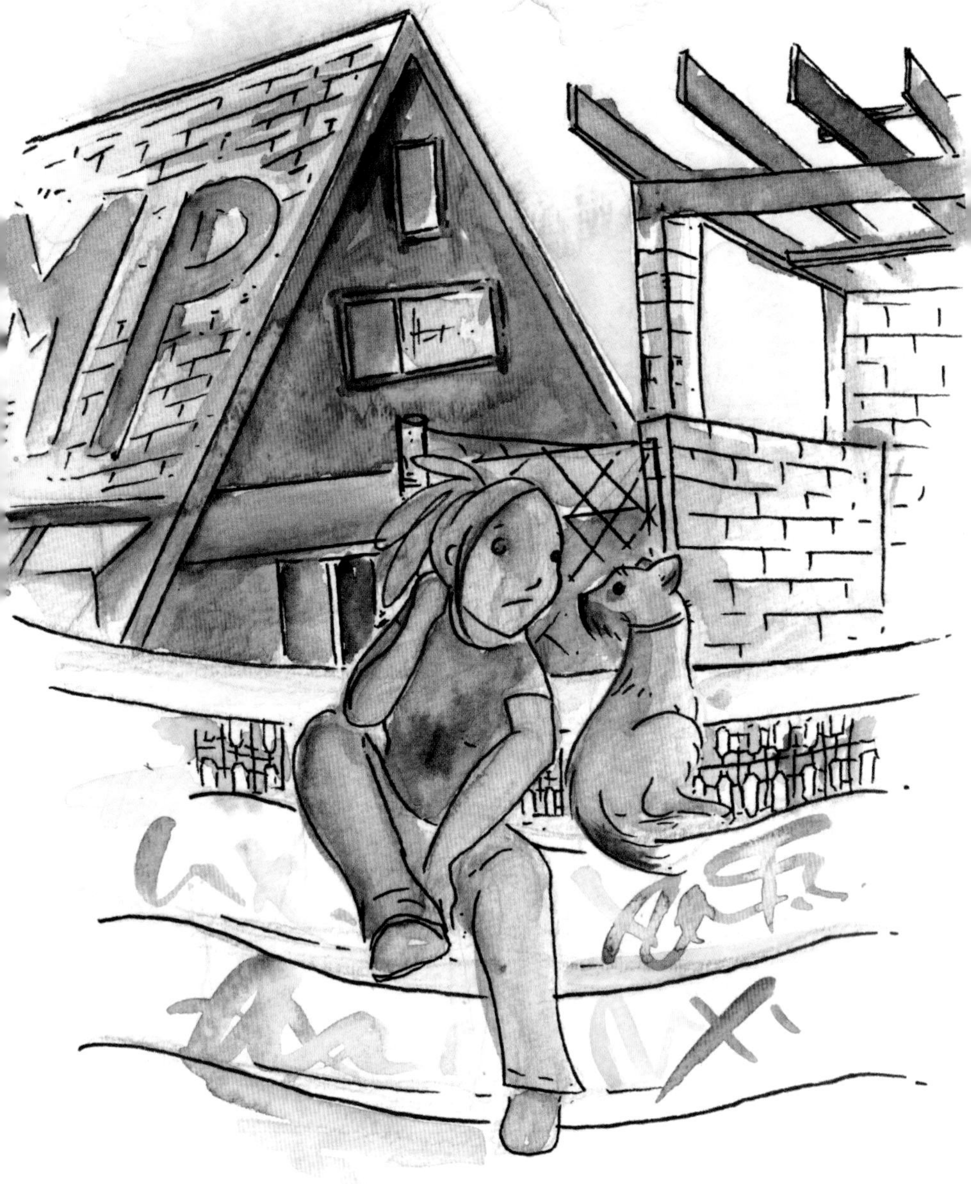

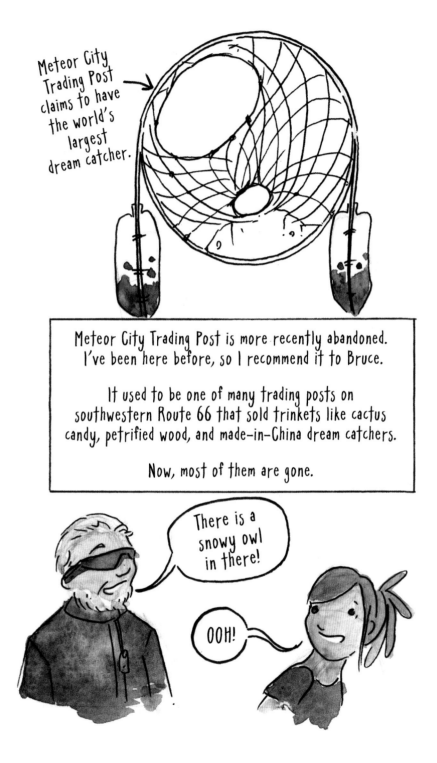

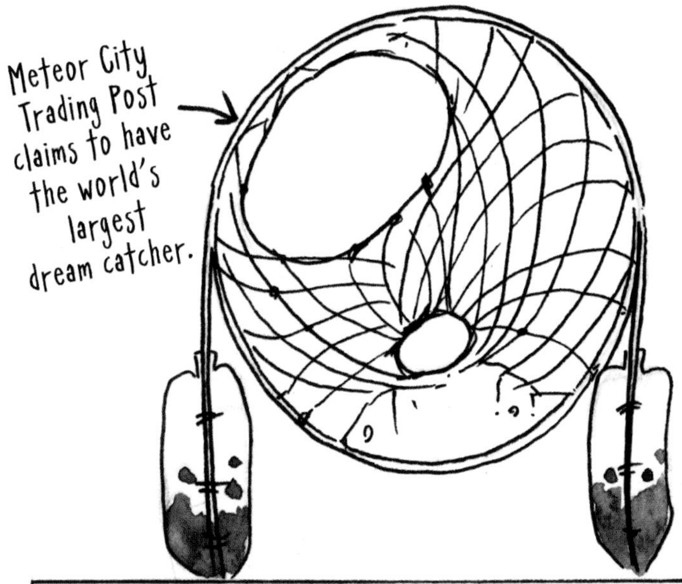
Meteor City Trading Post claims to have the world's largest dream catcher.

Meteor City Trading Post is more recently abandoned. I've been here before, so I recommend it to Bruce.

It used to be one of many trading posts on southwestern Route 66 that sold trinkets like cactus candy, petrified wood, and made-in-China dream catchers.

Now, most of them are gone.

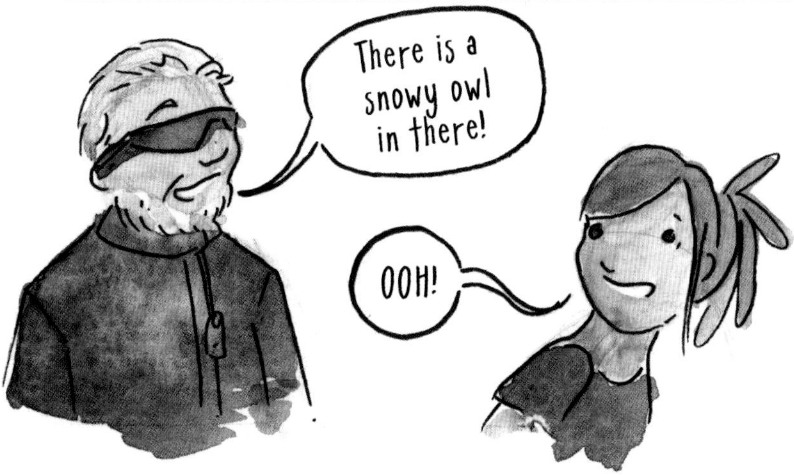
There is a snowy owl in there!
OOH!

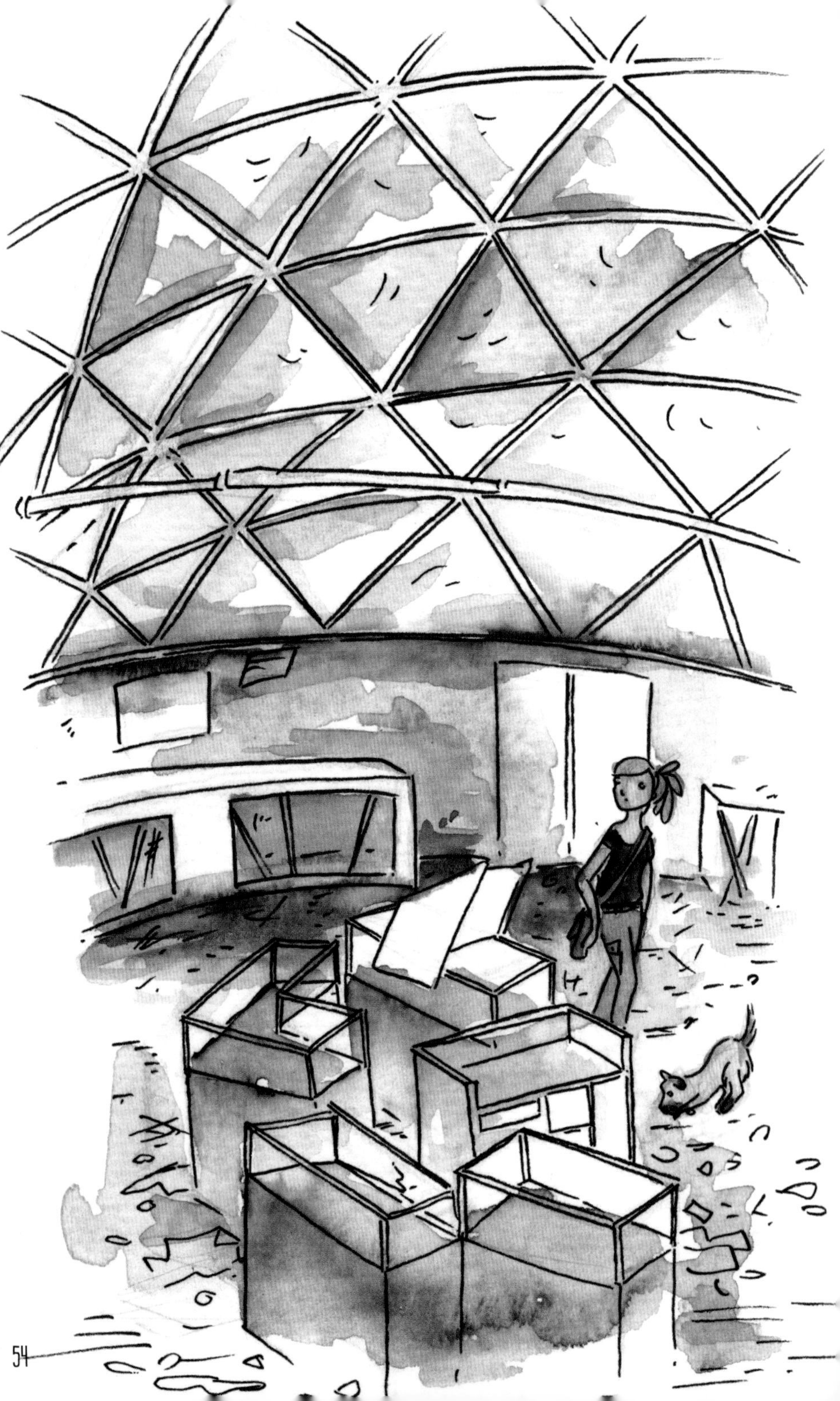

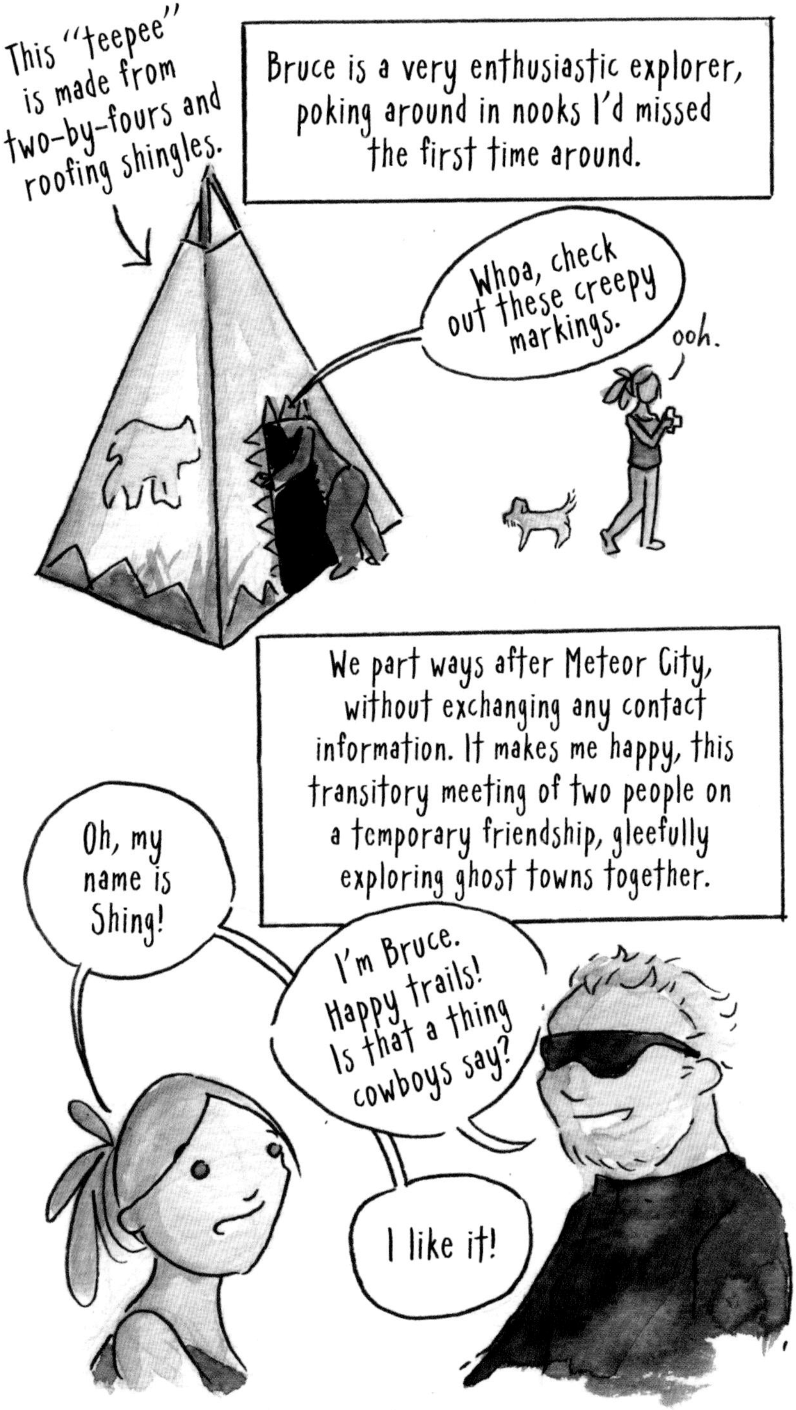

This "teepee" is made from two-by-fours and roofing shingles.
Bruce is a very enthusiastic explorer, poking around in nooks I'd missed the first time around.
Whoa, check out these creepy markings.
ooh.
We part ways after Meteor City, without exchanging any contact information. It makes me happy, this transitory meeting of two people on a temporary friendship, gleefully exploring ghost towns together.
Oh, my name is Shing!
I'm Bruce. Happy trails! Is that a thing cowboys say?
I like it!

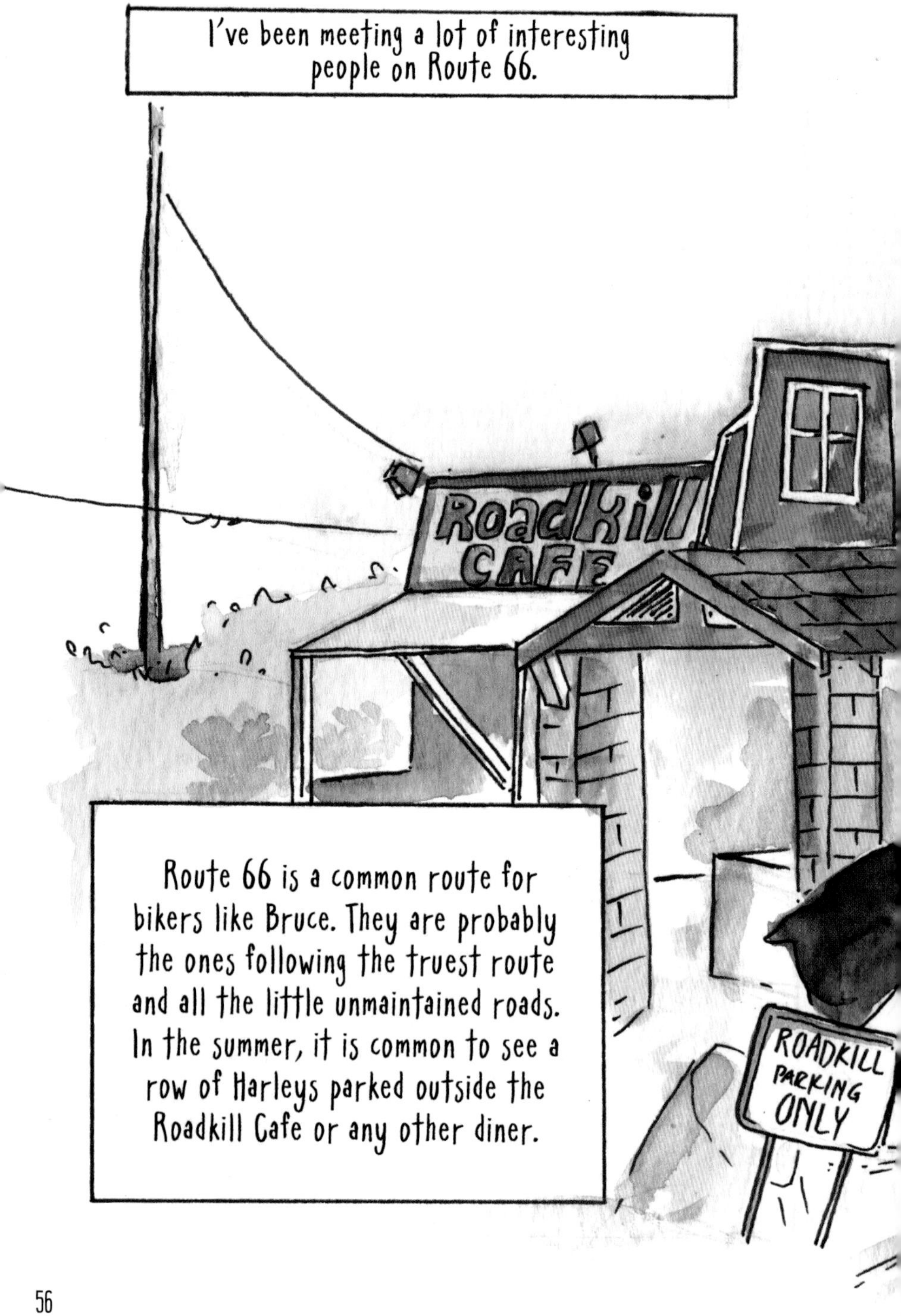
I've been meeting a lot of interesting people on Route 66.
RoadKill CAFE
Route 66 is a common route for bikers like Bruce. They are probably the ones following the truest route and all the little unmaintained roads. In the summer, it is common to see a row of Harleys parked outside the Roadkill Cafe or any other diner.
ROADKILL PARKING ONLY

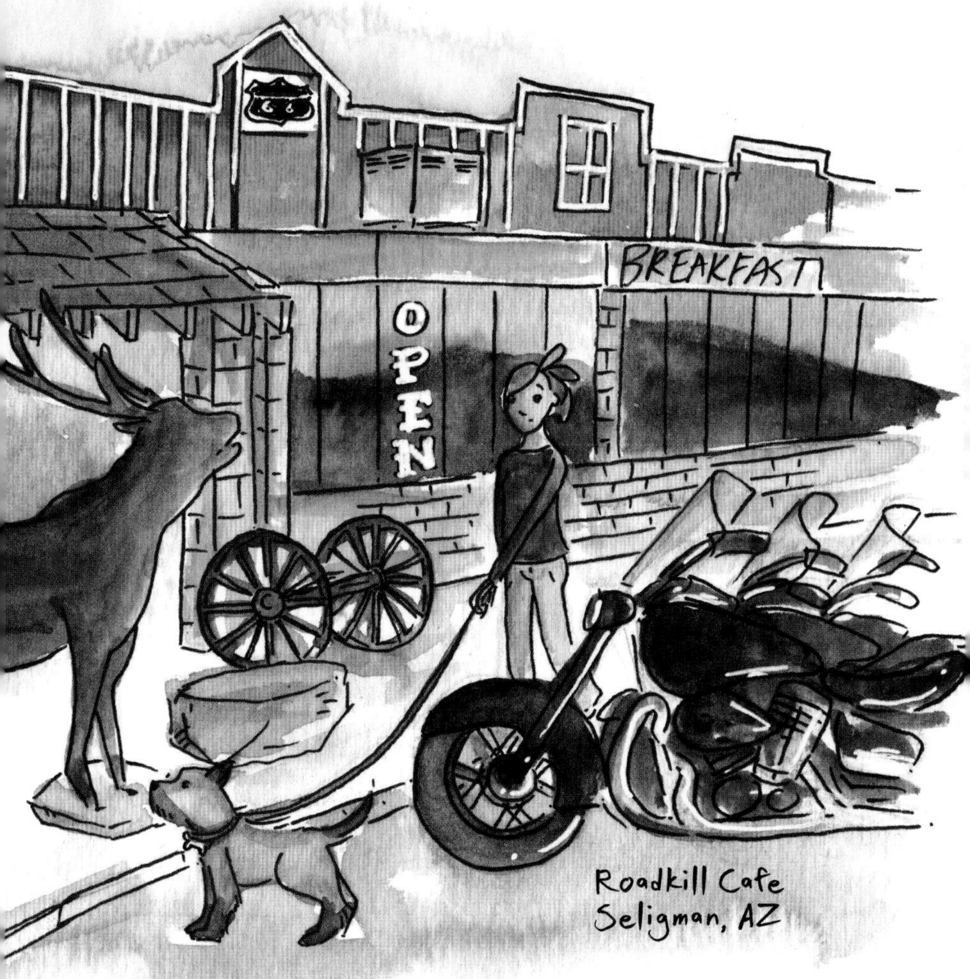

66
BREAKFAST
OPEN
Roadkill Cafe
Seligman, AZ

The route is also common among RVers, who are usually very nice. They are often retired older couples or families with good dogs.

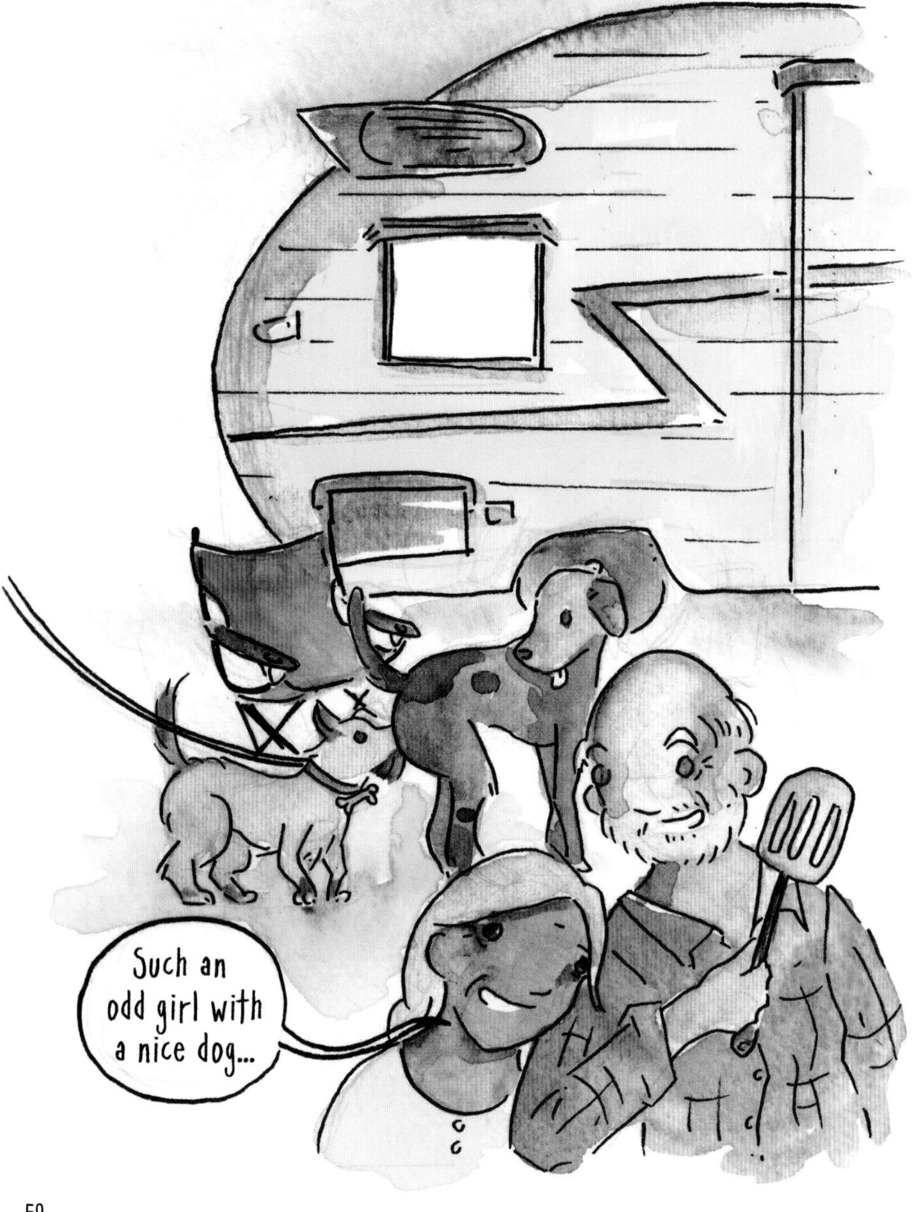
Such an odd girl with a nice dog...

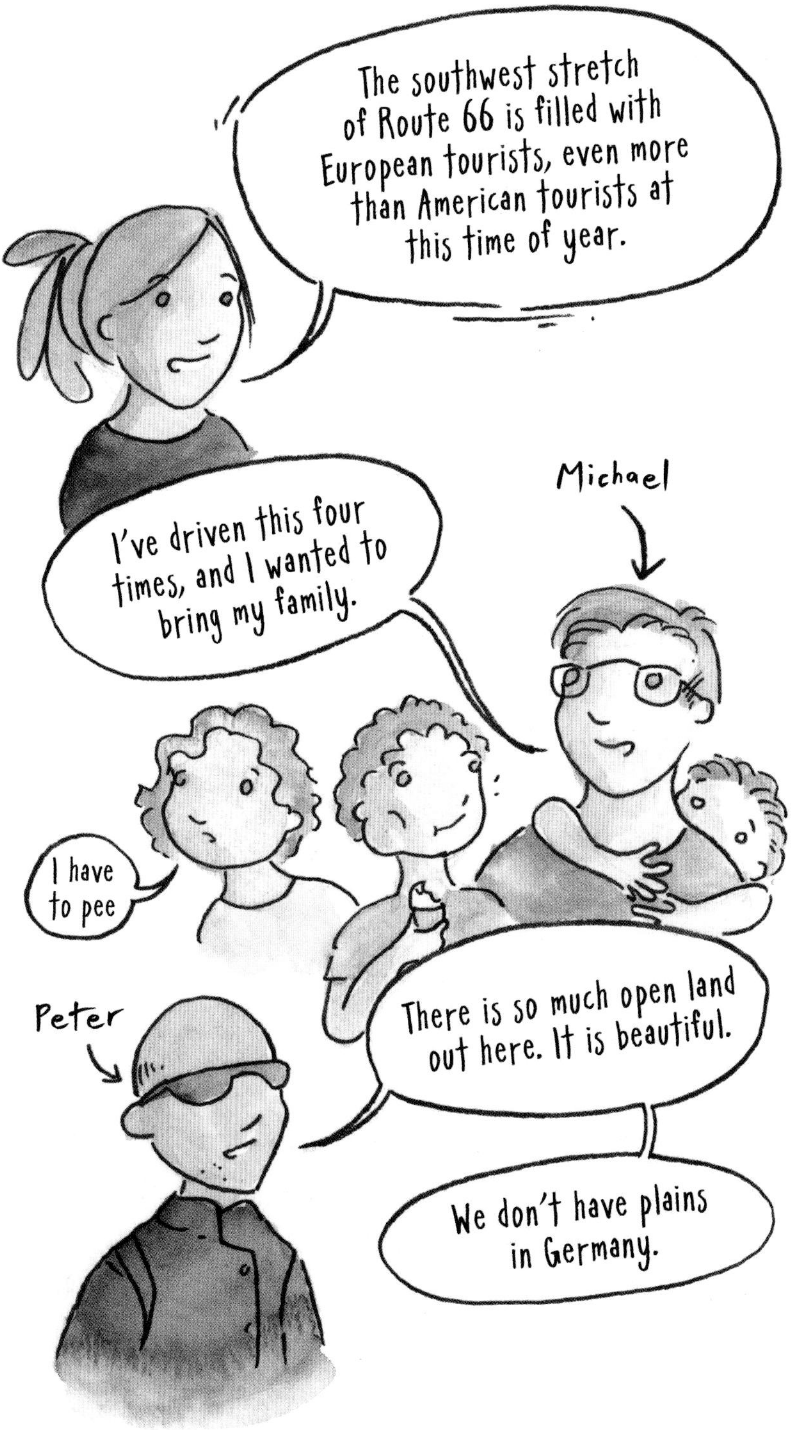
The southwest stretch of Route 66 is filled with European tourists, even more than American tourists at this time of year.
Michael
I've driven this four times, and I wanted to bring my family.
I have to pee
Peter
There is so much open land out here. It is beautiful.
We don't have plains in Germany.

And then there are the tour buses. They are large and air-conditioned and filled with people who really enjoy crowding around the Route 66 painted road markers for pictures.
Which is cute, except that this is an active road, and they are standing in the middle of it.

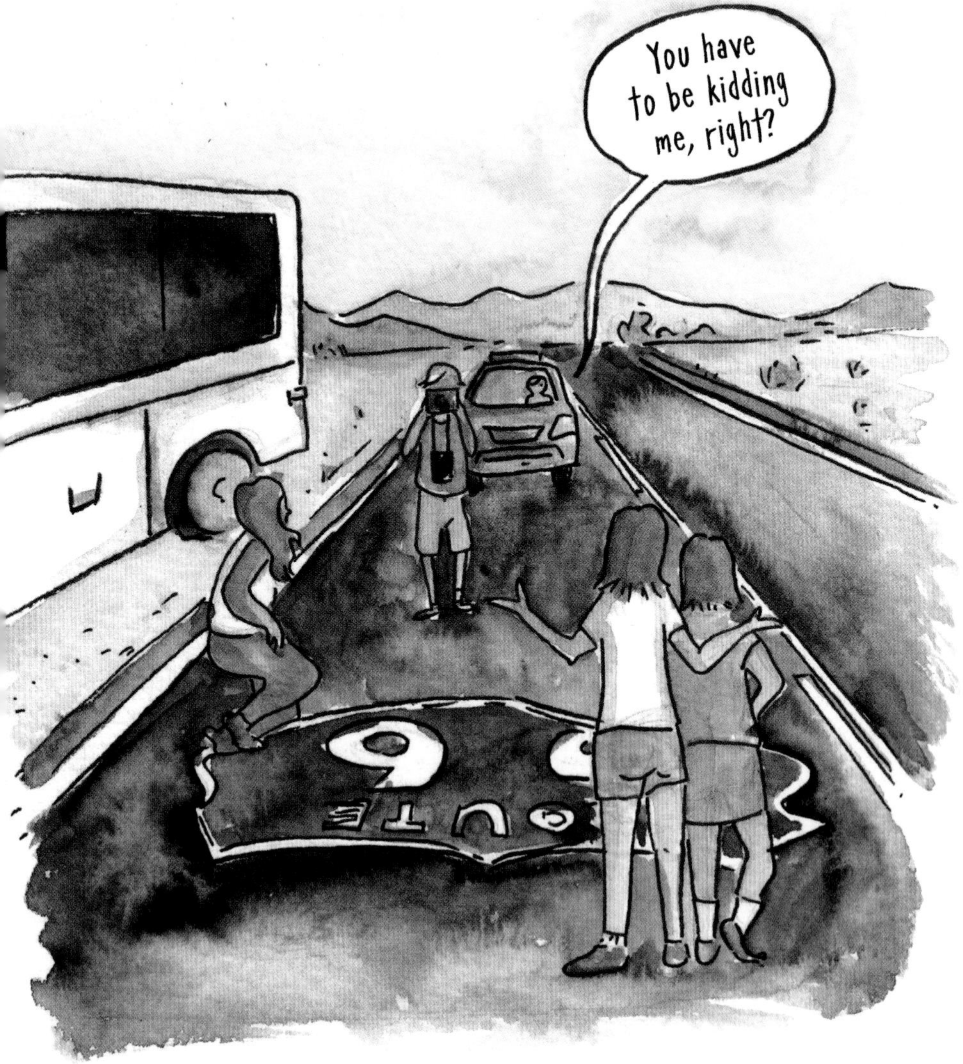
You have to be kidding me, right?
ROUTE 66

It is pretty annoying, but I am not comfortable with the false distinction between tourist and traveler.

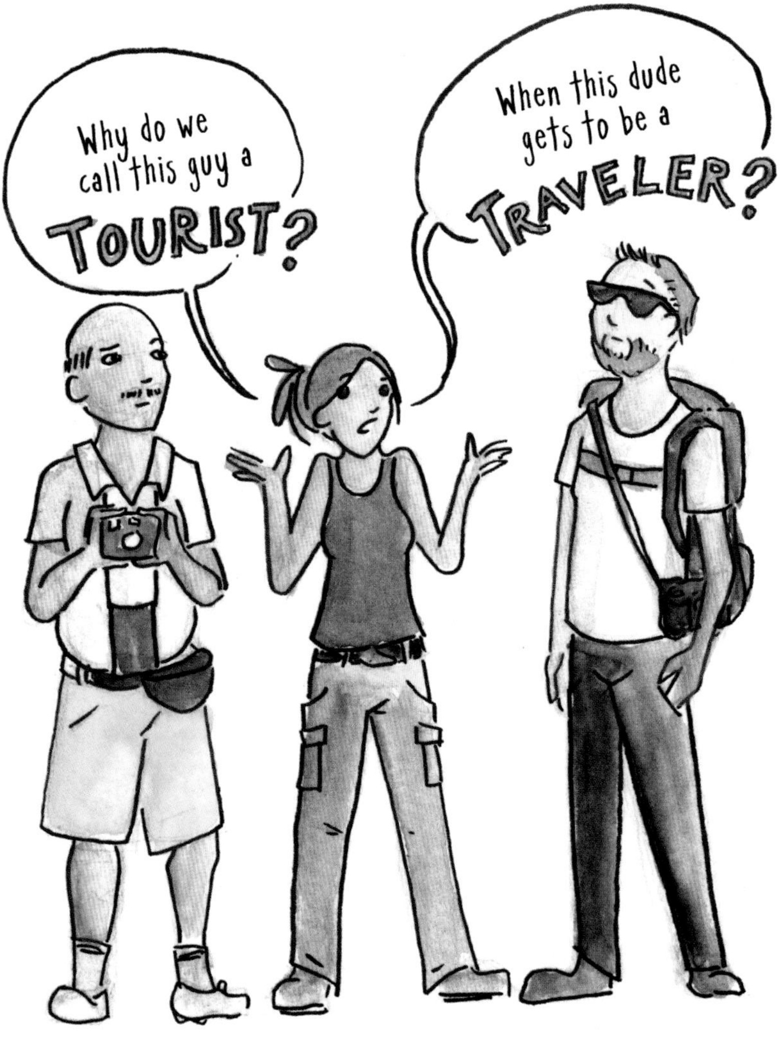
Why do we call this guy a TOURIST?
When this dude gets to be a TRAVELER?

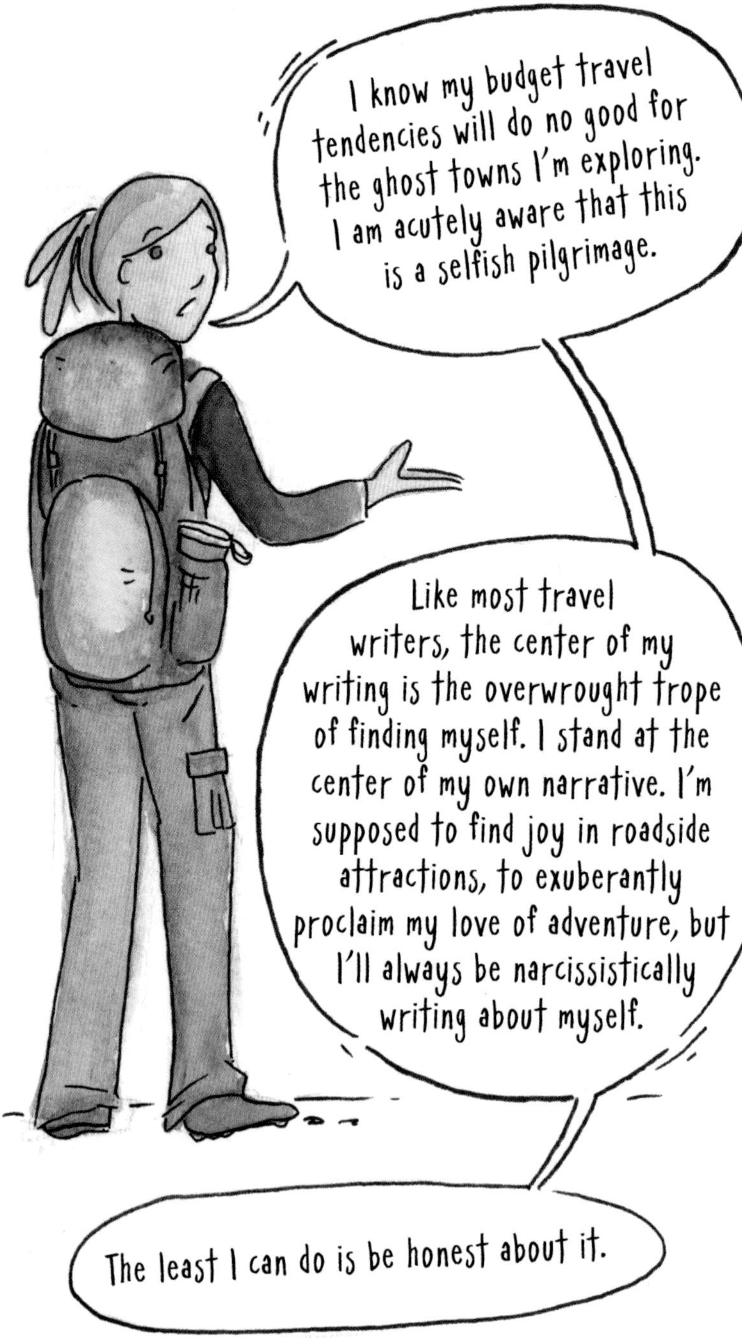
I know my budget travel tendencies will do no good for the ghost towns I'm exploring. I am acutely aware that this is a selfish pilgrimage.
Like most travel writers, the center of my writing is the overwrought trope of finding myself. I stand at the center of my own narrative. I'm supposed to find joy in roadside attractions, to exuberantly proclaim my love of adventure, but I'll always be narcissistically writing about myself.
The least I can do is be honest about it.

While I'm busy being excited about decay and deliberately overthinking the nature of tourism, Arizona is busy preserving its Route 66 history. Seligman, AZ, has an especially enthusiastic embrace of Route 66 kitsch.

The popularity of Disney's *Cars* has also resulted in some adaptation to that cartoonish aesthetic...

Snow Cap Drive-in
Seligman, AZ

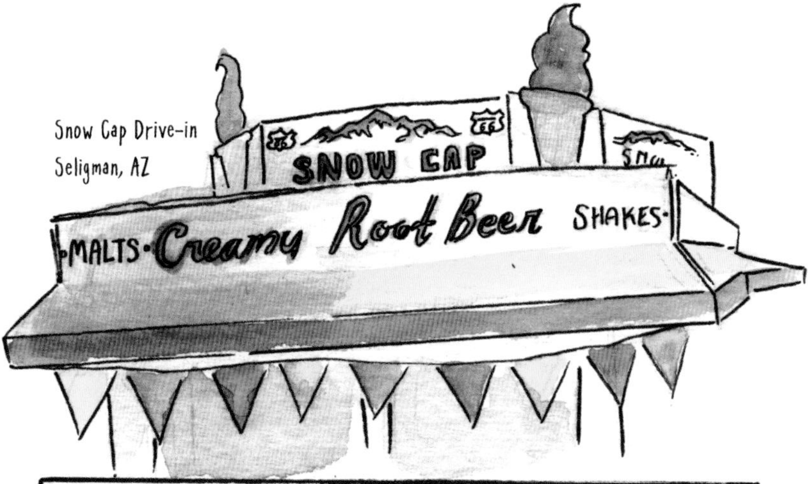
SNOW CAP
MALTS · Creamy Root Beer SHAKES ·

...the effect is actually slightly ghoulish.

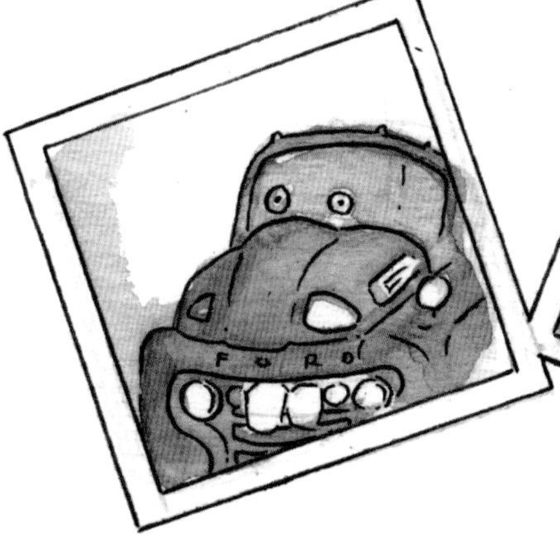
F O R D

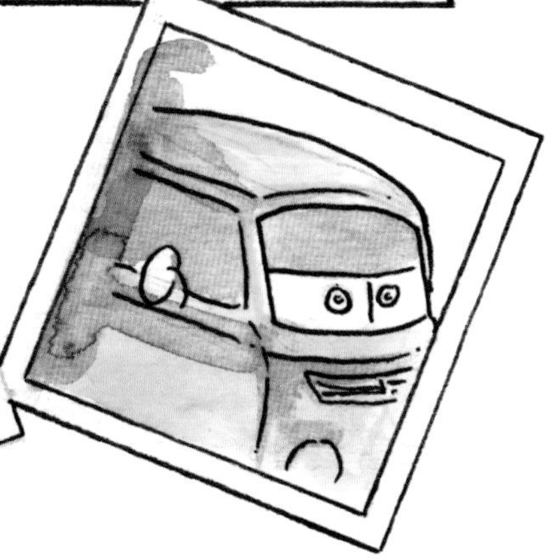

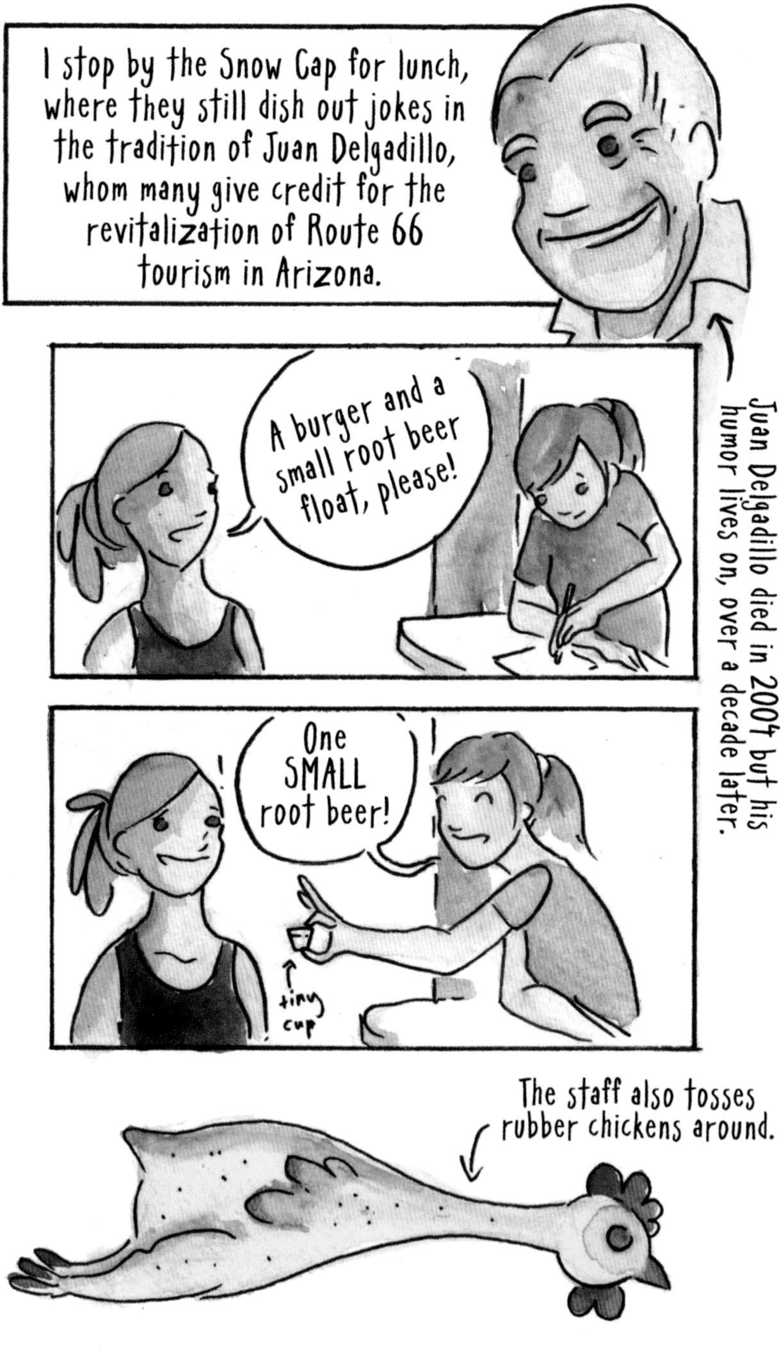
I stop by the Snow Cap for lunch, where they still dish out jokes in the tradition of Juan Delgadillo, whom many give credit for the revitalization of Route 66 tourism in Arizona.
Juan Delgadillo died in 2004 but his humor lives on, over a decade later.
A burger and a small root beer float, please!
One SMALL root beer!
tiny cup
The staff also tosses rubber chickens around.

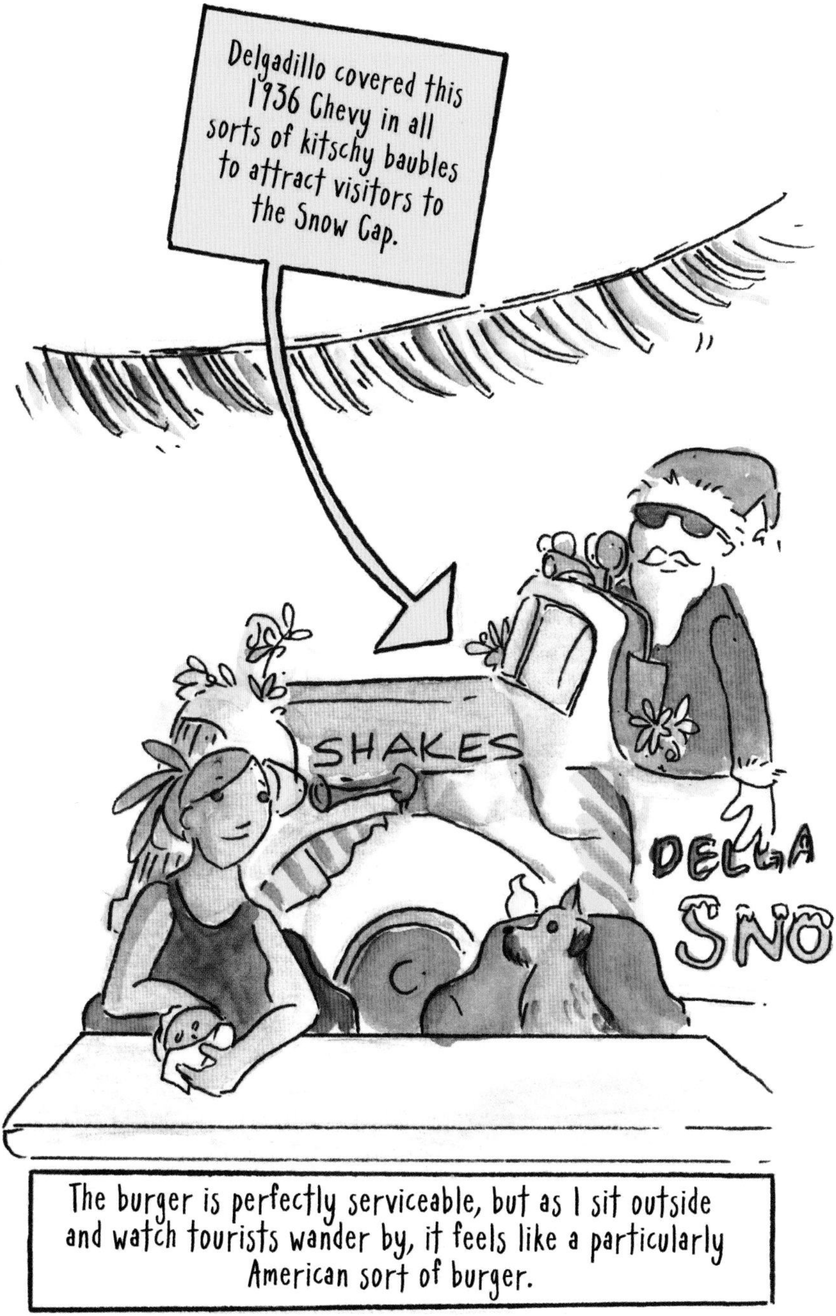
Delgadillo covered this 1936 Chevy in all sorts of kitschy baubles to attract visitors to the Snow Cap.
SHAKES
DELGA
SNO
The burger is perfectly serviceable, but as I sit outside and watch tourists wander by, it feels like a particularly American sort of burger.

I take a small detour to visit my friends Royce and Nita, artists who live near Prescott, Arizona. Bug visits her first creek!

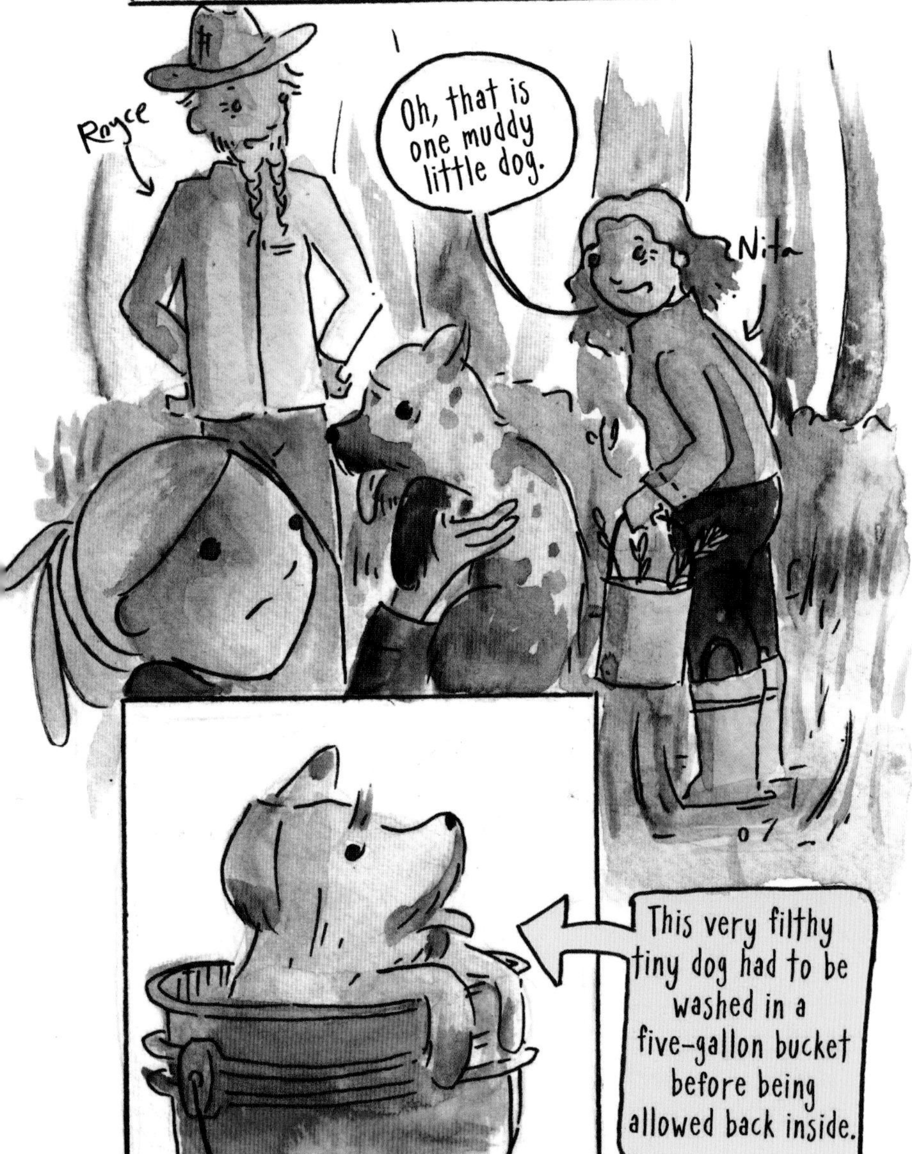
Royce
Oh, that is one muddy little dog.
Nita
This very filthy tiny dog had to be washed in a five-gallon bucket before being allowed back inside.

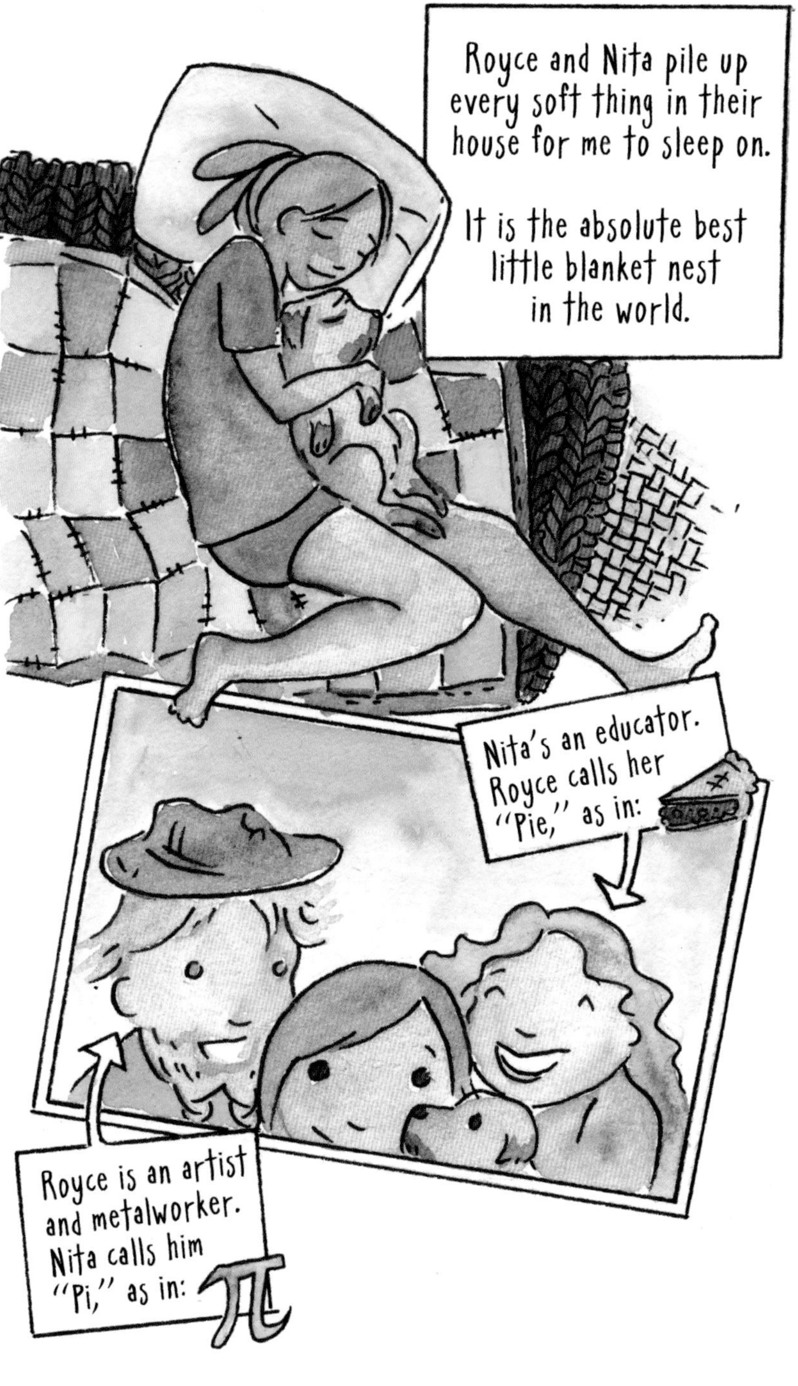
Royce and Nita pile up every soft thing in their house for me to sleep on.
It is the absolute best little blanket nest in the world.
Nita's an educator. Royce calls her "Pie," as in:
Royce is an artist and metalworker. Nita calls him "Pi," as in:
π

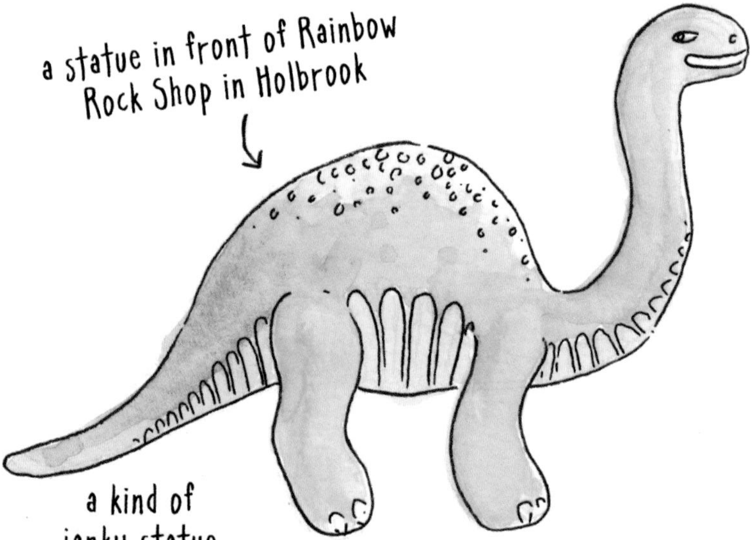
a statue in front of Rainbow Rock Shop in Holbrook

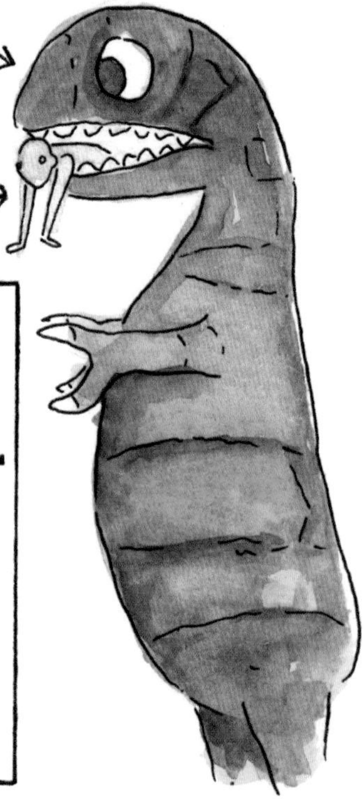
a kind of janky statue at Stewart's Petrified Wood in Holbrook
poor mannequin

*take me back to* DINOSAUR CITY

# HOLBROOK, AZ

One of my favorite things about Arizona is the panoply of roadside dinosaur statues!

Some are handmade.

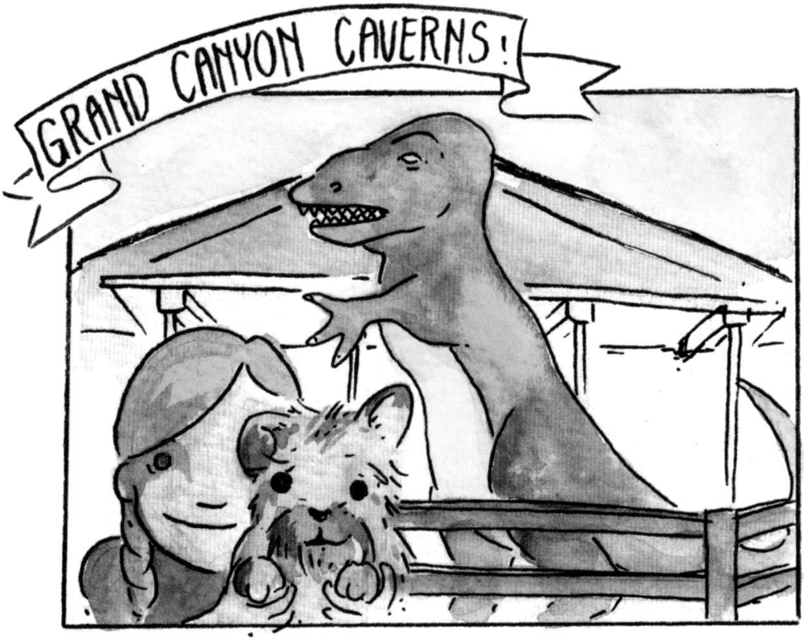
GRAND CANYON CAVERNS!

Peach Springs, AZ

The statues are almost all inaccurate, and
most of these dinosaurs were definitely
not discovered in Arizona.

I'm still a total sucker for their ridiculousness.

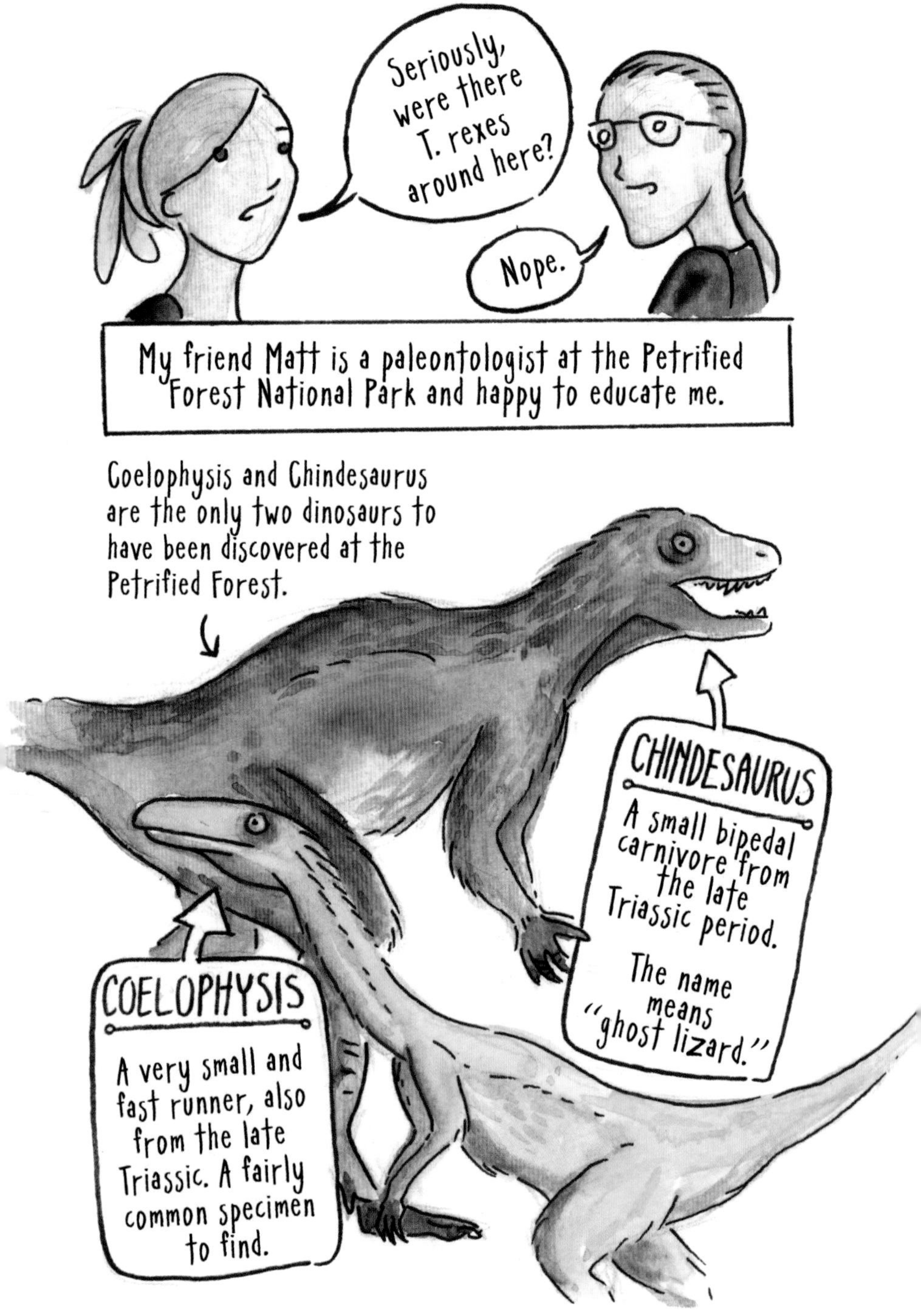
Seriously, were there T. rexes around here?
Nope.
My friend Matt is a paleontologist at the Petrified Forest National Park and happy to educate me.
Coelophysis and Chindesaurus are the only two dinosaurs to have been discovered at the Petrified Forest.
CHINDESAURUS
A small bipedal carnivore from the late Triassic period.
The name means "ghost lizard."
COELOPHYSIS
A very small and fast runner, also from the late Triassic. A fairly common specimen to find.

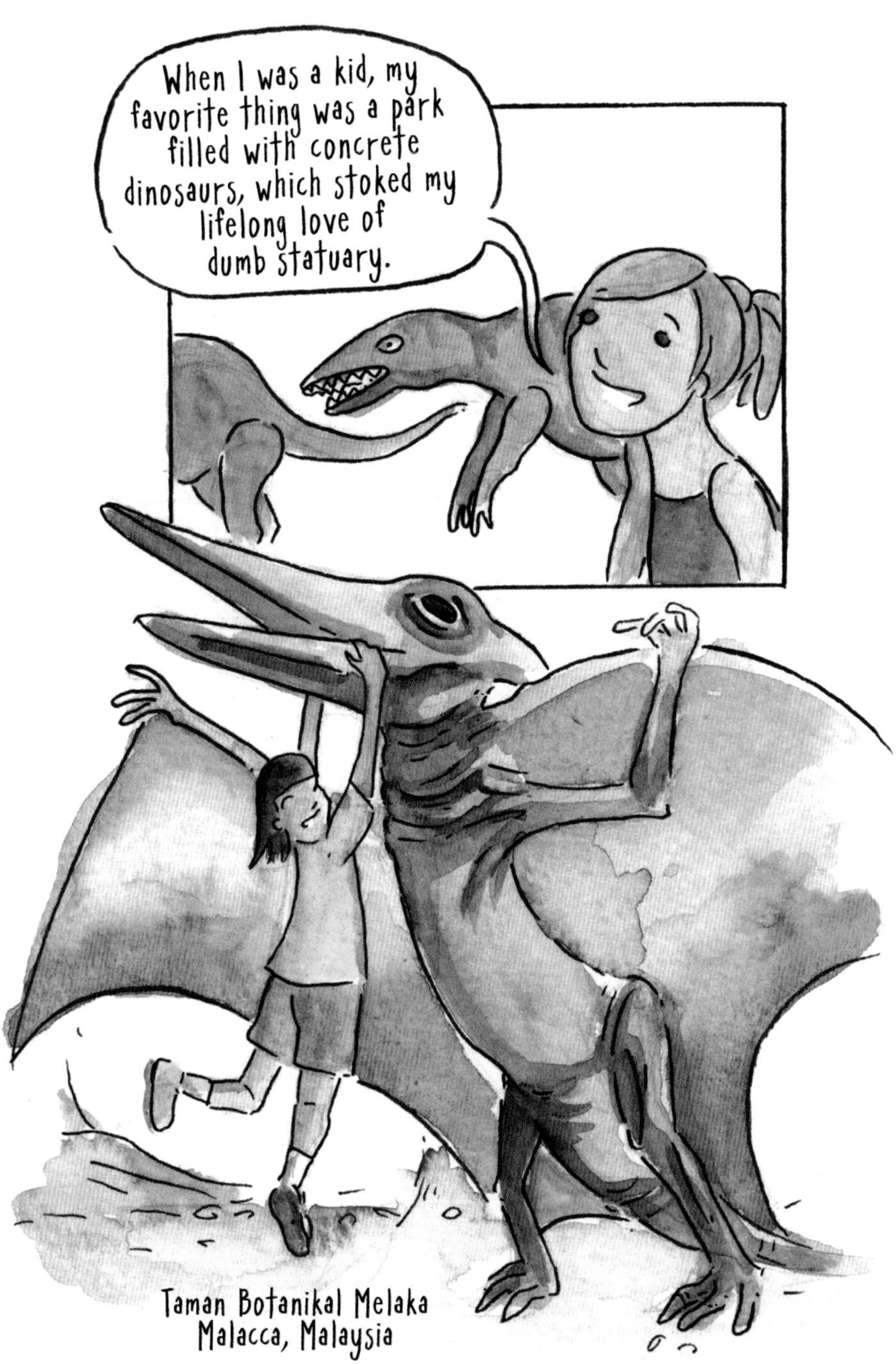
When I was a kid, my favorite thing was a park filled with concrete dinosaurs, which stoked my lifelong love of dumb statuary.
Taman Botanikal Melaka
Malacca, Malaysia

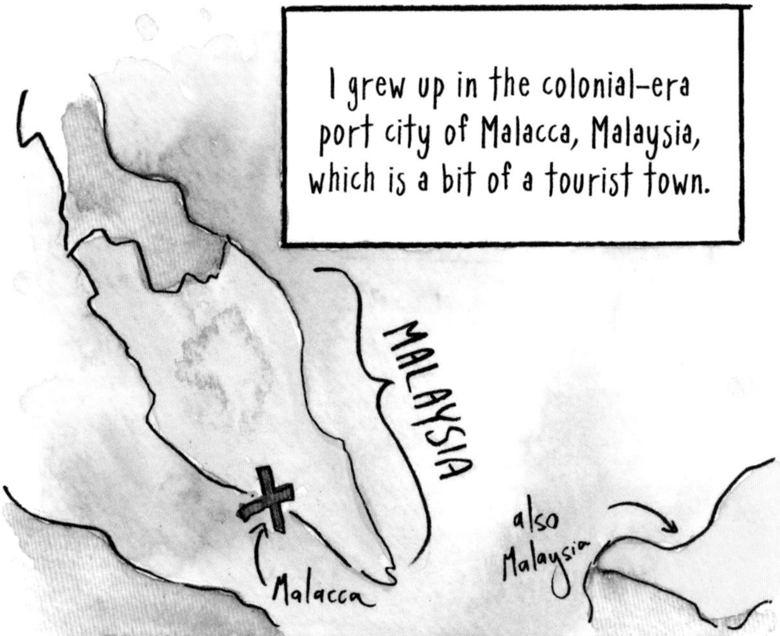
I grew up in the colonial-era port city of Malacca, Malaysia, which is a bit of a tourist town.
MALAYSIA
Malacca
also Malaysia

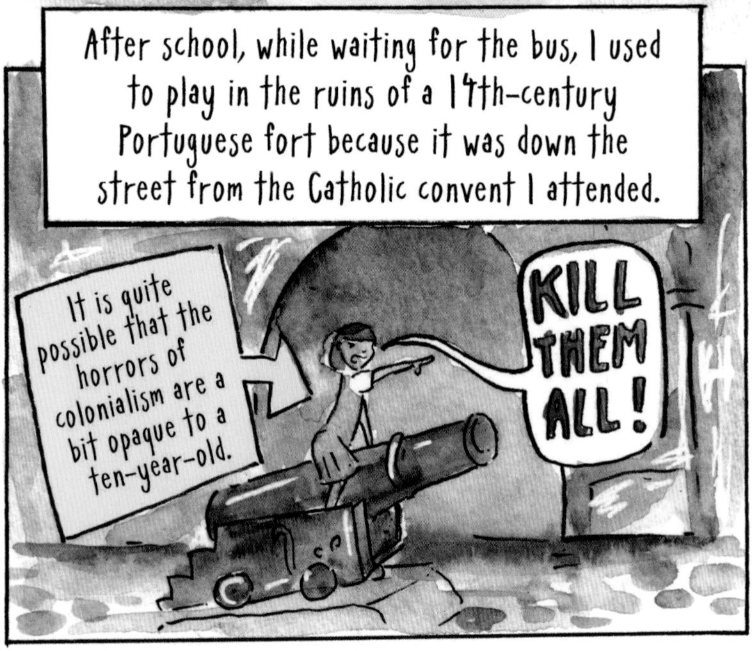
After school, while waiting for the bus, I used to play in the ruins of a 14th-century Portuguese fort because it was down the street from the Catholic convent I attended.
It is quite possible that the horrors of colonialism are a bit opaque to a ten-year-old.
KILL THEM ALL!

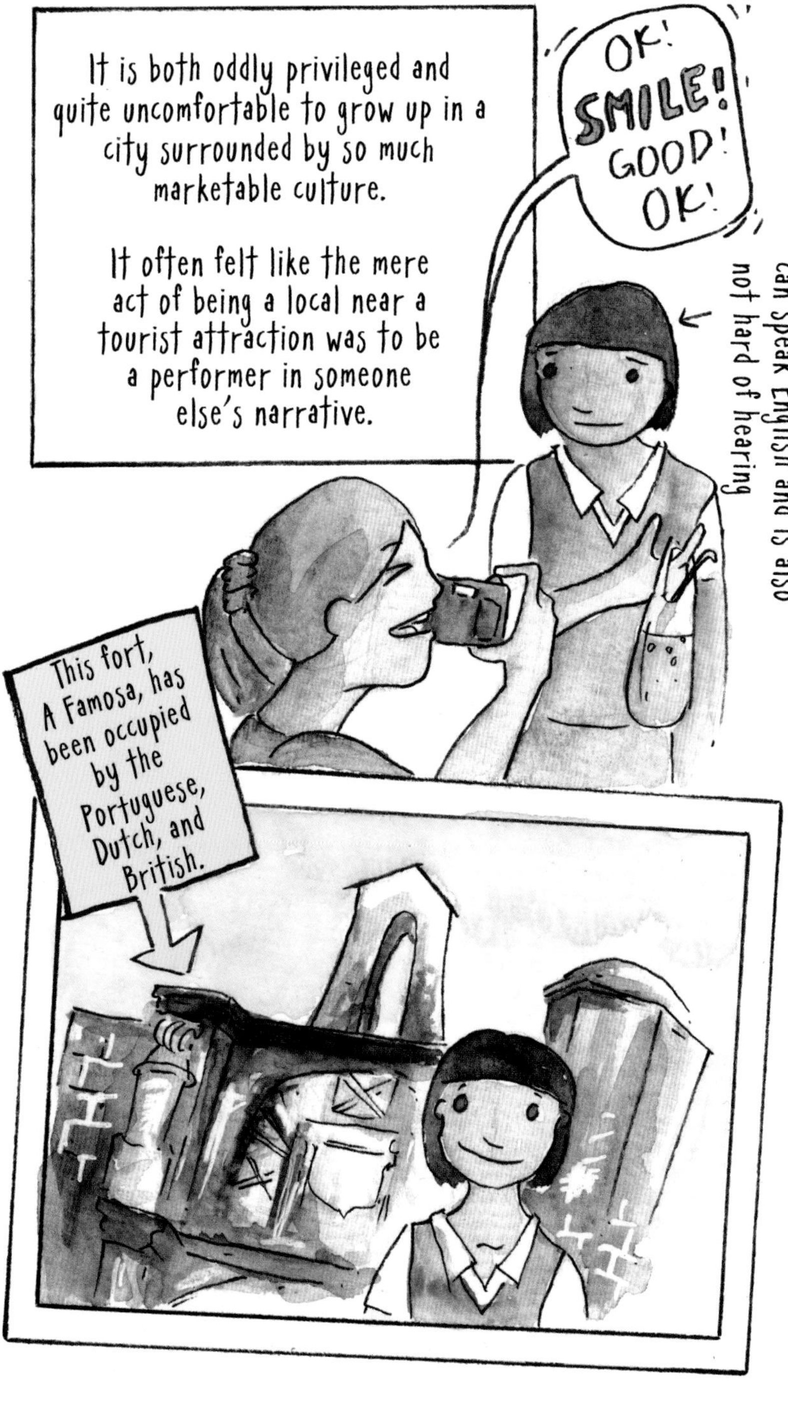
It is both oddly privileged and quite uncomfortable to grow up in a city surrounded by so much marketable culture.
It often felt like the mere act of being a local near a tourist attraction was to be a performer in someone else's narrative.
OK! SMILE! GOOD! OK!
can speak English and is also not hard of hearing
This fort, A Famosa, has been occupied by the Portuguese, Dutch, and British.

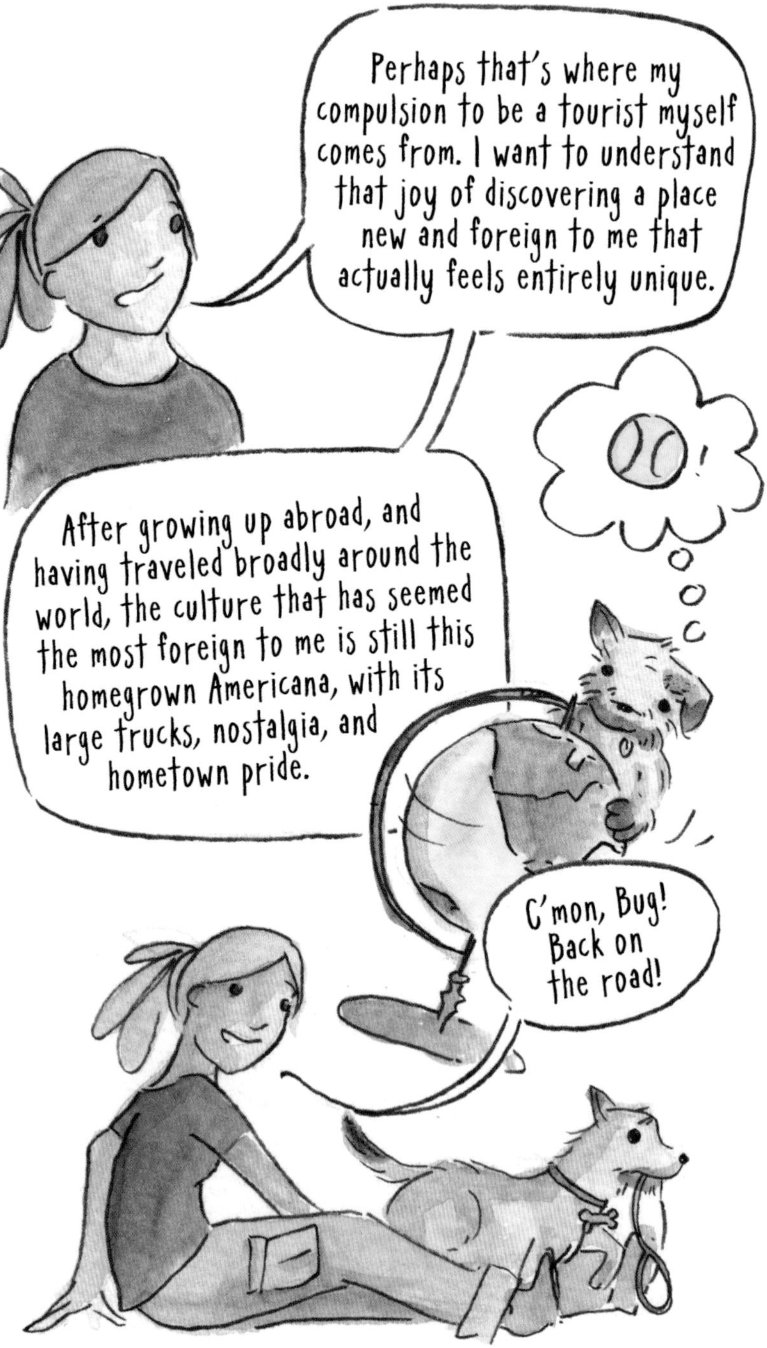
Perhaps that's where my compulsion to be a tourist myself comes from. I want to understand that joy of discovering a place new and foreign to me that actually feels entirely unique.
After growing up abroad, and having traveled broadly around the world, the culture that has seemed the most foreign to me is still this homegrown Americana, with its large trucks, nostalgia, and hometown pride.
!
C'mon, Bug! Back on the road!

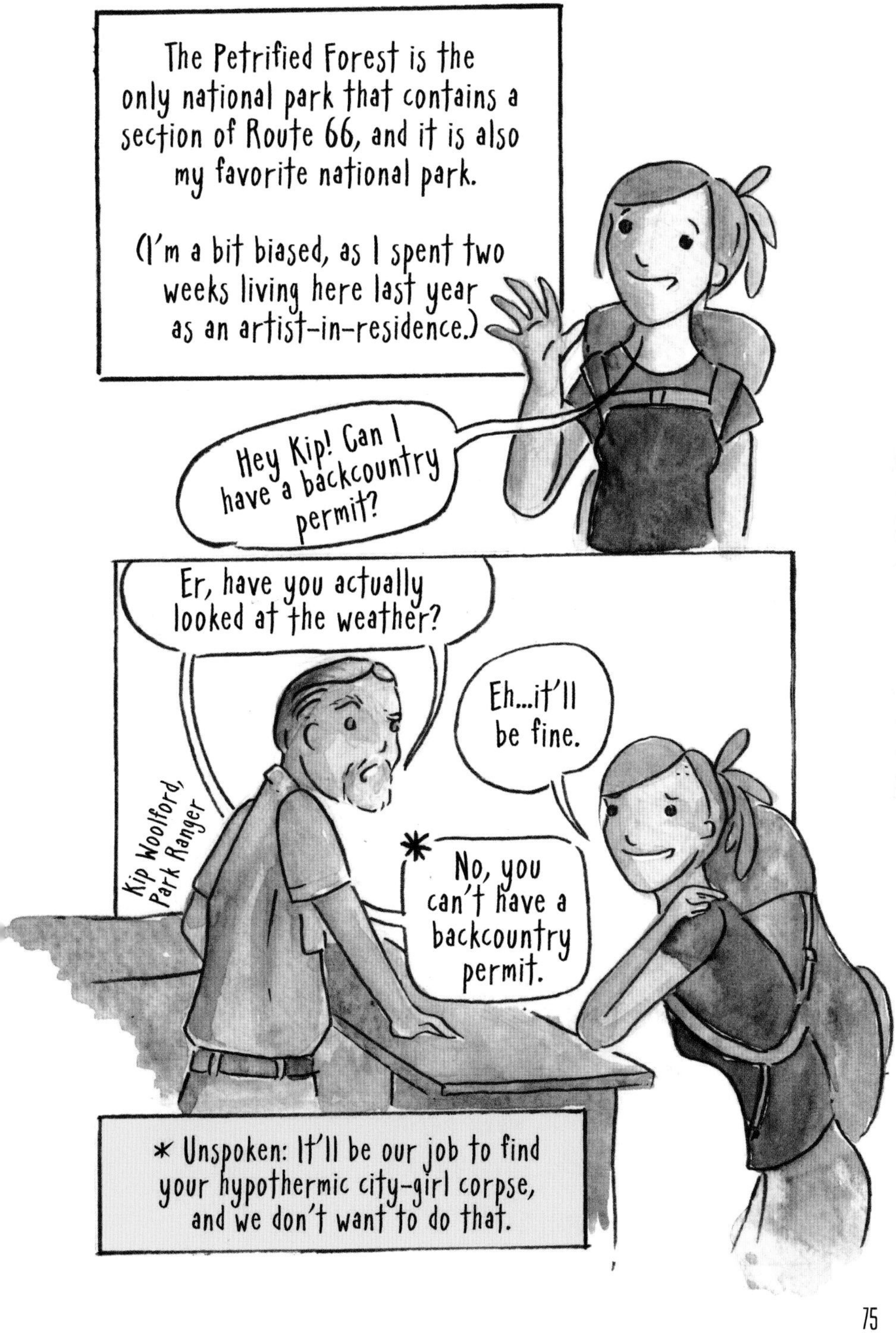

The Petrified Forest is the only national park that contains a section of Route 66, and it is also my favorite national park.
(I'm a bit biased, as I spent two weeks living here last year as an artist-in-residence.)
Hey Kip! Can I have a backcountry permit?
Er, have you actually looked at the weather?
Eh...it'll be fine.
Kip Woolford, Park Ranger
* No, you can't have a backcountry permit.
* Unspoken: It'll be our job to find your hypothermic city-girl corpse, and we don't want to do that.

I pay a visit to Bill Parker, the Chief of Science at the Petrified Forest. He's a paleontologist by training and a historian by passion, and he loves the park.

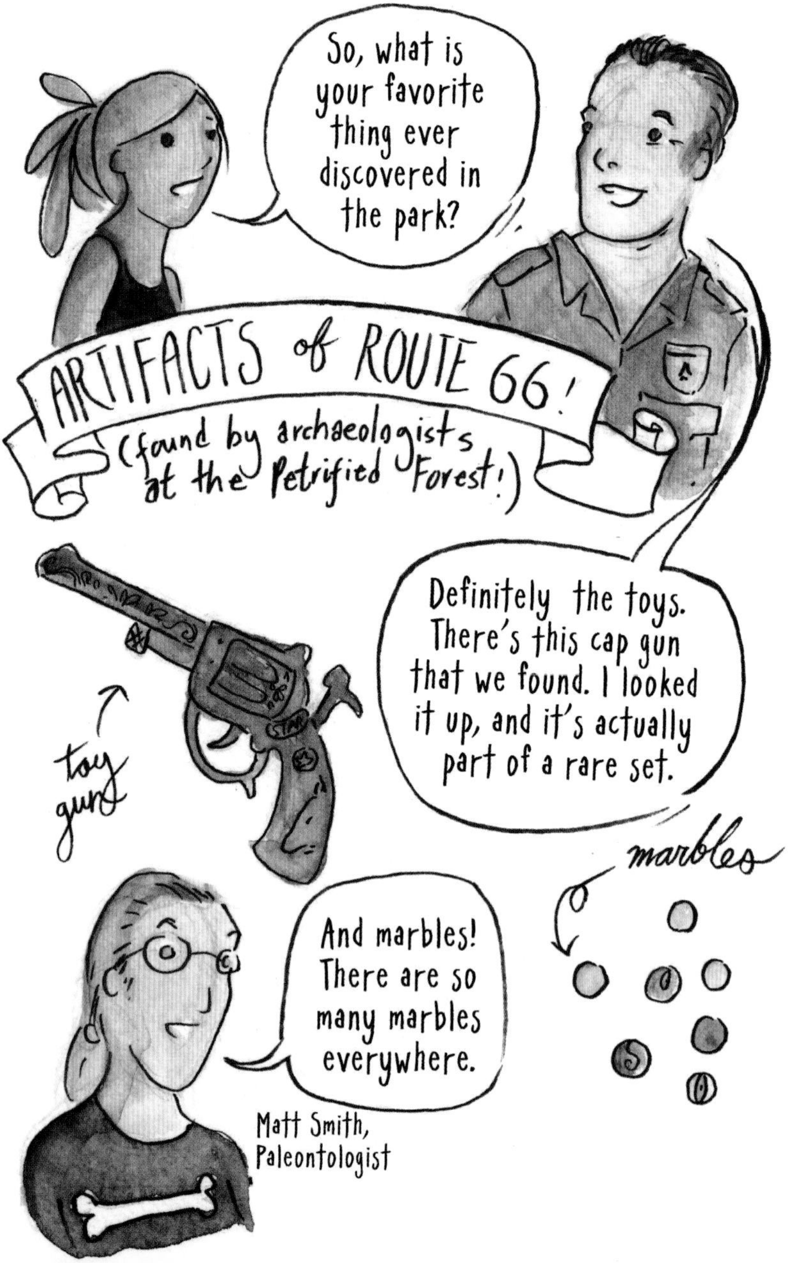
So, what is your favorite thing ever discovered in the park?
ARTIFACTS of ROUTE 66!
(found by archaeologists at the Petrified Forest!)
Definitely the toys. There's this cap gun that we found. I looked it up, and it's actually part of a rare set.
toy gun
STAR
marbles
And marbles! There are so many marbles everywhere.
Matt Smith, Paleontologist

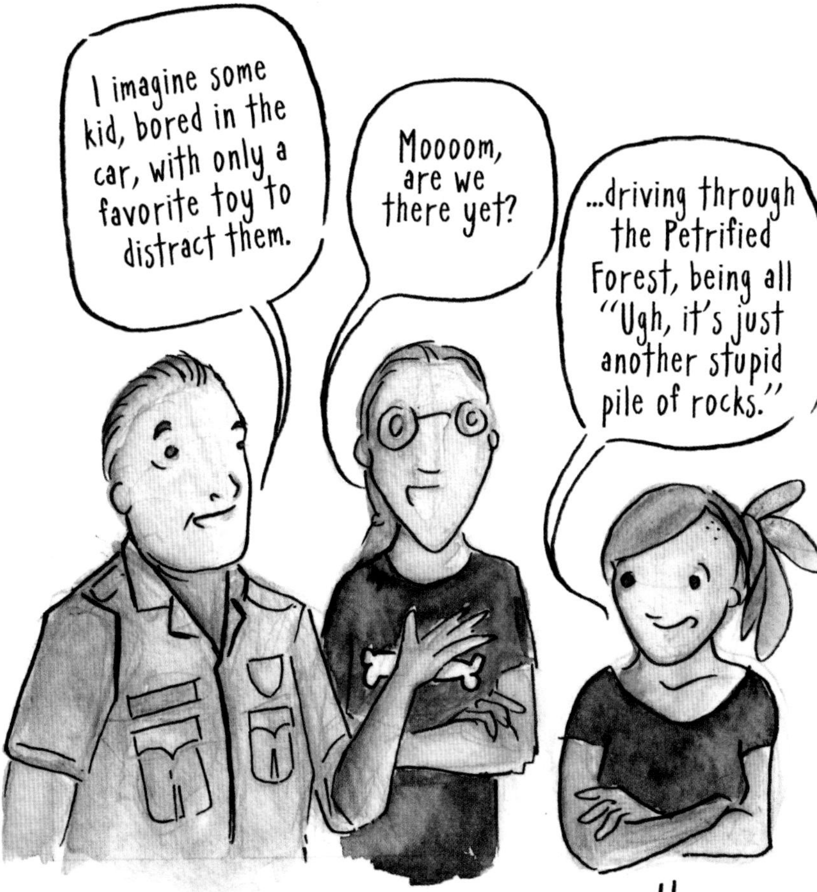
I imagine some kid, bored in the car, with only a favorite toy to distract them.
Moooom, are we there yet?
...driving through the Petrified Forest, being all "Ugh, it's just another stupid pile of rocks."

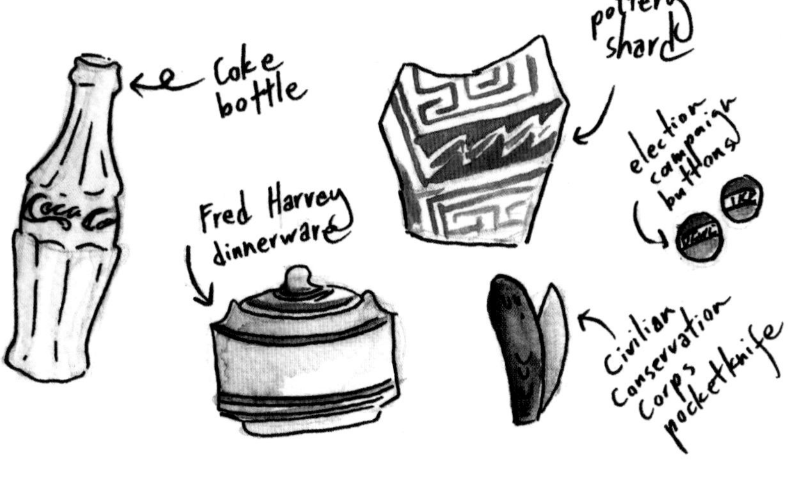
Coke bottle
pottery shard
election campaign buttons
Fred Harvey dinnerware
Civilian Conservation Corps pocketknife

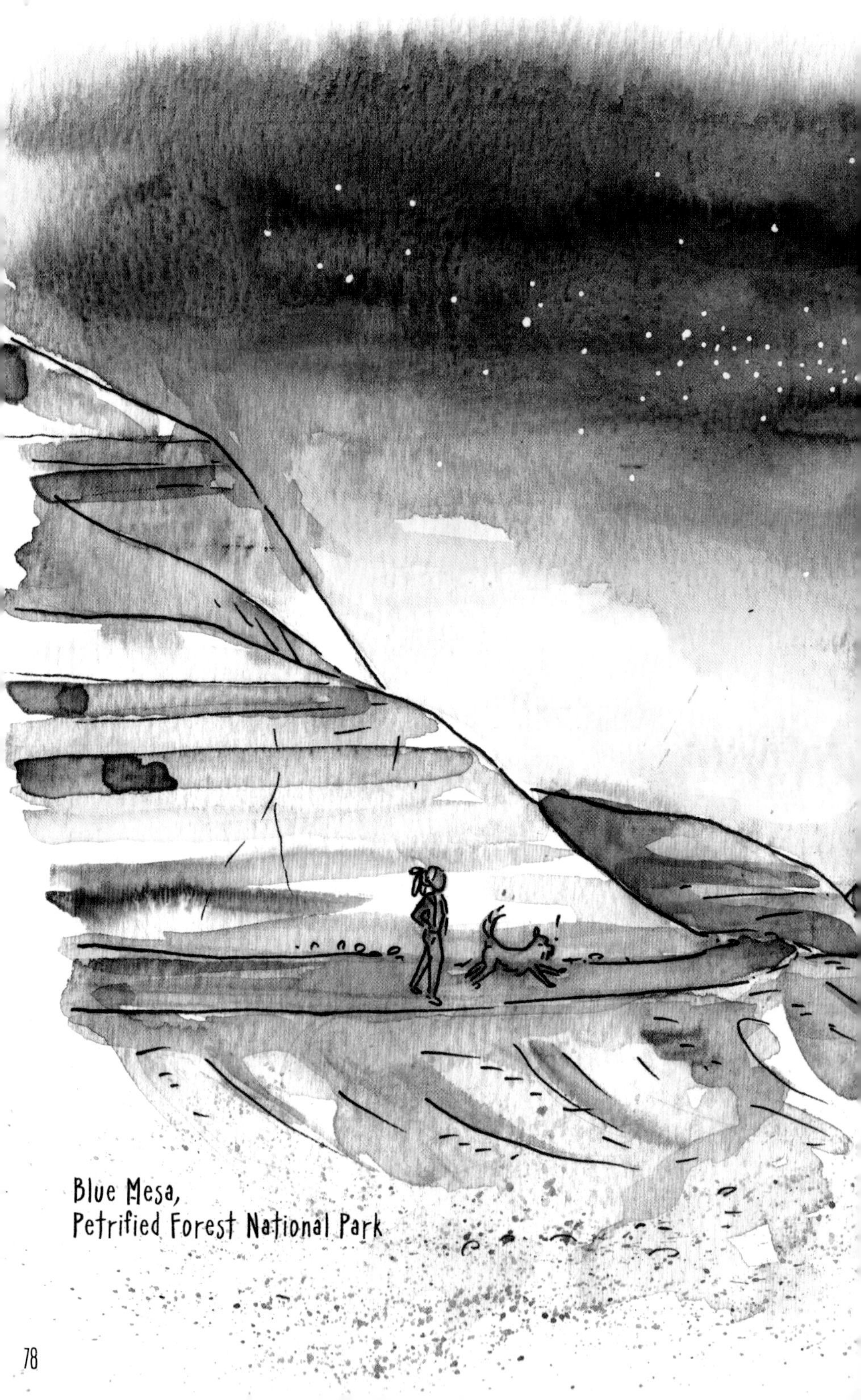

Blue Mesa,
Petrified Forest National Park

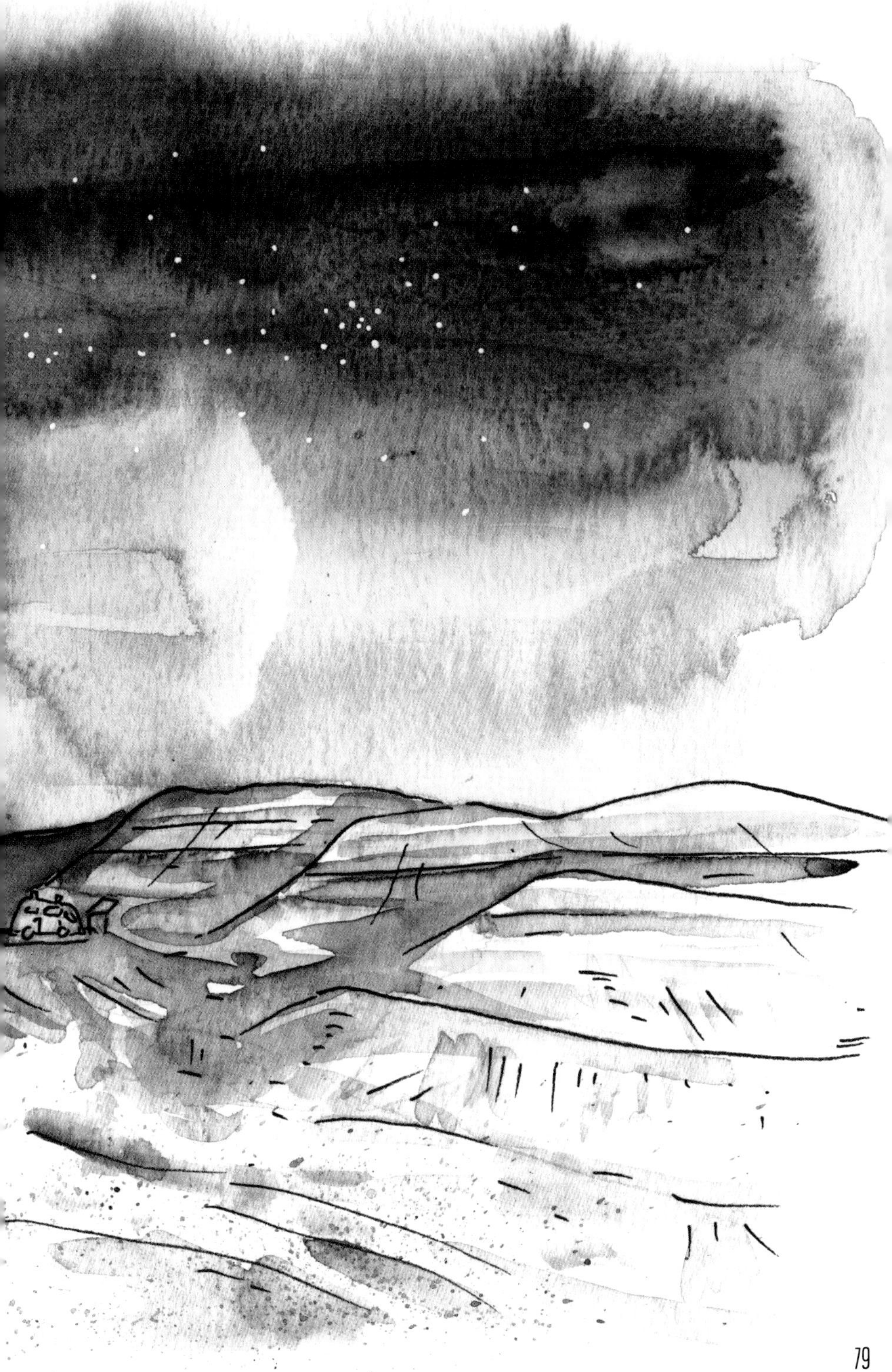

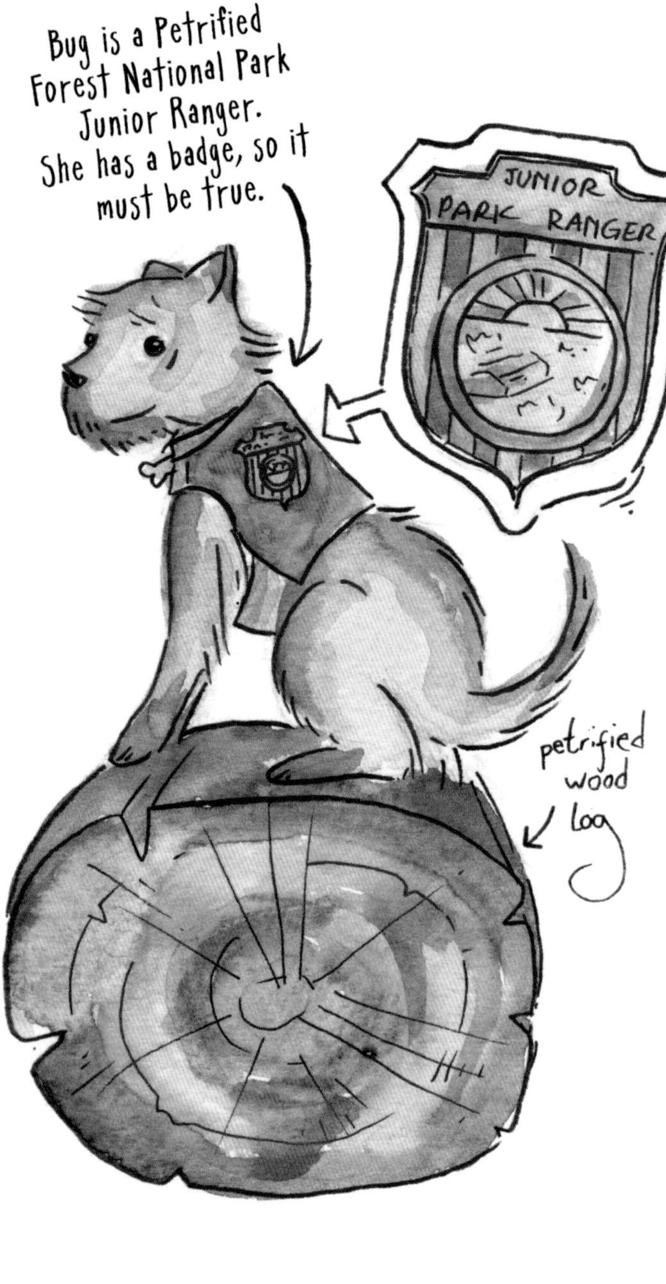
Bug is a Petrified Forest National Park Junior Ranger. She has a badge, so it must be true.
JUNIOR PARK RANGER
petrified wood log

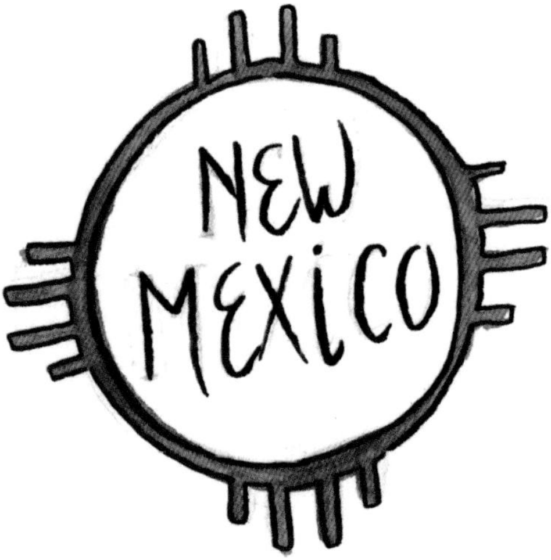
NEW
MEXICO

I already love New Mexico.

For me, it is the perfect blend of kitschy Americana, with a strong helping of Native American art and just enough city.

It's also where I've heard one of the best sentences ever said to me: "Would you like green or red chile?"

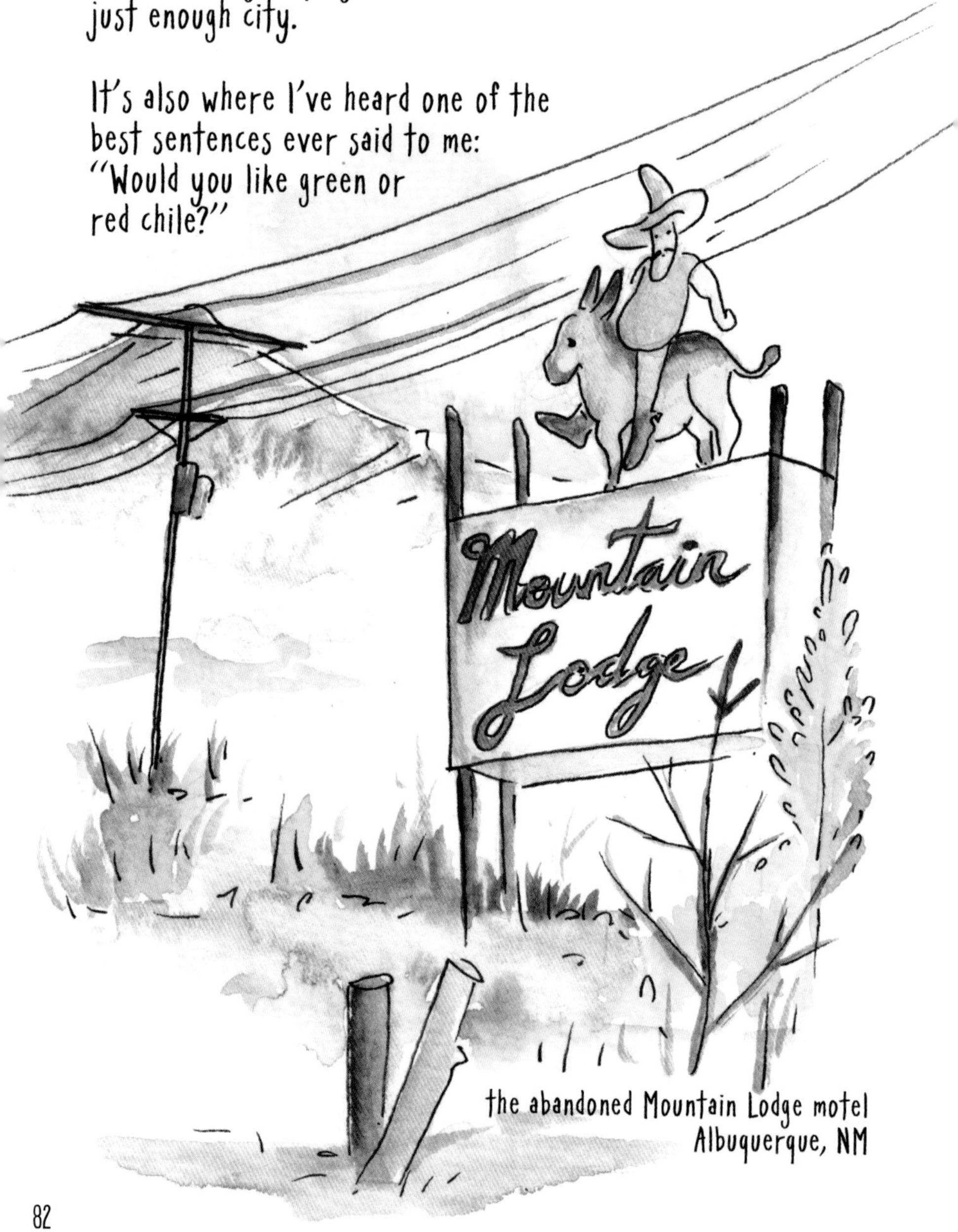
Mountain
Lodge

the abandoned Mountain Lodge motel
Albuquerque, NM

(The correct answer is "Christmas!")

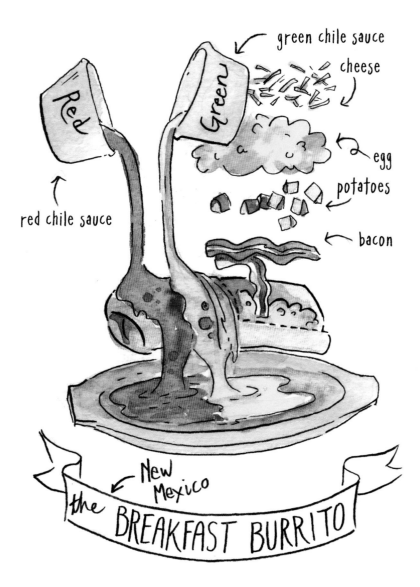

green chile sauce

cheese

egg

potatoes

bacon

red chile sauce

New Mexico

the BREAKFAST BURRITO

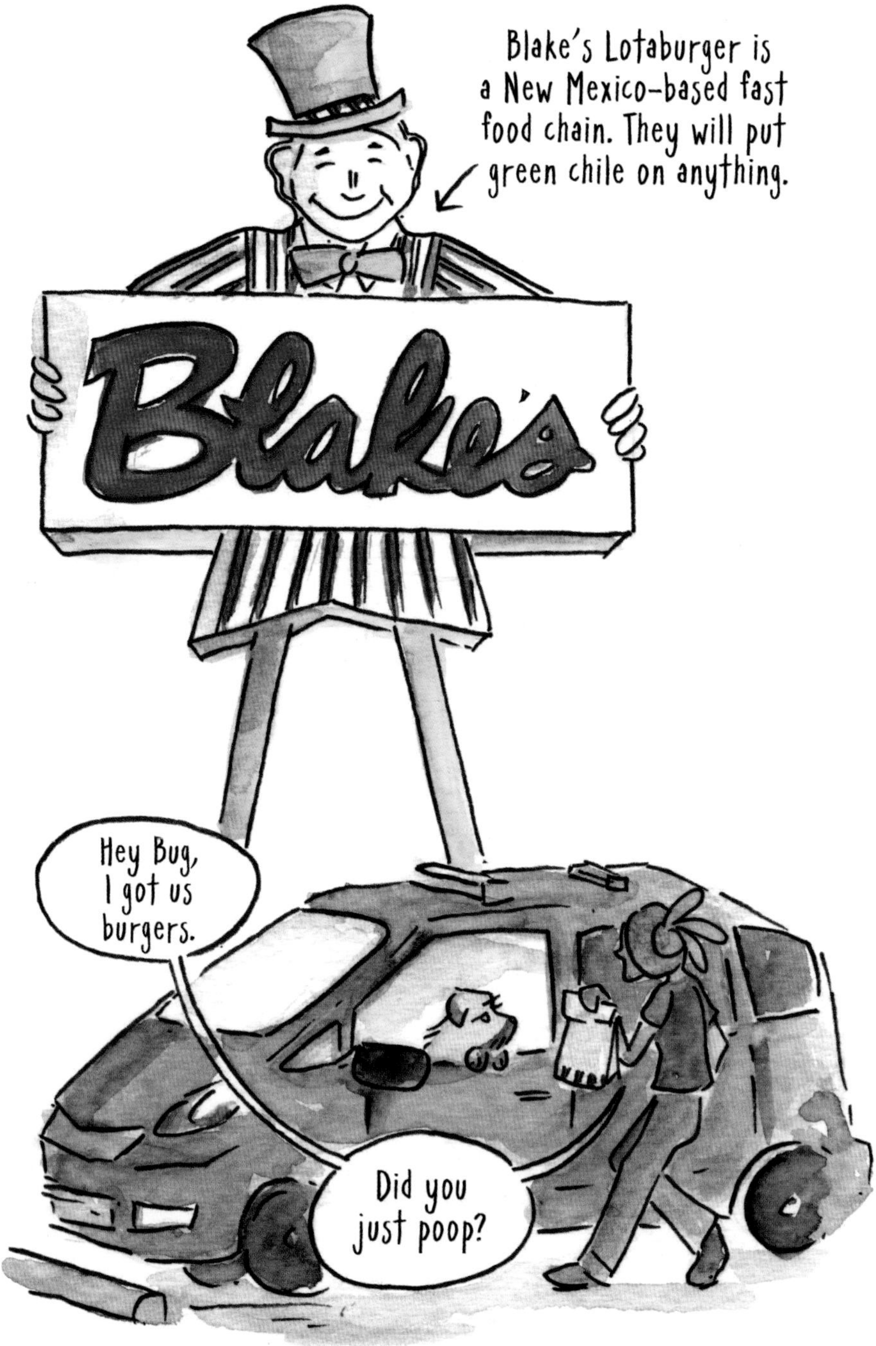
Blake's Lotaburger is a New Mexico-based fast food chain. They will put green chile on anything.
Blake's
Hey Bug, I got us burgers.
Did you just poop?

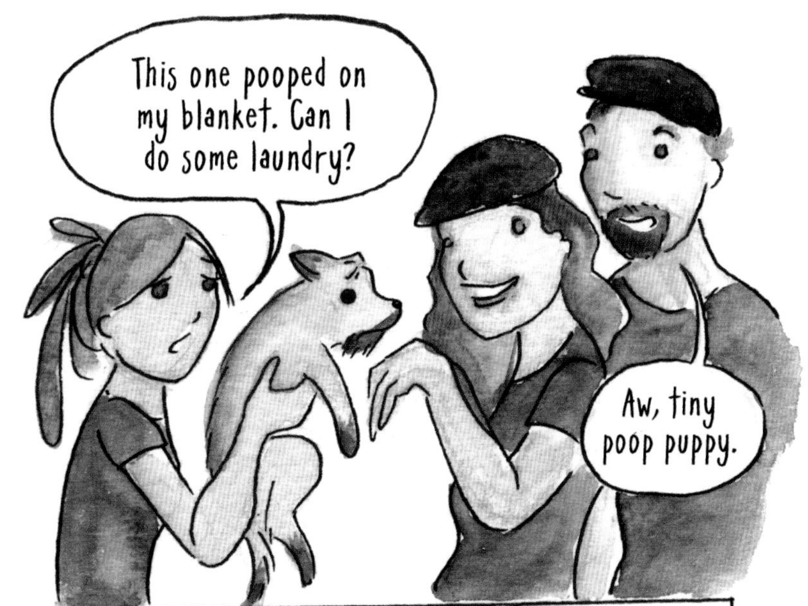
This one pooped on my blanket. Can I do some laundry?
Aw, tiny poop puppy.

My artist friends Brandt and Kathie live in Albuquerque and I've visited them a few times. They run an art gallery on Central Avenue, which is part of historic Route 66, and they have a very comfortable couch.

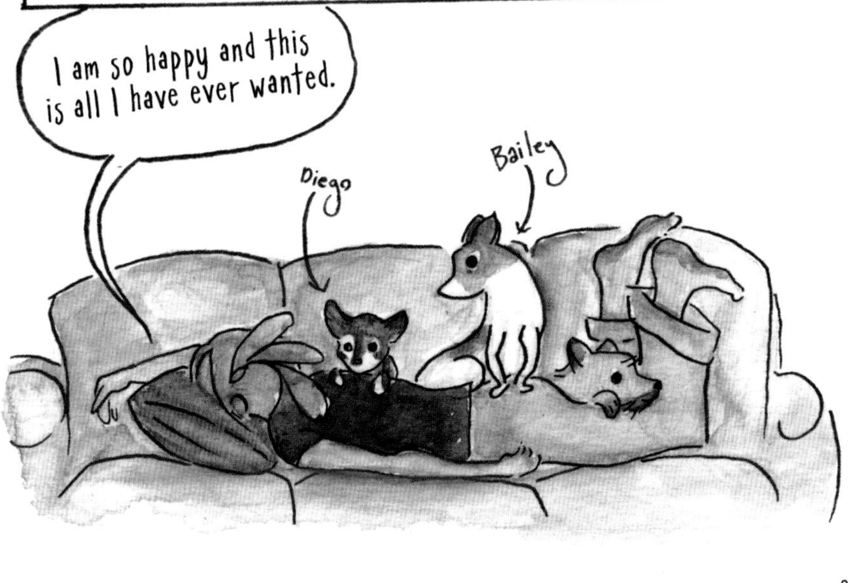
I am so happy and this is all I have ever wanted.
Diego
Bailey

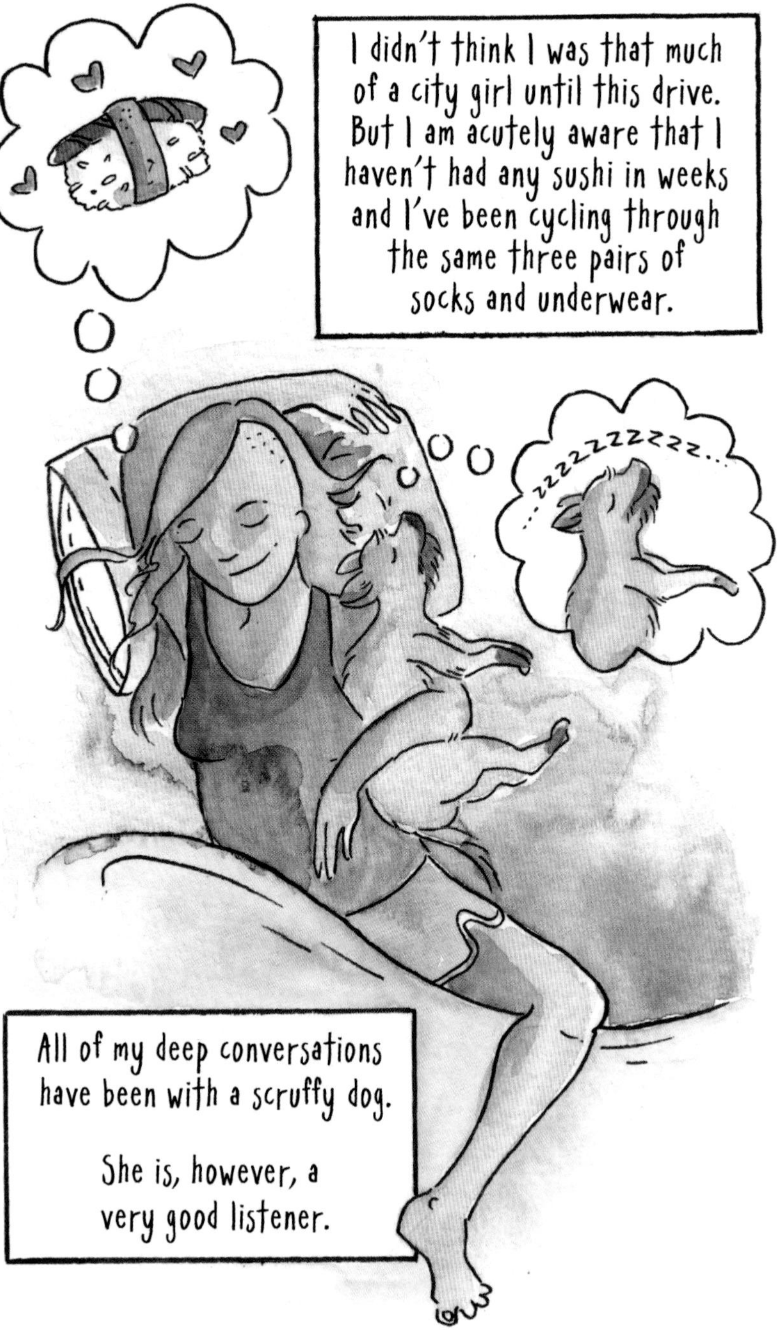
I didn't think I was that much of a city girl until this drive. But I am acutely aware that I haven't had any sushi in weeks and I've been cycling through the same three pairs of socks and underwear.
ZZZZZZZZZZZZ...
All of my deep conversations have been with a scruffy dog.
She is, however, a very good listener.

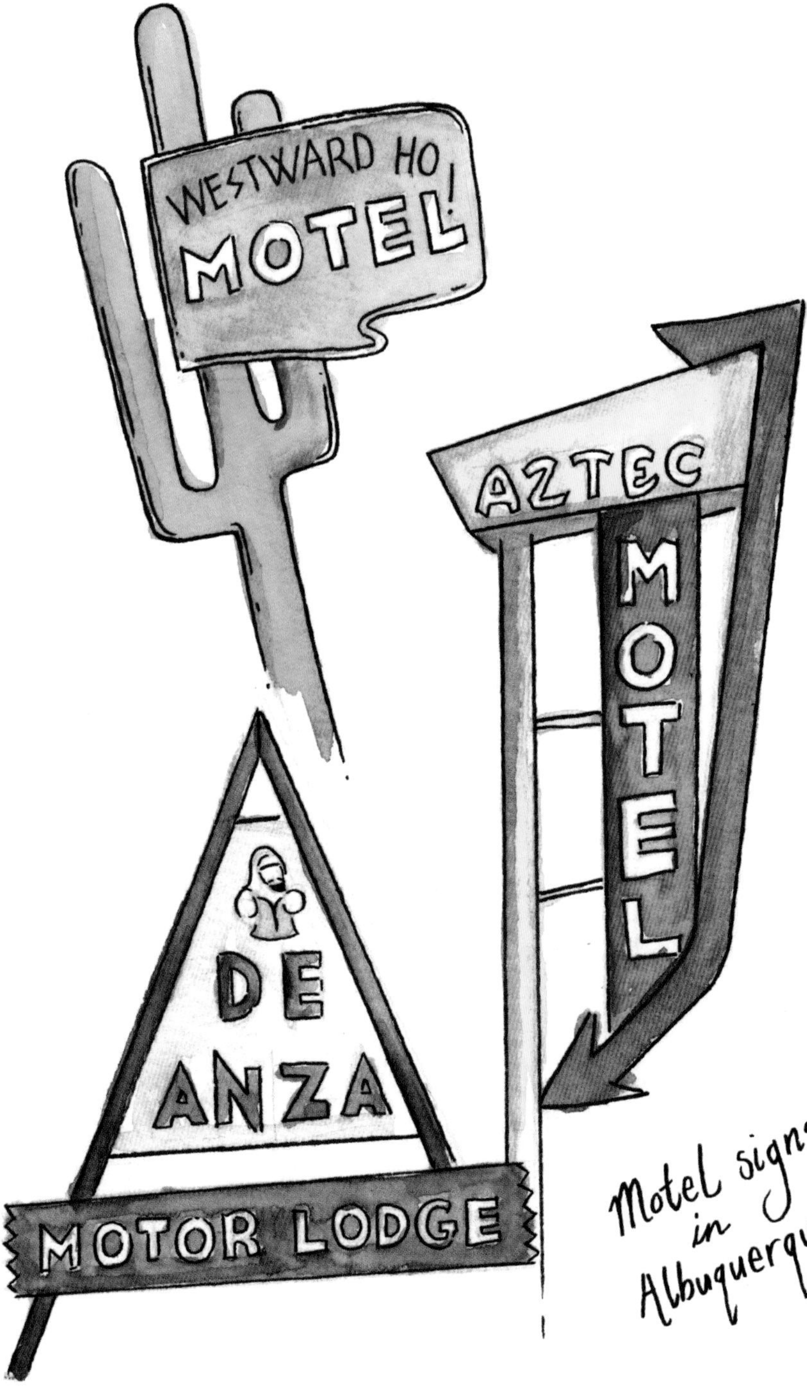
WESTWARD HO!
MOTEL
AZTEC
MOTEL
DE
ANZA
MOTOR LODGE

Motel signs in Albuquerque

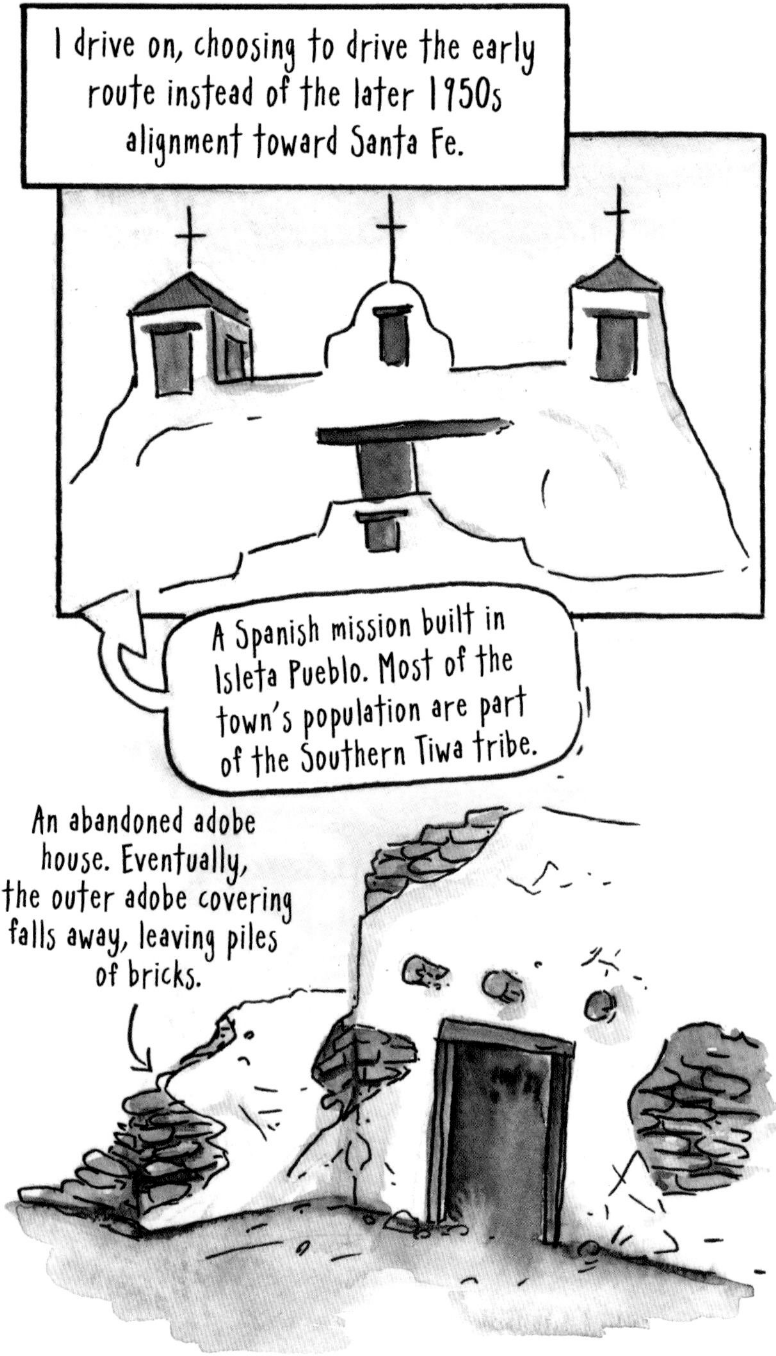
I drive on, choosing to drive the early route instead of the later 1950s alignment toward Santa Fe.
A Spanish mission built in Isleta Pueblo. Most of the town's population are part of the Southern Tiwa tribe.
An abandoned adobe house. Eventually, the outer adobe covering falls away, leaving piles of bricks.

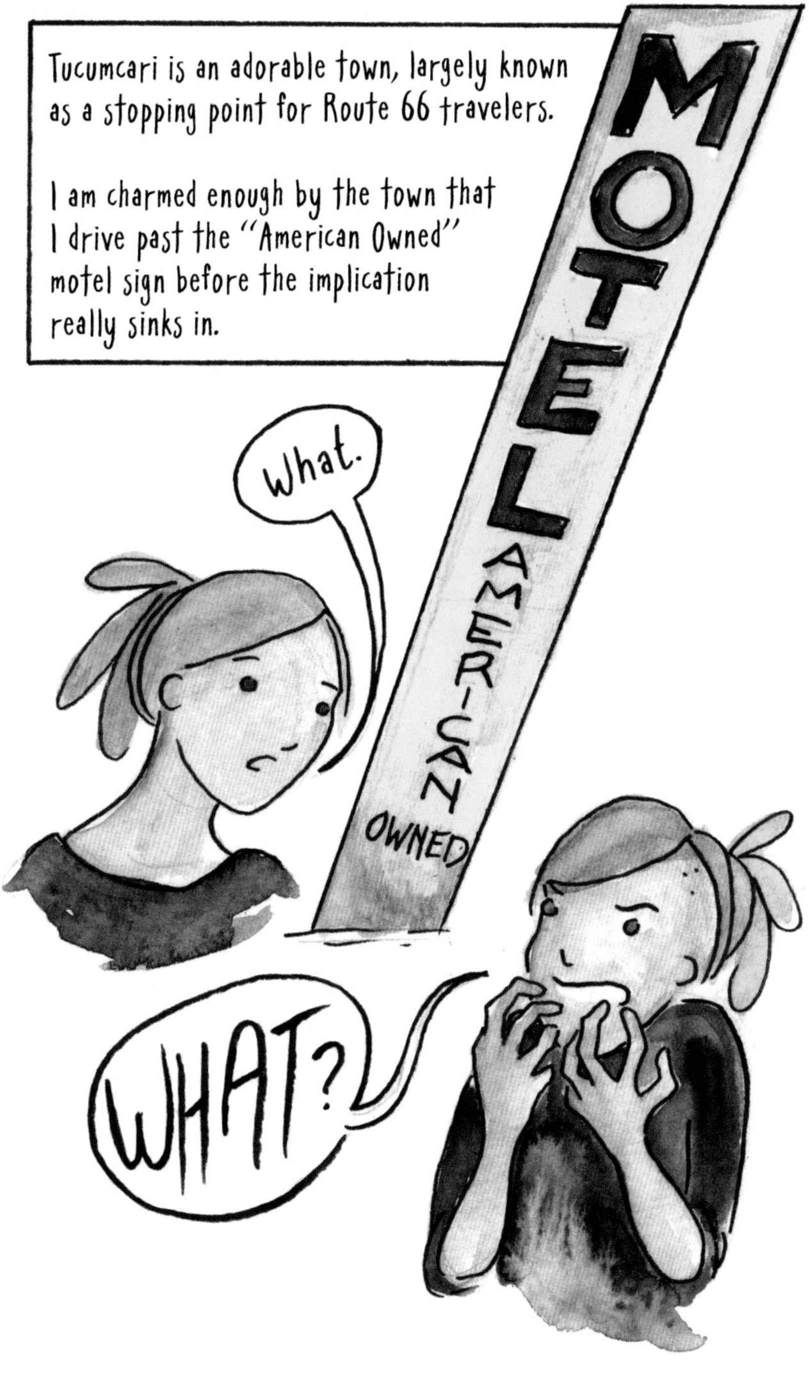
Tucumcari is an adorable town, largely known as a stopping point for Route 66 travelers.
I am charmed enough by the town that I drive past the "American Owned" motel sign before the implication really sinks in.
MOTEL
AMER-ICAN
OWNED
What.
WHAT?

American owned. AMERICAN owned. It might not mean anything to most people, but as a brown American, I know exactly what that means. The term "Patel Motel" is used as a pejorative, a play on the term "no-tell motel," but with an extra helping of racism.

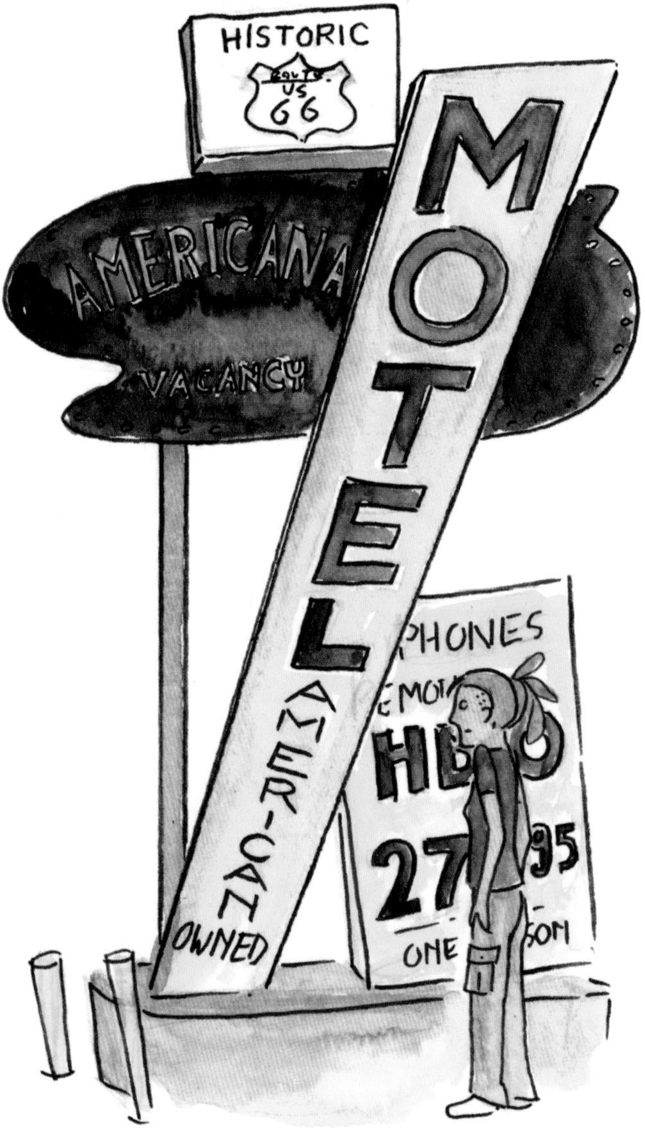
HISTORIC
ROUTE
US
66
AMERICANA
VACANCY
MOTEL
AMER-ICAN
OWNED
PHONES
HBO
27 95
ONE

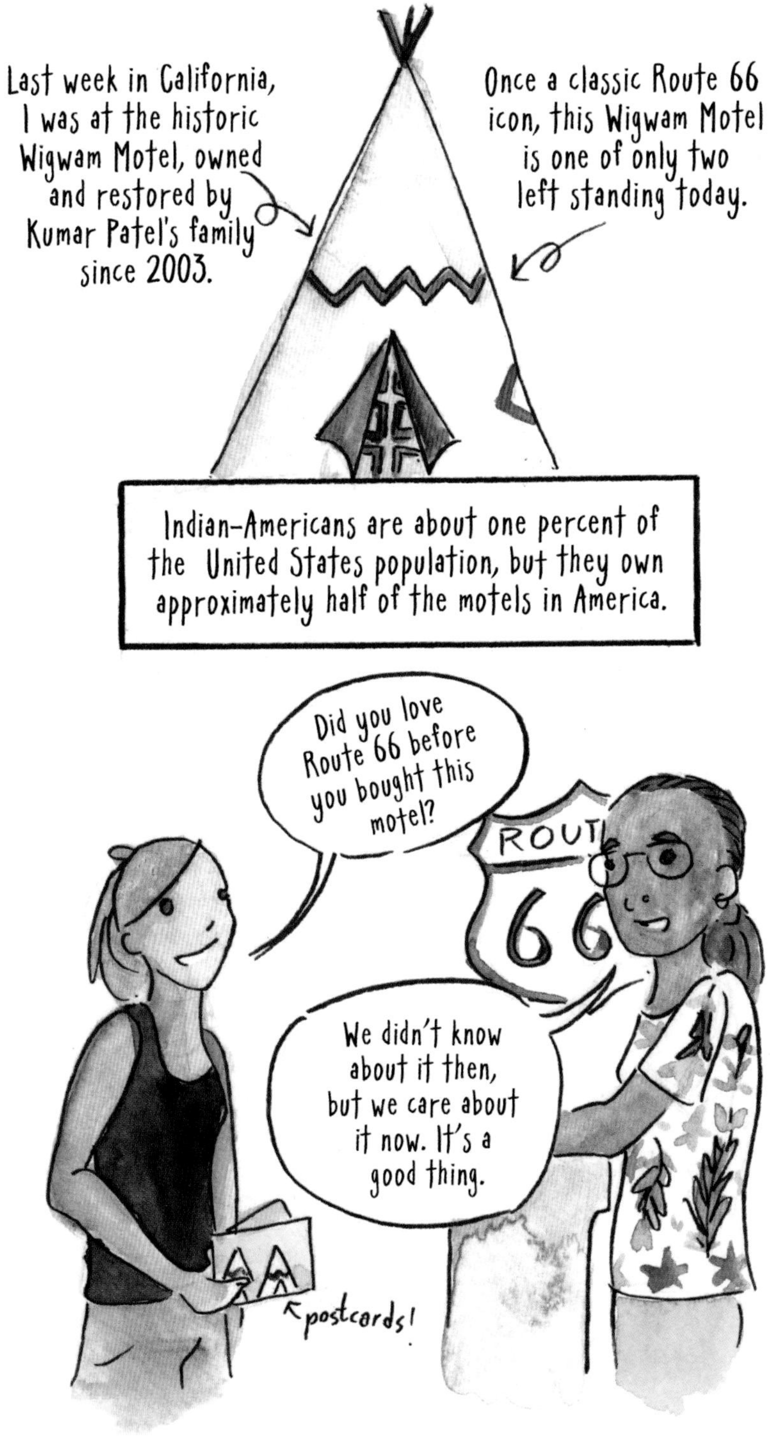
Last week in California, I was at the historic Wigwam Motel, owned and restored by Kumar Patel's family since 2003.
Once a classic Route 66 icon, this Wigwam Motel is one of only two left standing today.
Indian-Americans are about one percent of the United States population, but they own approximately half of the motels in America.
Did you love Route 66 before you bought this motel?
ROUT
66
We didn't know about it then, but we care about it now. It's a good thing.
postcards!

San Bernadino, CA

WIGWAM MOTEL!

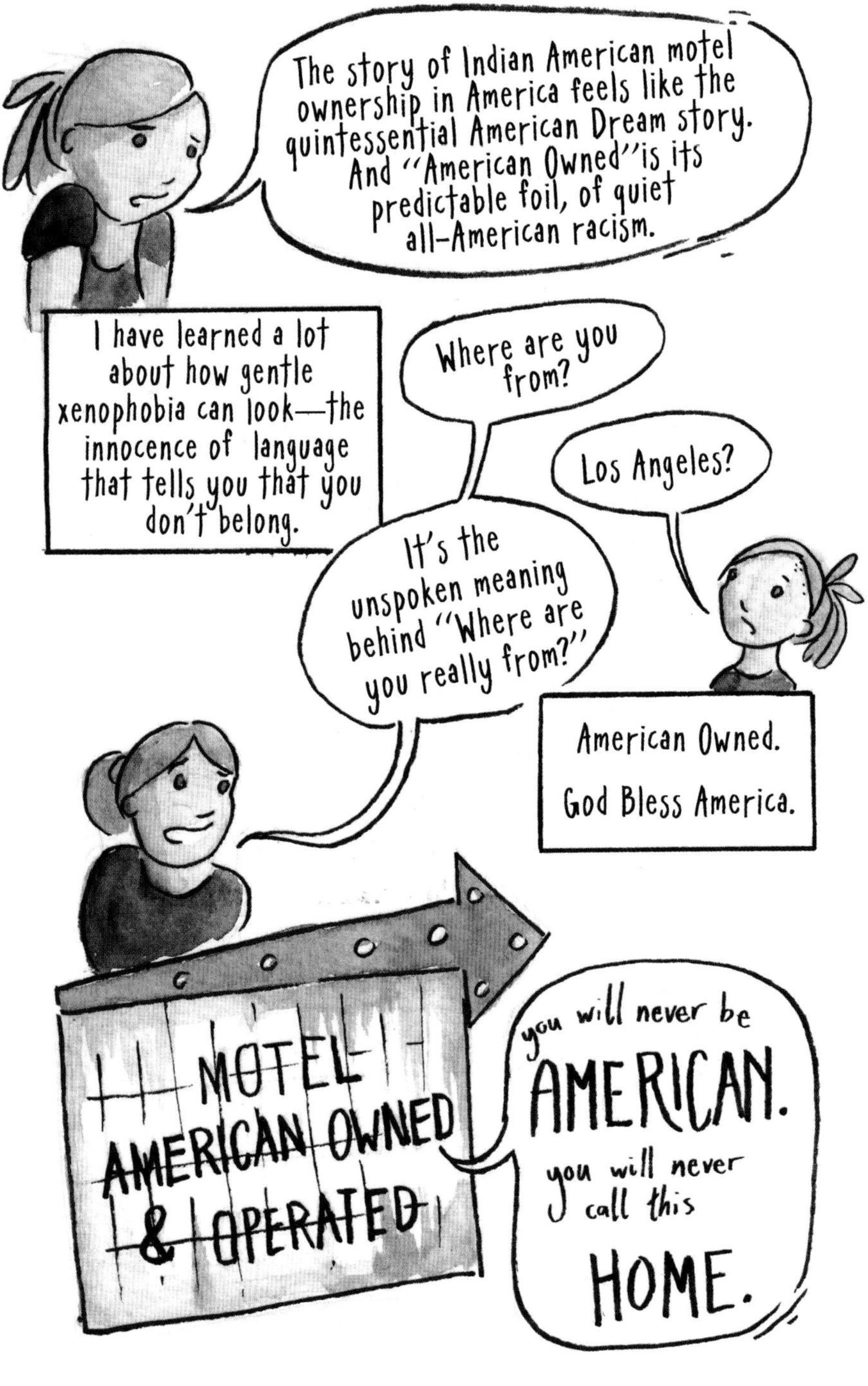

The story of Indian American motel ownership in America feels like the quintessential American Dream story. And "American Owned" is its predictable foil, of quiet all-American racism.
I have learned a lot about how gentle xenophobia can look—the innocence of language that tells you that you don't belong.
Where are you from?
Los Angeles?
It's the unspoken meaning behind "Where are you really from?"
American Owned.
God Bless America.
MOTEL
AMERICAN OWNED
& OPERATED
you will never be AMERICAN.
you will never call this HOME.

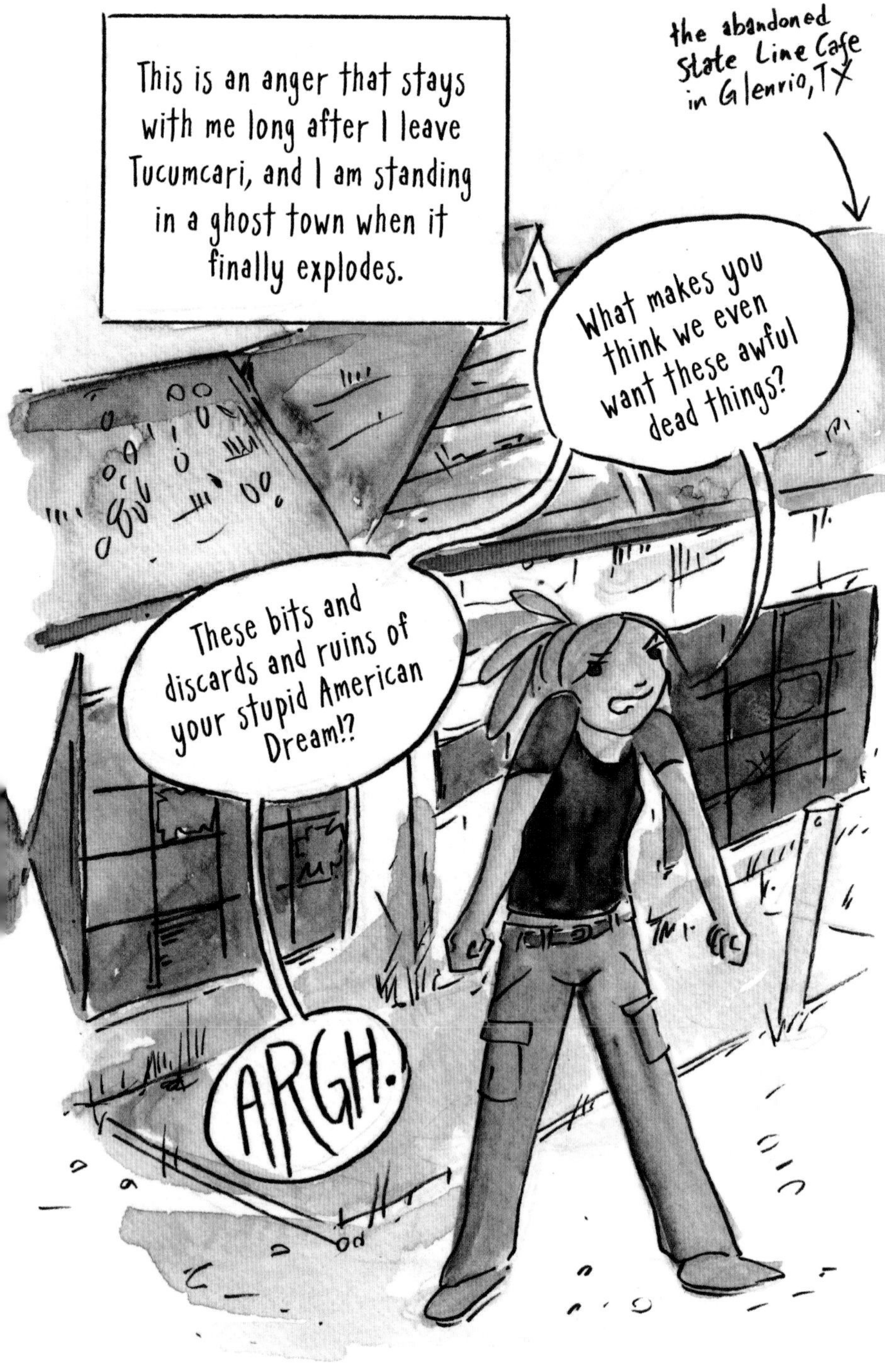
This is an anger that stays with me long after I leave Tucumcari, and I am standing in a ghost town when it finally explodes.
the abandoned State Line Cafe in Glenrio, TX
What makes you think we even want these awful dead things?
These bits and discards and ruins of your stupid American Dream!?
ARGH.

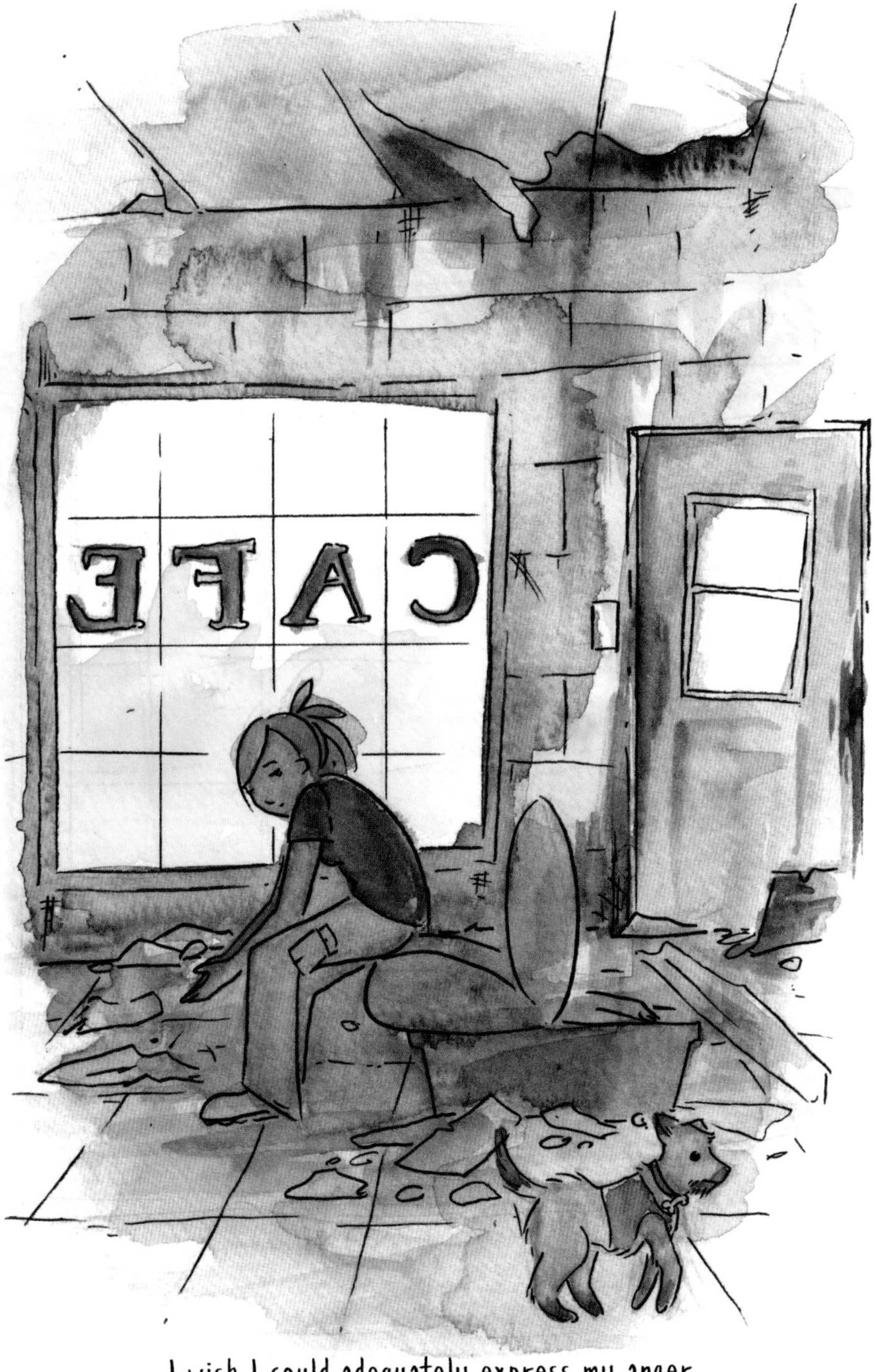
CAFE

I wish I could adequately express my anger.
For now, I'll drive on.

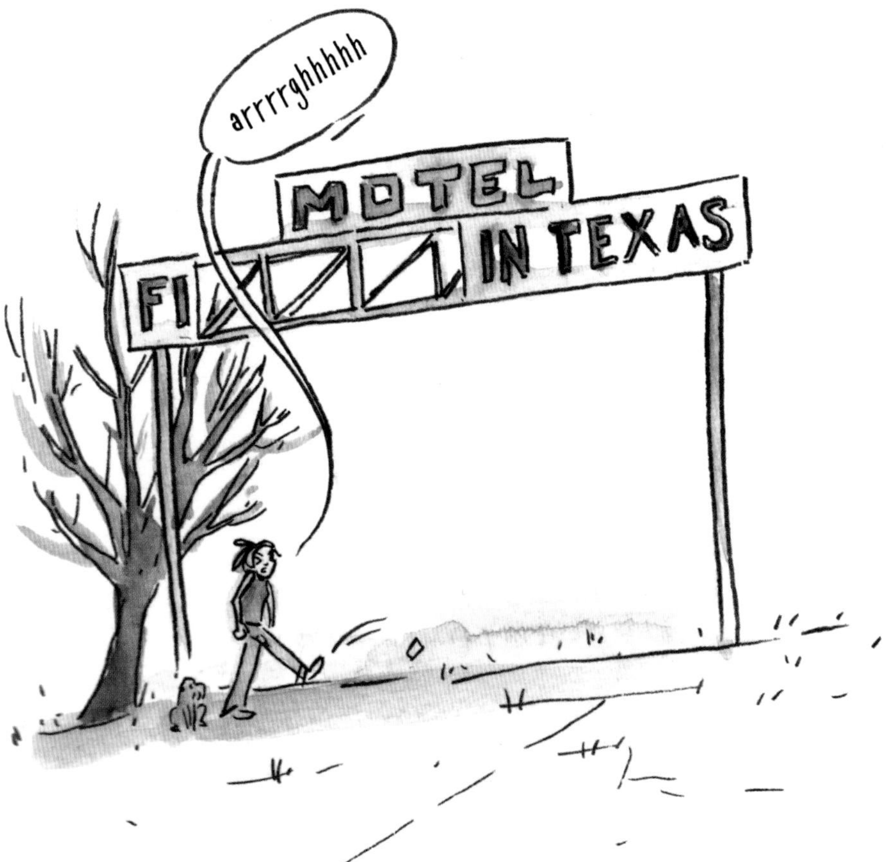
arrrrghhhhh
MOTEL
FI
IN TEXAS

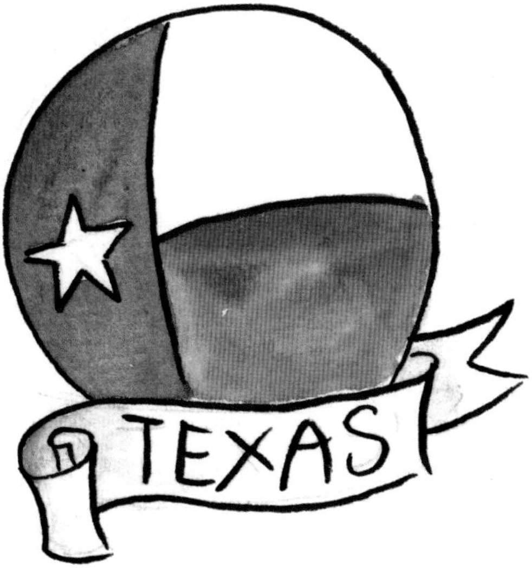
TEXAS

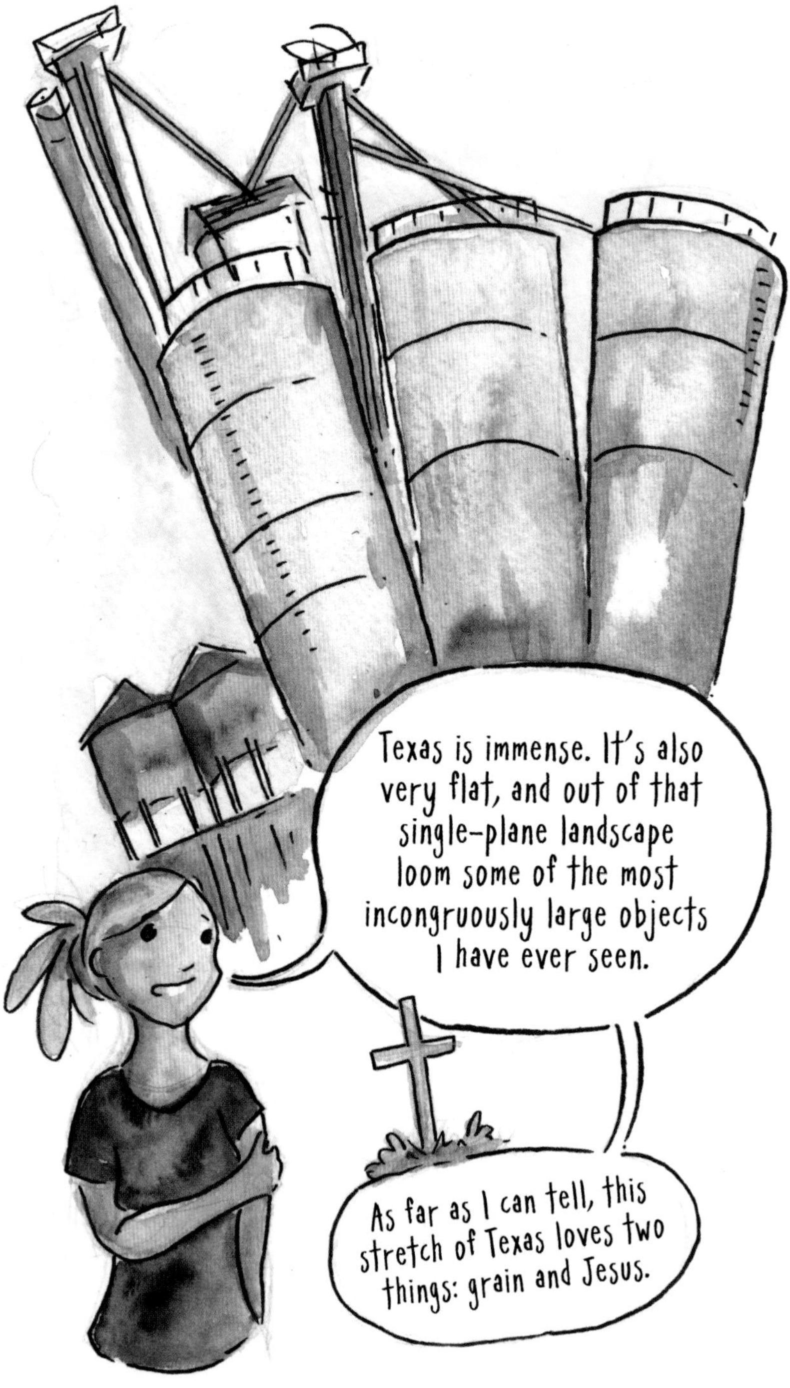
Texas is immense. It's also very flat, and out of that single-plane landscape loom some of the most incongruously large objects I have ever seen.
As far as I can tell, this stretch of Texas loves two things: grain and Jesus.

I can only find one radio station here, and it is playing Jesus Rock, which gives me youth group flashbacks. The religion here itches under my skin and makes me feel especially out of place.

Age 6. Attended Catholic convent.

Hail MARY full of GRACE...

Age 12. Went to Buddhist temples with family.

Na Mo A Mi Tuo Fo...

i dont really care if they label me a JESUS FREAK!

Age 16. Accepted Jesus at a youth retreat.

I was raised in and with a variety of religions and even spent some time in the embrace of a chosen church community. I shouldn't feel that awkward.

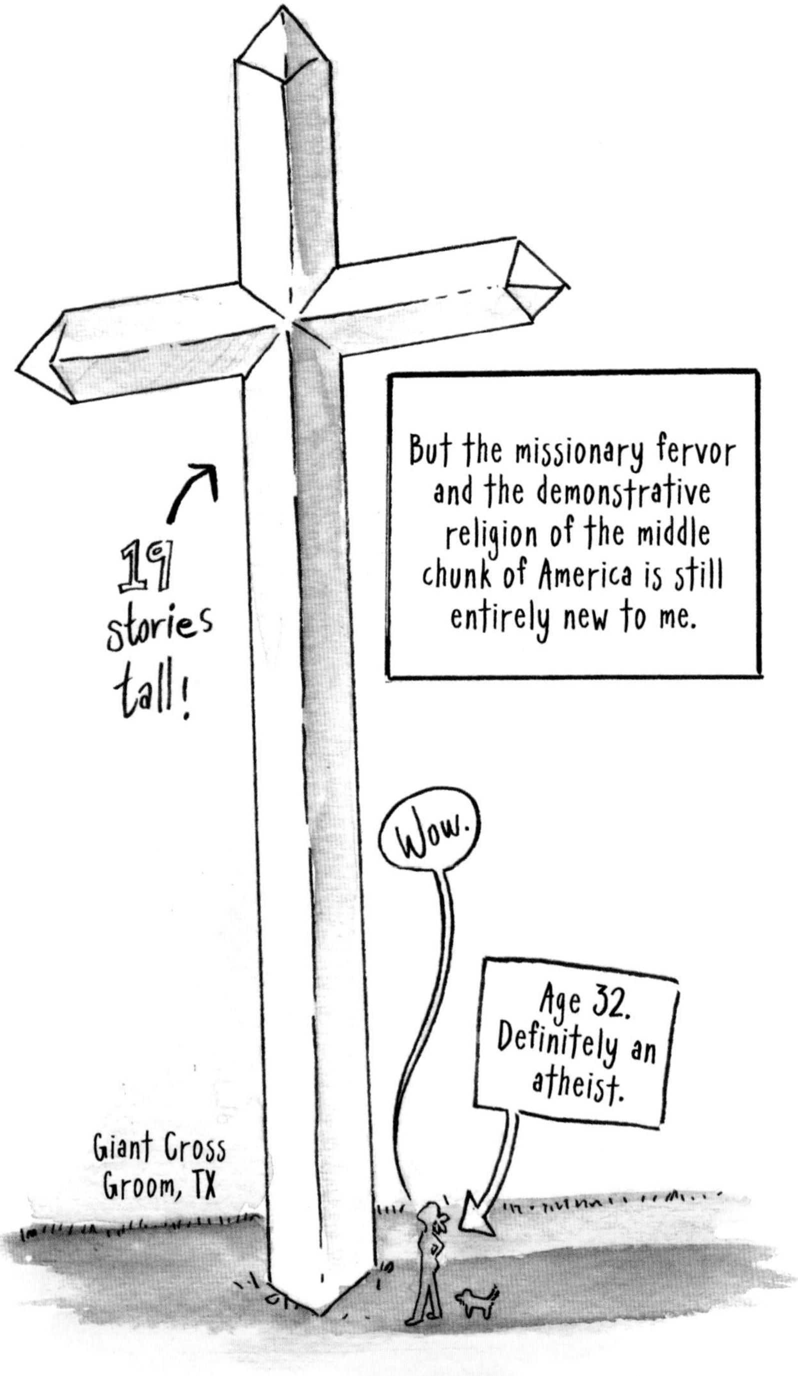
But the missionary fervor and the demonstrative religion of the middle chunk of America is still entirely new to me.
19 stories tall!
Wow.
Age 32. Definitely an atheist.
Giant Cross Groom, TX

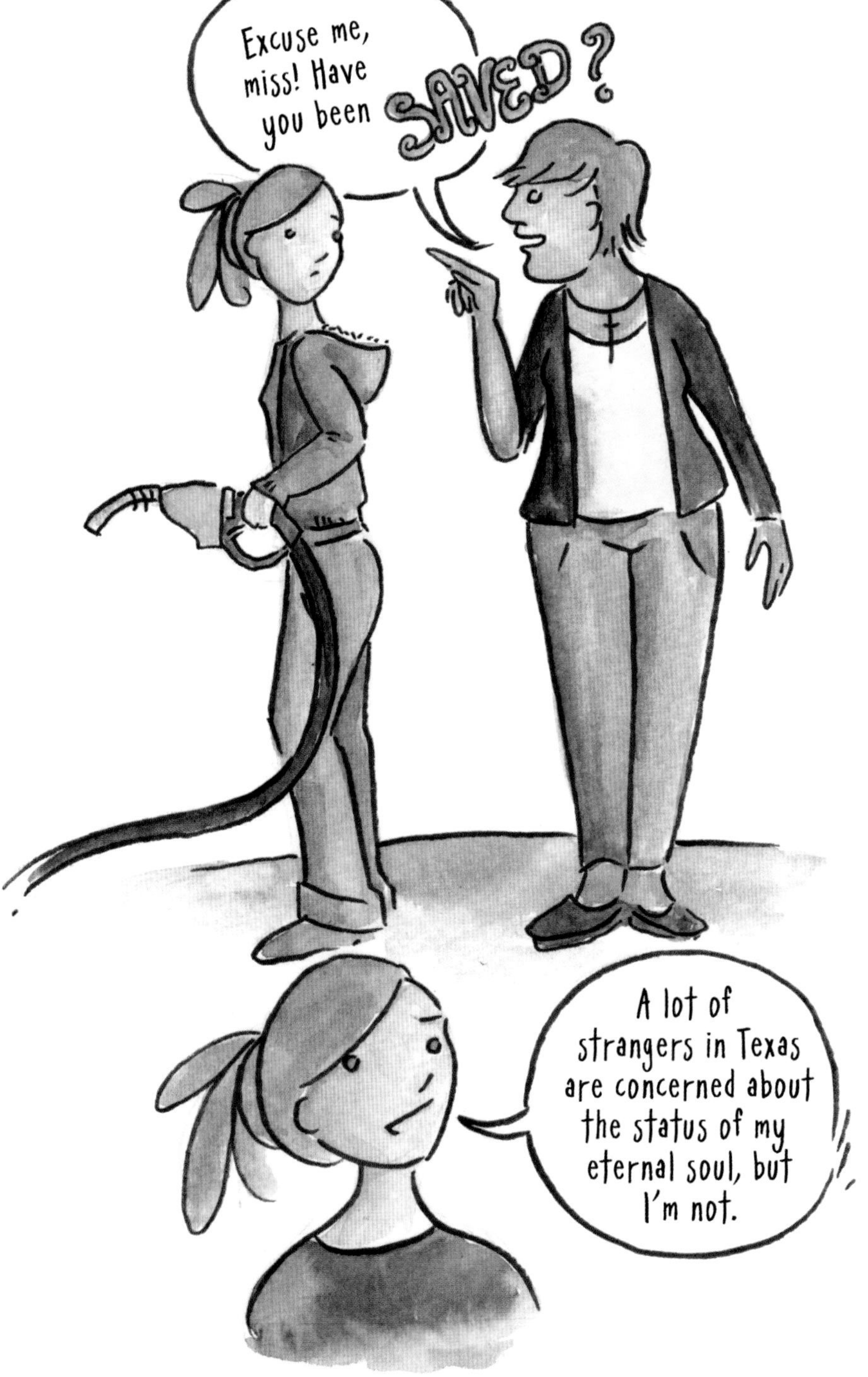
Excuse me, miss! Have you been SAVED?
A lot of strangers in Texas are concerned about the status of my eternal soul, but I'm not.

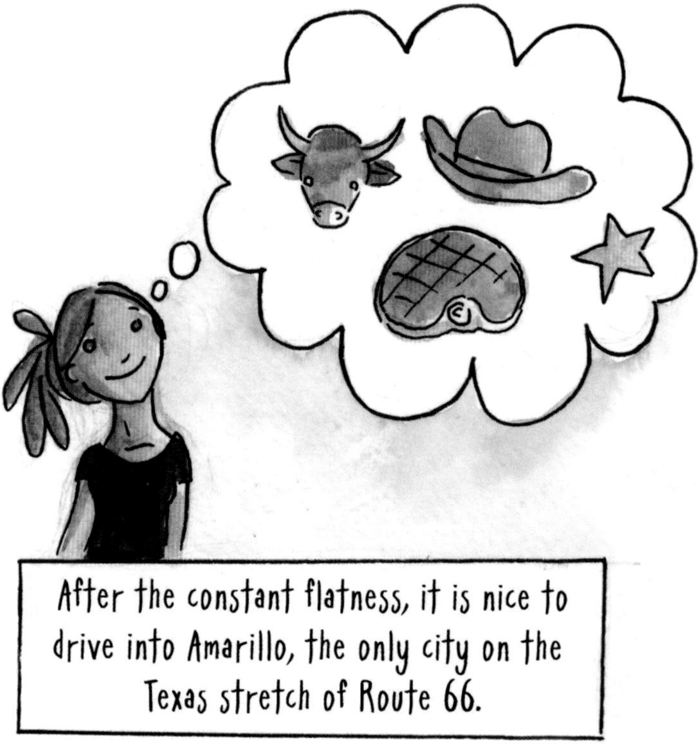
After the constant flatness, it is nice to drive into Amarillo, the only city on the Texas stretch of Route 66.

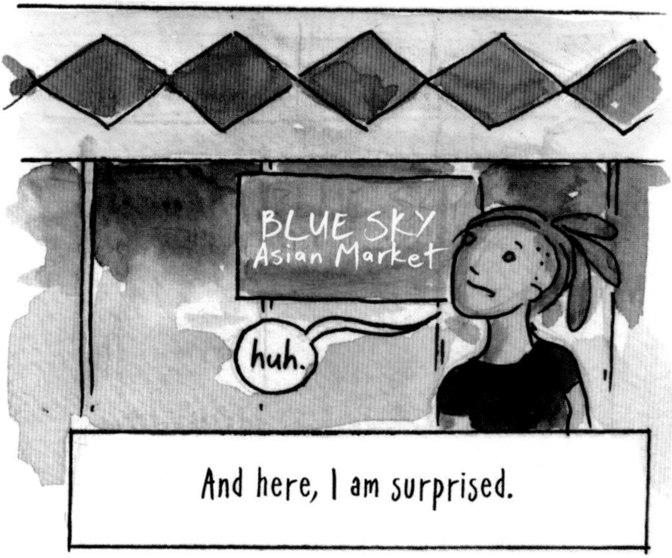
BLUE SKY
Asian Market
huh.
And here, I am surprised.

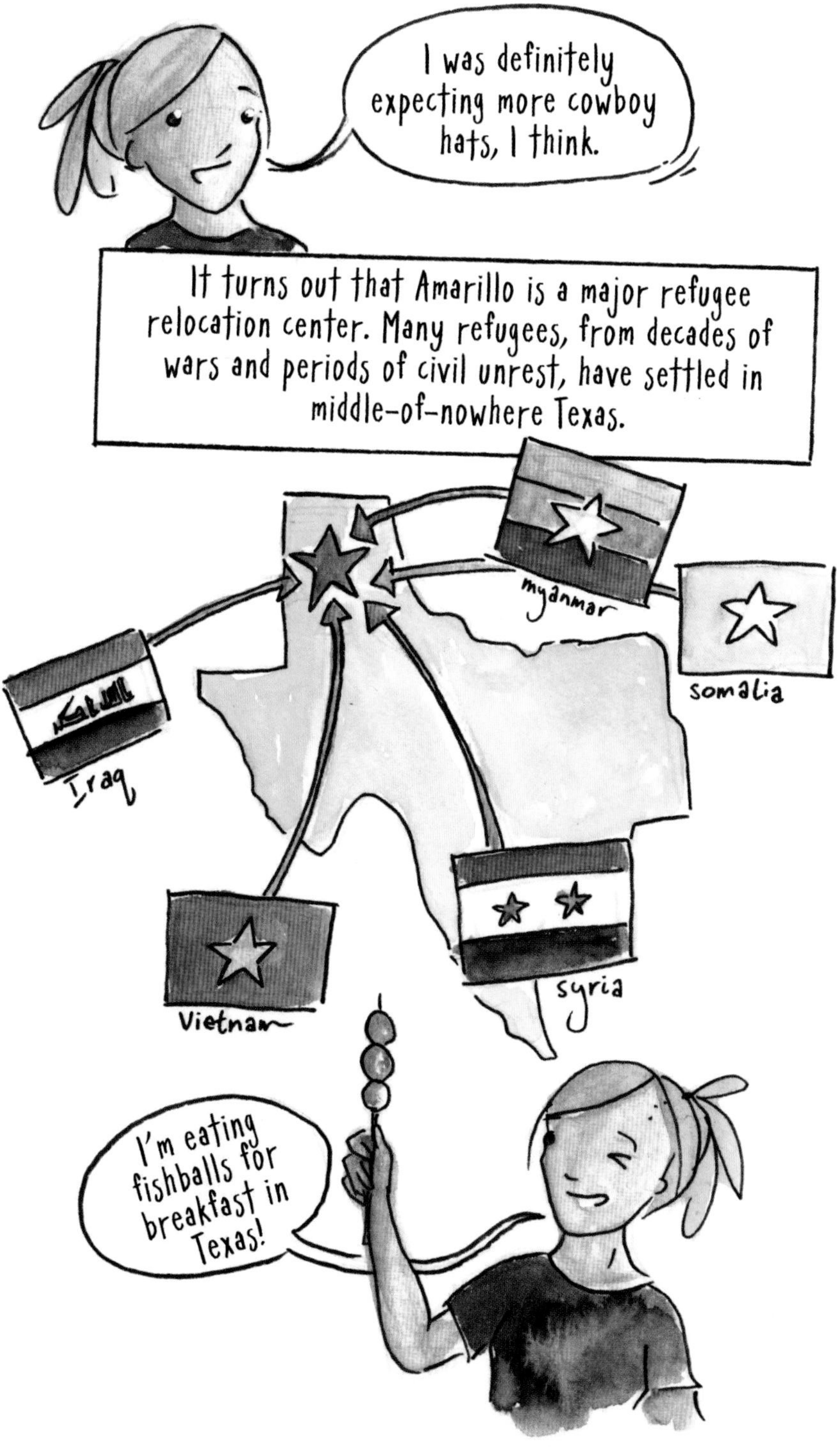
I was definitely expecting more cowboy hats, I think.
It turns out that Amarillo is a major refugee relocation center. Many refugees, from decades of wars and periods of civil unrest, have settled in middle-of-nowhere Texas.
Myanmar
Somalia
Iraq
Vietnam
Syria
I'm eating fishballs for breakfast in Texas!

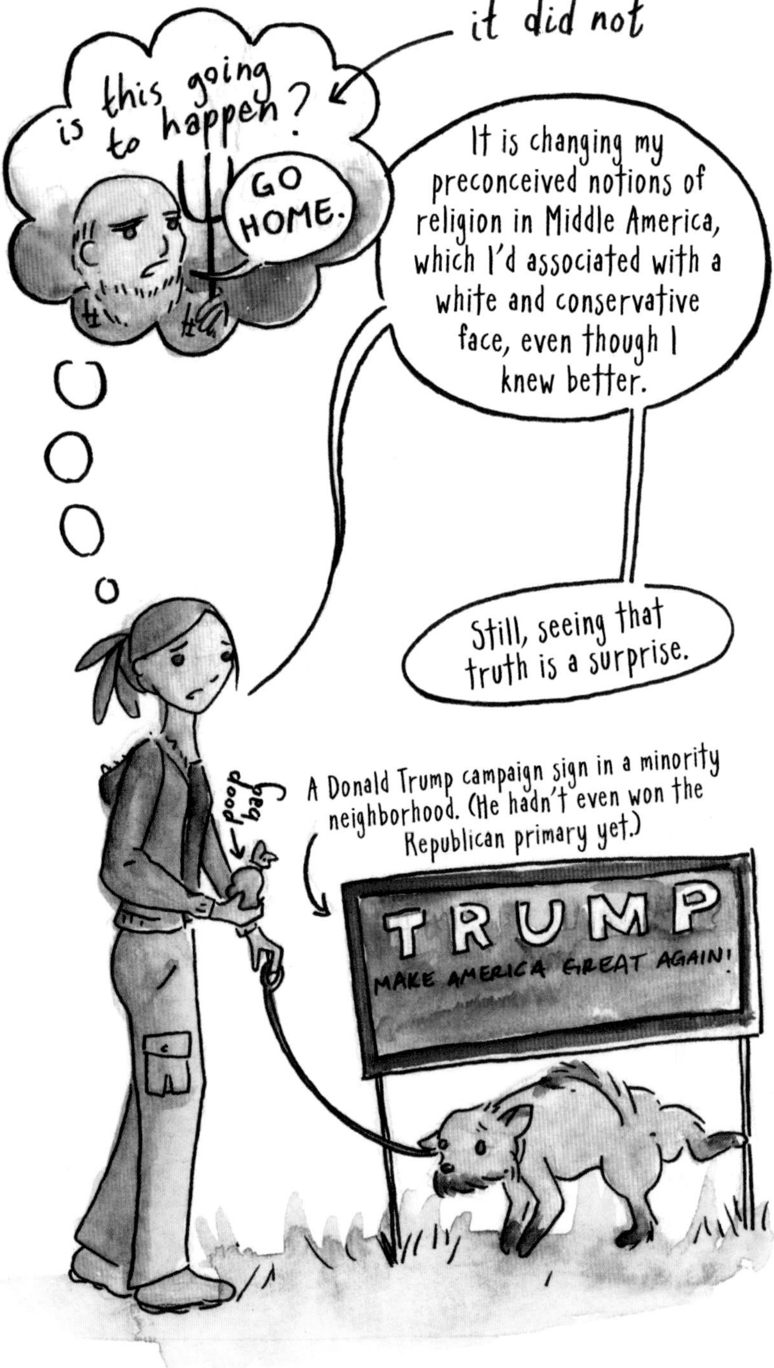
is this going to happen?
GO HOME.
it did not
It is changing my preconceived notions of religion in Middle America, which I'd associated with a white and conservative face, even though I knew better.
Still, seeing that truth is a surprise.
A Donald Trump campaign sign in a minority neighborhood. (He hadn't even won the Republican primary yet.)
poop bag
TRUMP
MAKE AMERICA GREAT AGAIN!

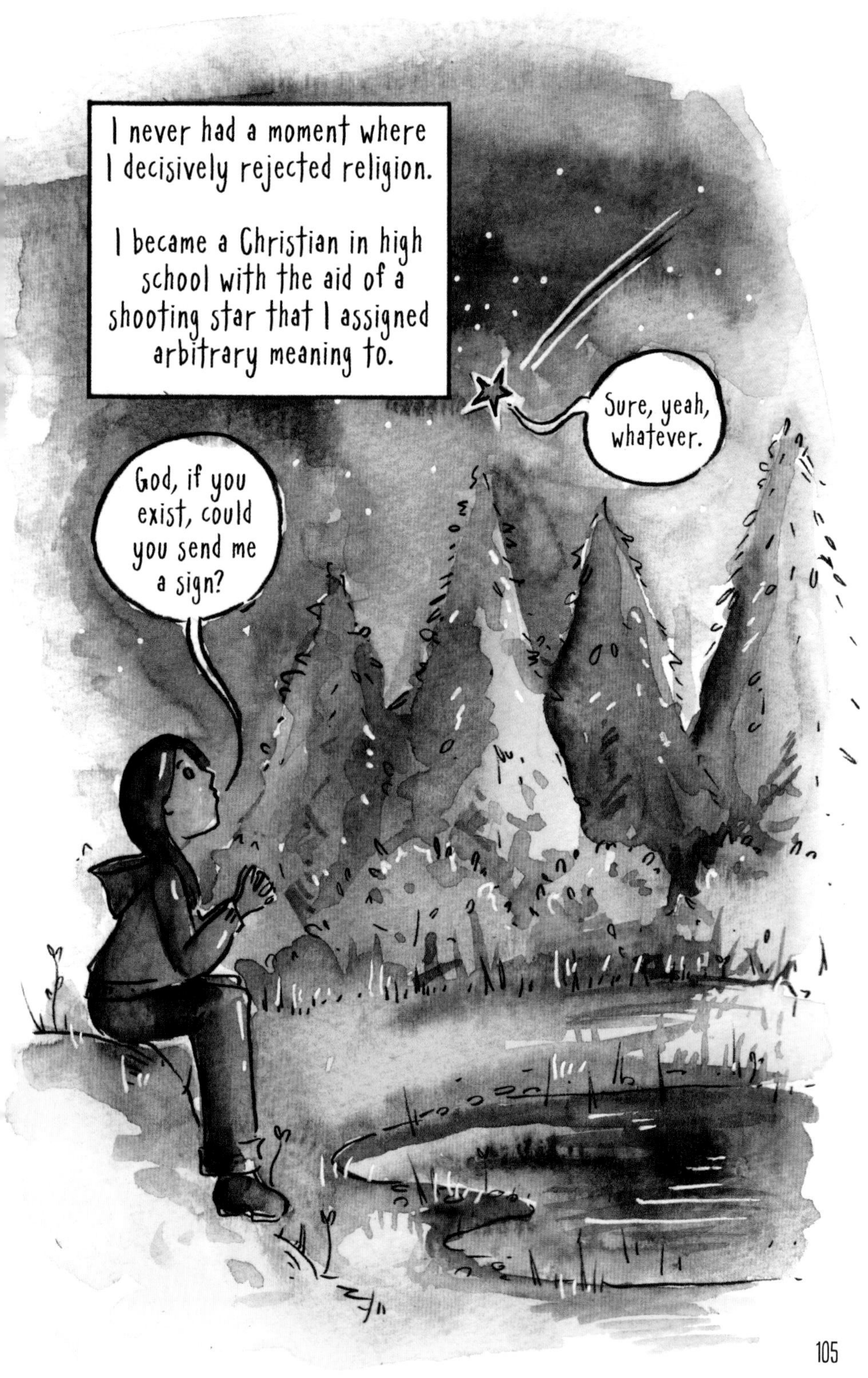
I never had a moment where I decisively rejected religion.
I became a Christian in high school with the aid of a shooting star that I assigned arbitrary meaning to.
God, if you exist, could you send me a sign?
Sure, yeah, whatever.

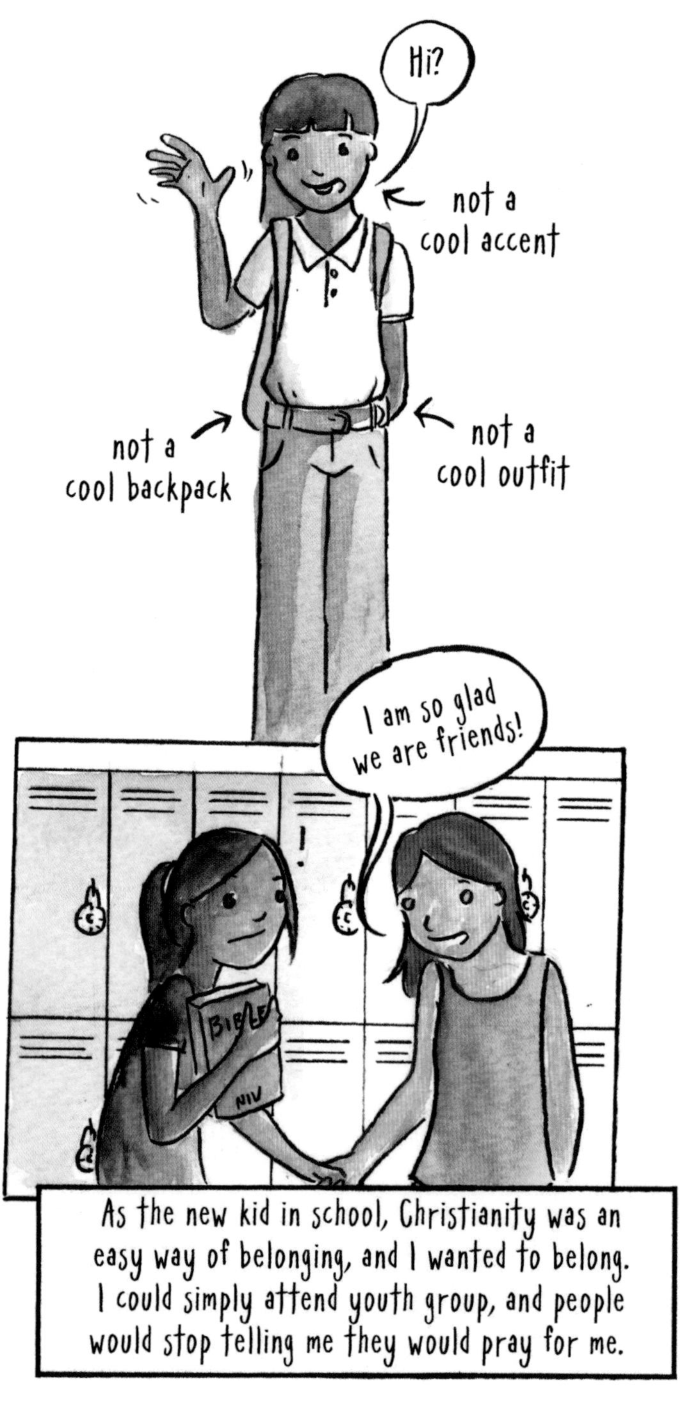

Hi?
not a cool accent
not a cool backpack
not a cool outfit
I am so glad we are friends!
BIBLE
NIV
As the new kid in school, Christianity was an easy way of belonging, and I wanted to belong. I could simply attend youth group, and people would stop telling me they would pray for me.

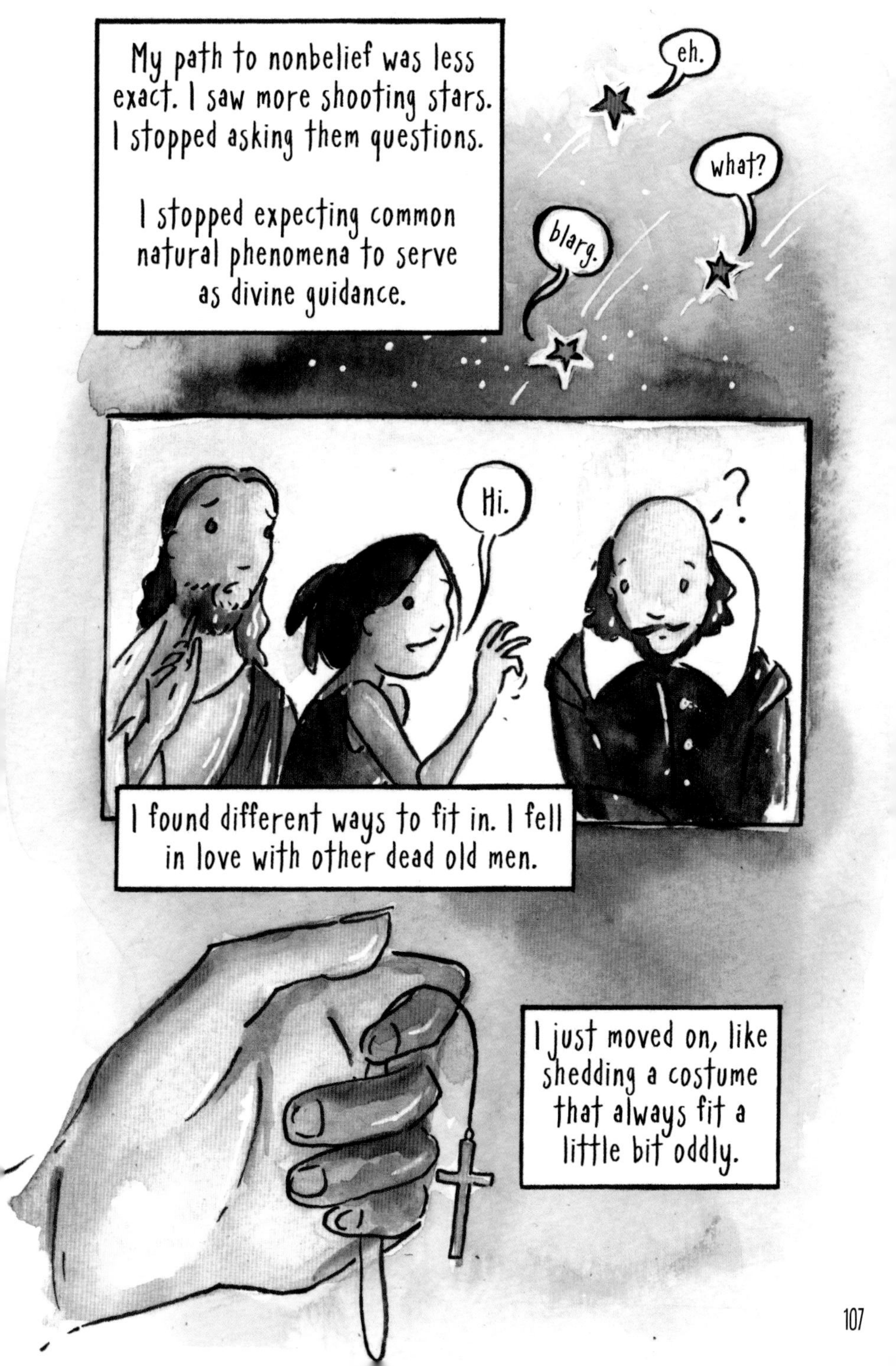
My path to nonbelief was less exact. I saw more shooting stars. I stopped asking them questions.
I stopped expecting common natural phenomena to serve as divine guidance.
eh.
what?
blarg.
Hi.
?
I found different ways to fit in. I fell in love with other dead old men.
I just moved on, like shedding a costume that always fit a little bit oddly.

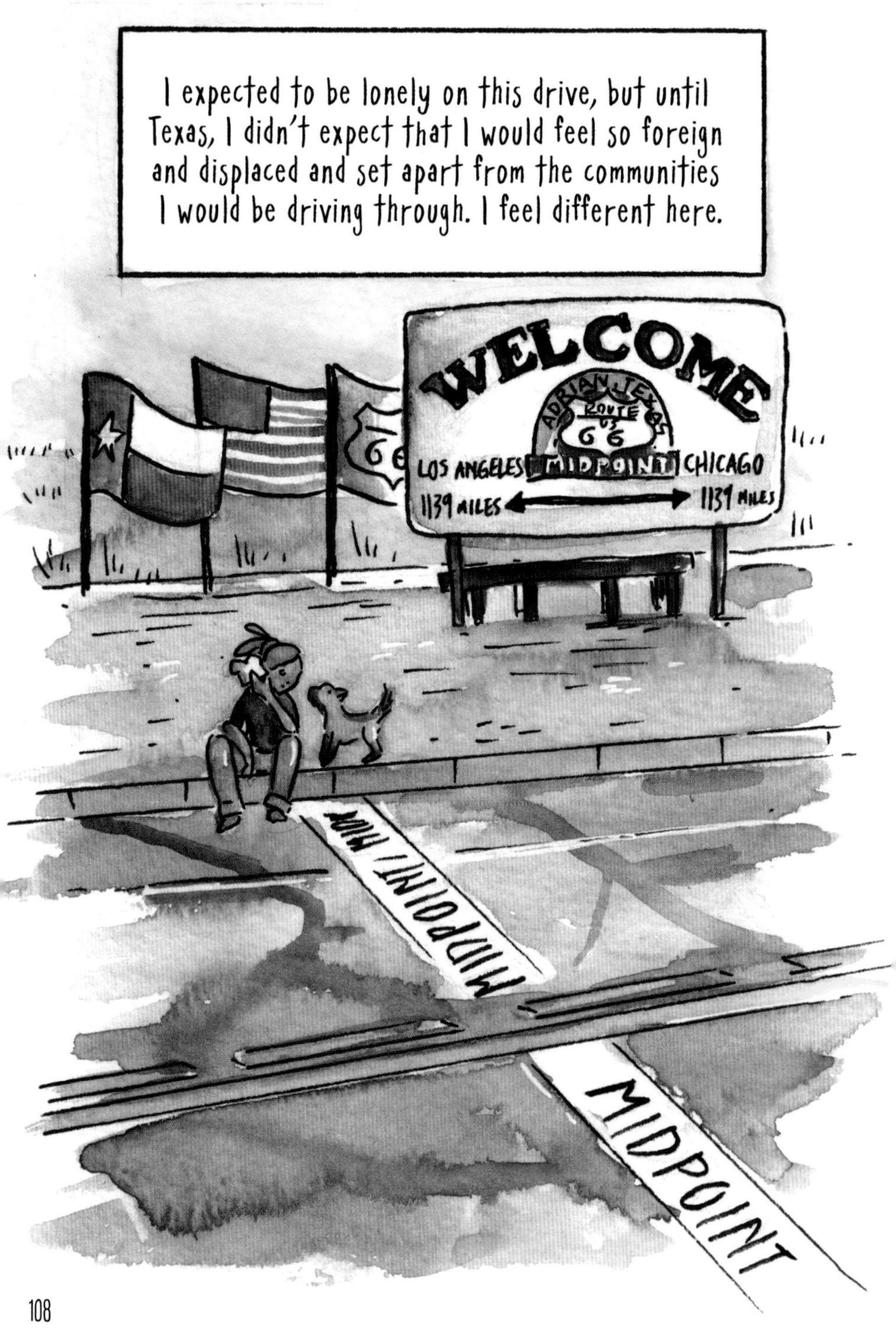
I expected to be lonely on this drive, but until Texas, I didn't expect that I would feel so foreign and displaced and set apart from the communities I would be driving through. I feel different here.
WELCOME
ADRIAN, TEXAS
ROUTE
66
LOS ANGELES
MIDPOINT
CHICAGO
1139 MILES
1139 MILES
66
MIDPOINT

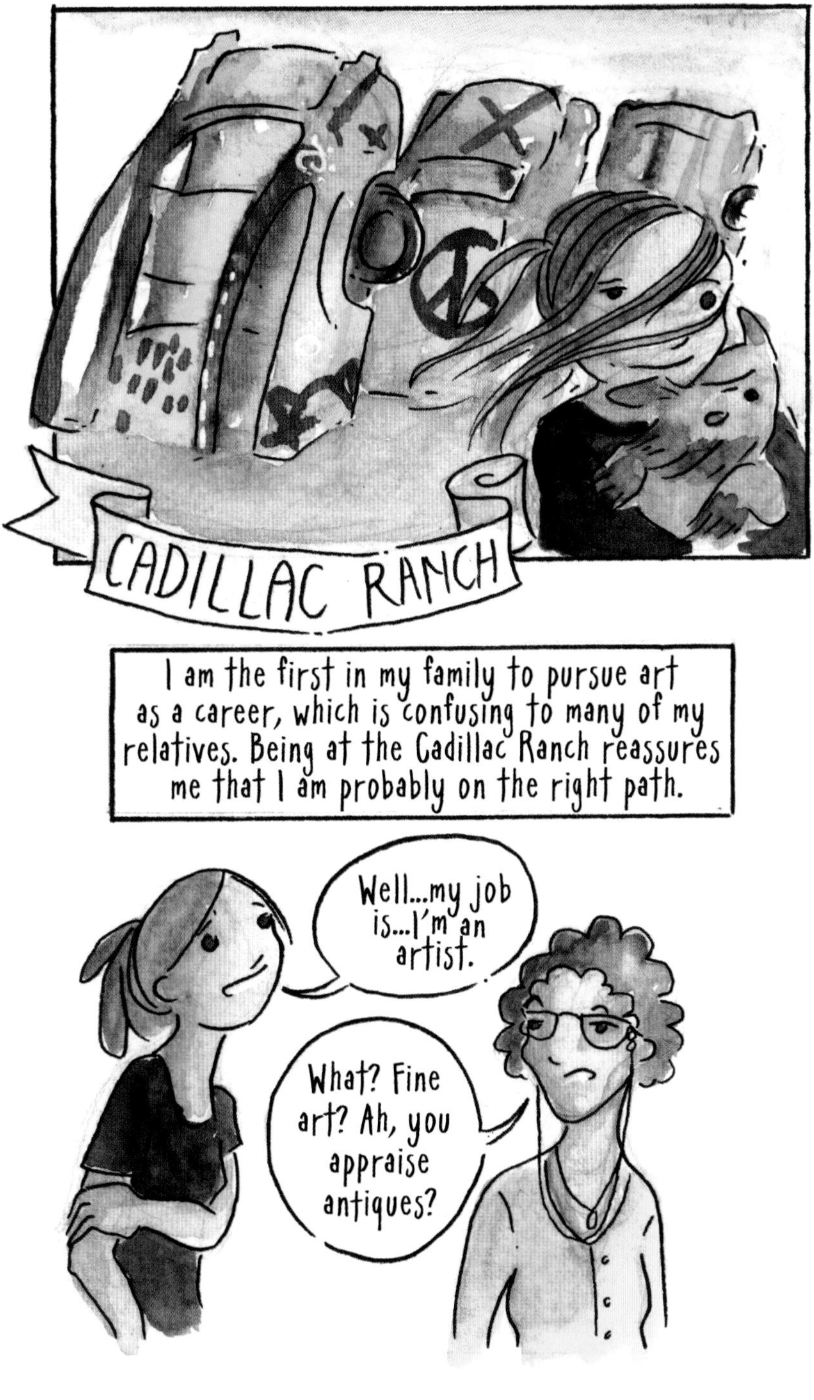
CADILLAC RANCH
I am the first in my family to pursue art as a career, which is confusing to many of my relatives. Being at the Cadillac Ranch reassures me that I am probably on the right path.
Well...my job is...I'm an artist.
What? Fine art? Ah, you appraise antiques?

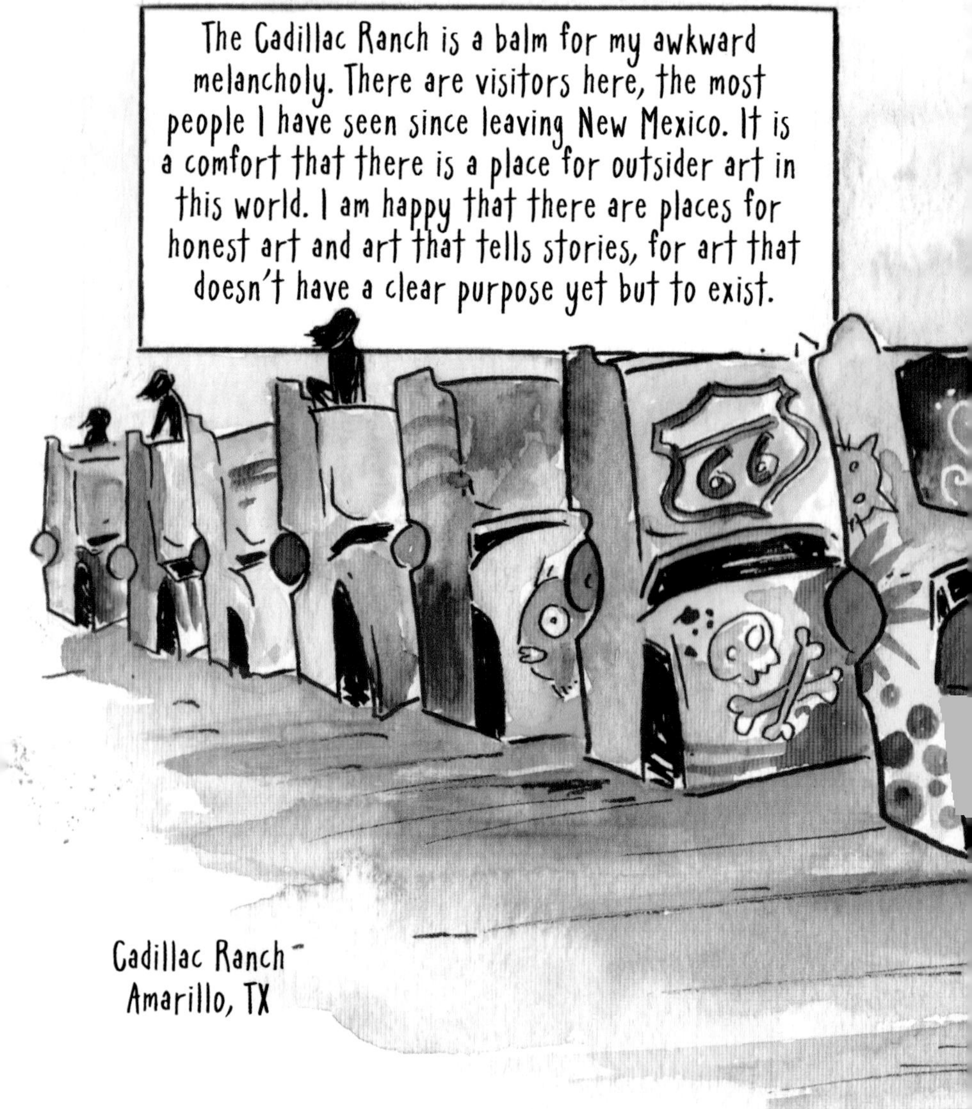
The Cadillac Ranch is a balm for my awkward melancholy. There are visitors here, the most people I have seen since leaving New Mexico. It is a comfort that there is a place for outsider art in this world. I am happy that there are places for honest art and art that tells stories, for art that doesn't have a clear purpose yet but to exist.
66
Cadillac Ranch
Amarillo, TX

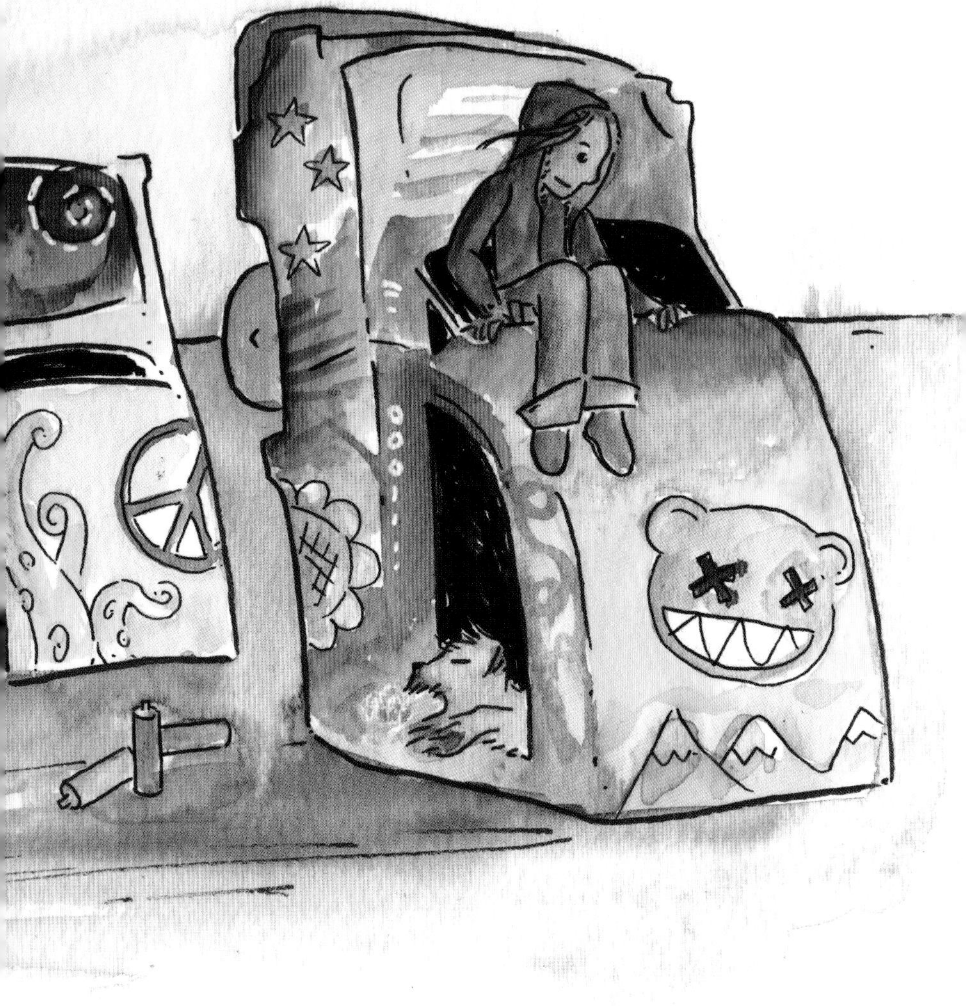

Cowboy Motel Sign
Amarillo, TX

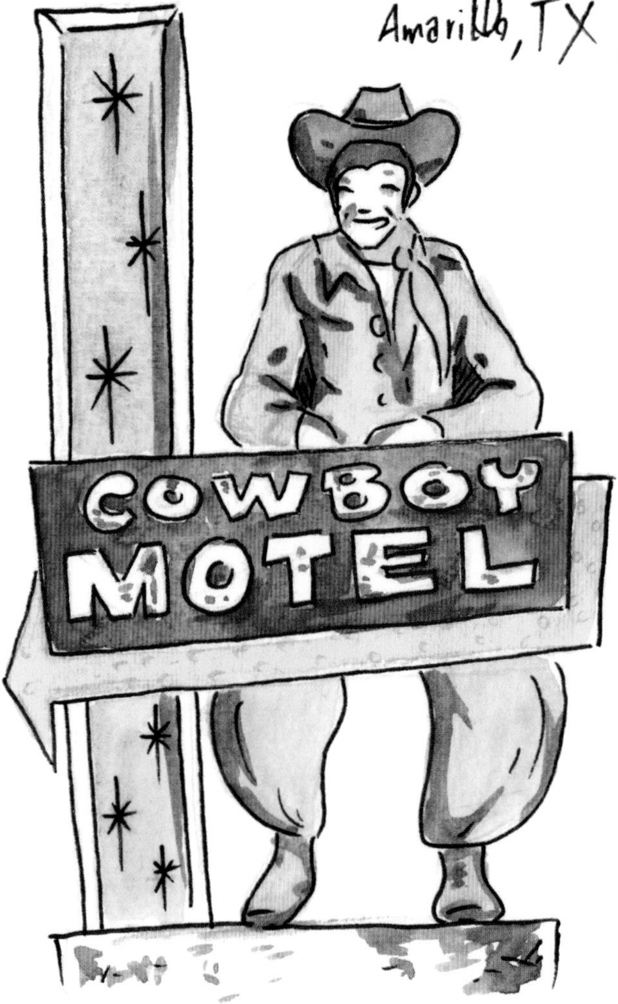
COWBOY
MOTEL

OKLAHOMA

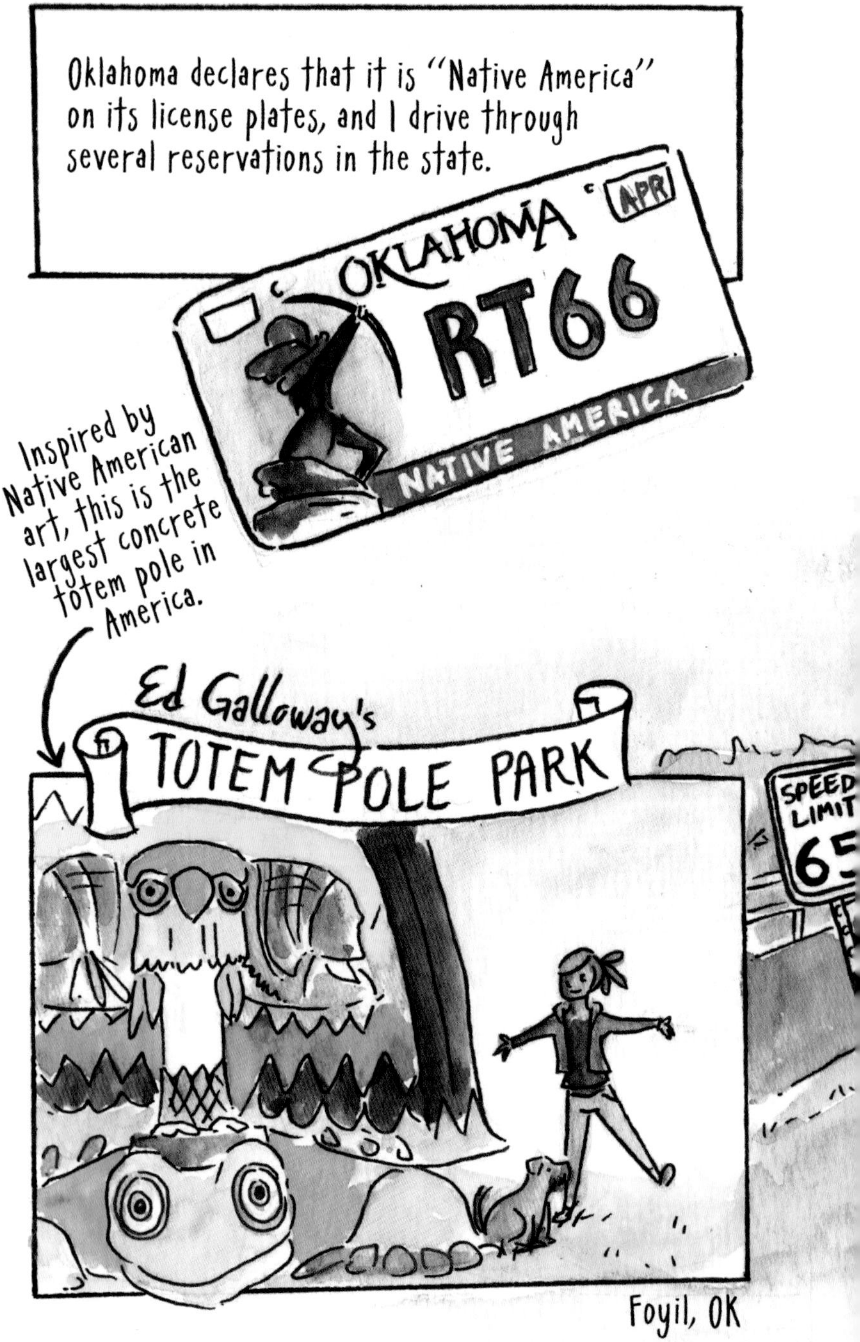
Oklahoma declares that it is "Native America" on its license plates, and I drive through several reservations in the state.
OKLAHOMA
APR
RT66
NATIVE AMERICA
Inspired by Native American art, this is the largest concrete totem pole in America.
Ed Galloway's
TOTEM POLE PARK
SPEED LIMIT
65
Foyil, OK

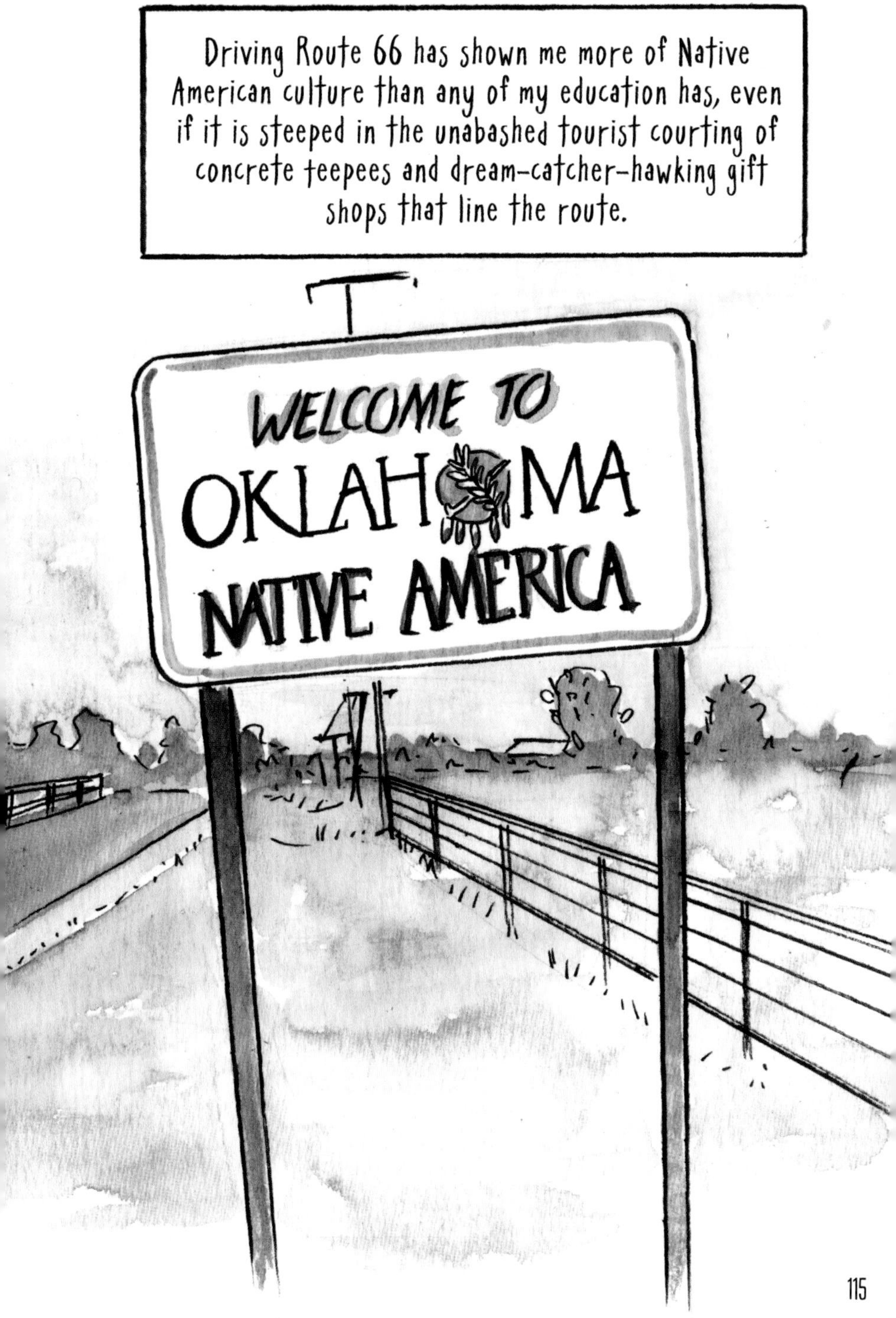
Driving Route 66 has shown me more of Native American culture than any of my education has, even if it is steeped in the unabashed tourist courting of concrete teepees and dream-catcher-hawking gift shops that line the route.
WELCOME TO
OKLAHOMA
NATIVE AMERICA

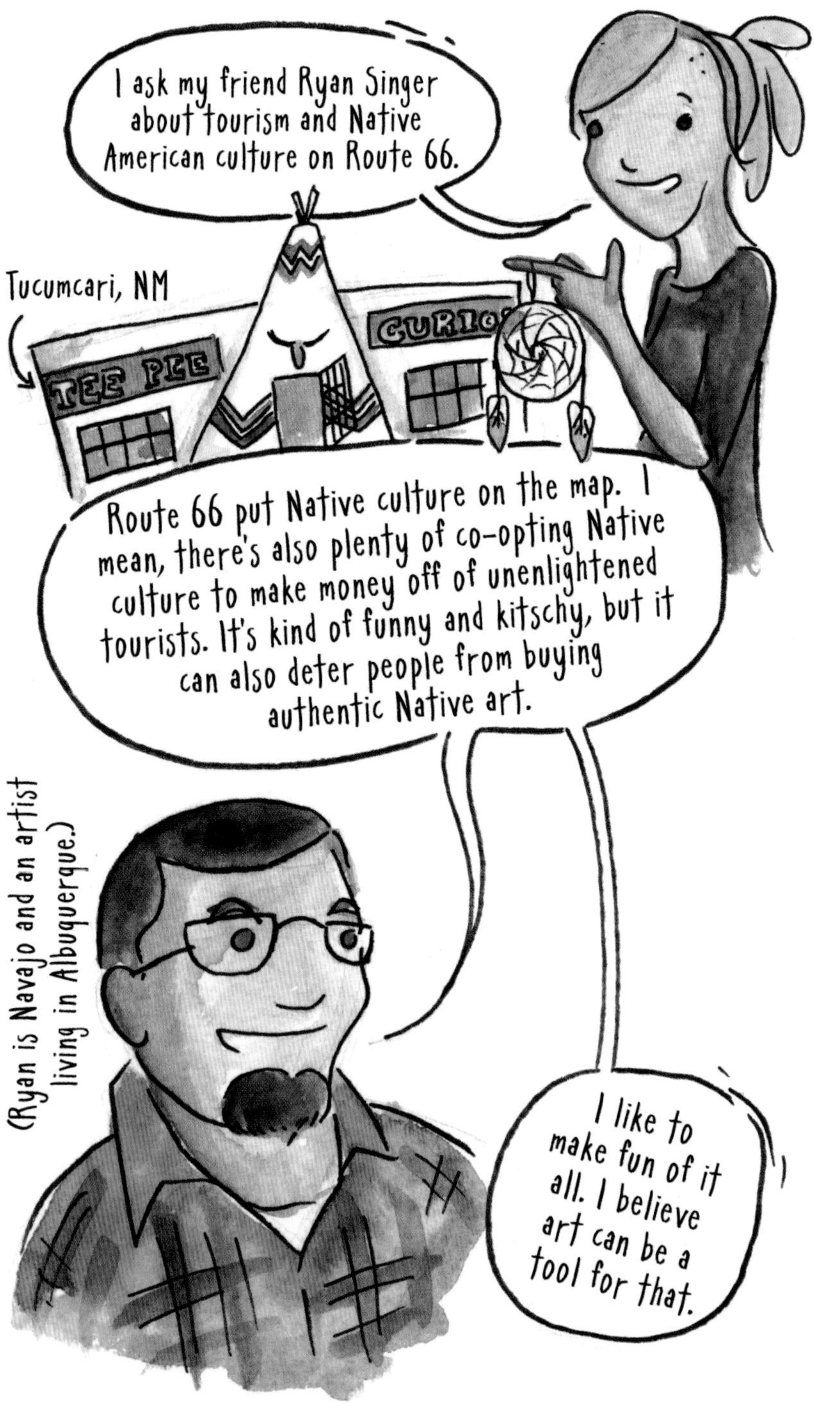
I ask my friend Ryan Singer about tourism and Native American culture on Route 66.
Tucumcari, NM
TEE PEE
CURIOS
Route 66 put Native culture on the map. I mean, there's also plenty of co-opting Native culture to make money off of unenlightened tourists. It's kind of funny and kitschy, but it can also deter people from buying authentic Native art.
(Ryan is Navajo and an artist living in Albuquerque.)
I like to make fun of it all. I believe art can be a tool for that.

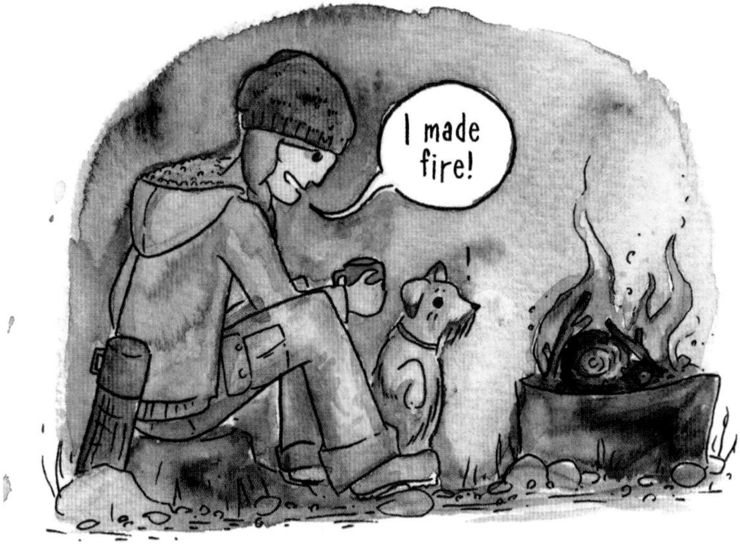
I made fire!

It is rainy and wet in Oklahoma, and my dedication to camping is wearing thin. In the drier states, I could bask in my (minimal) wilderness accomplishments.

Here, I am cold and wet and pooping in holes.

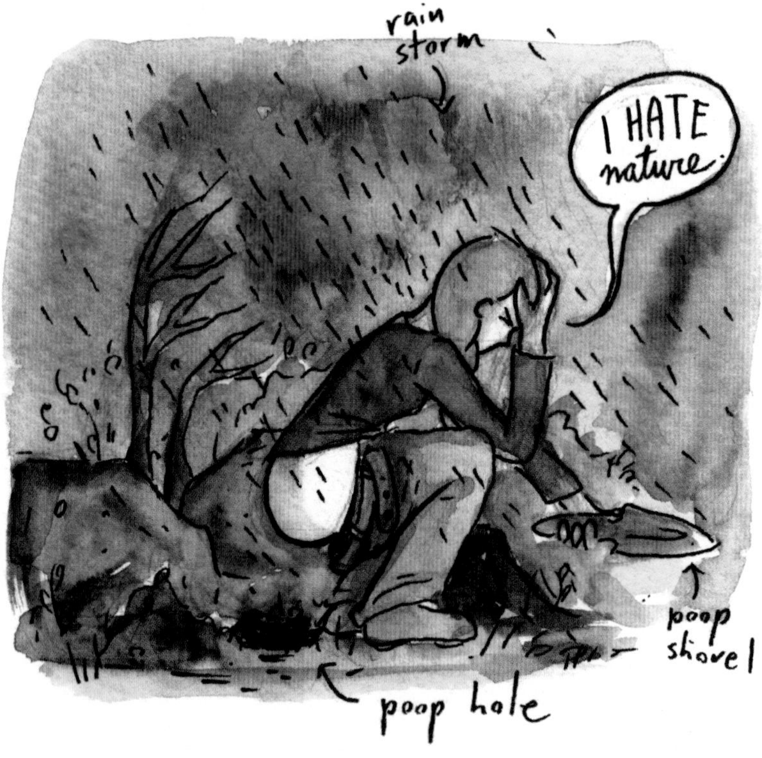
rain storm
I HATE nature.
poop shovel
poop hole

# HOW to POOP in NATURE

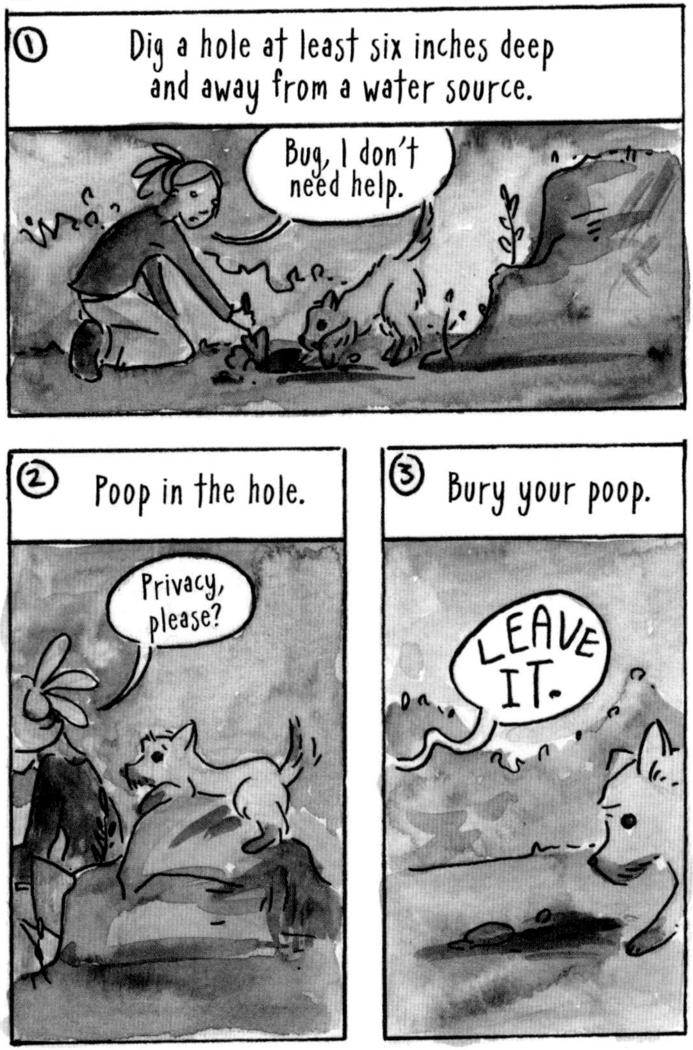
① Dig a hole at least six inches deep and away from a water source.
Bug, I don't need help.
② Poop in the hole.
Privacy, please?
③ Bury your poop.
LEAVE IT.

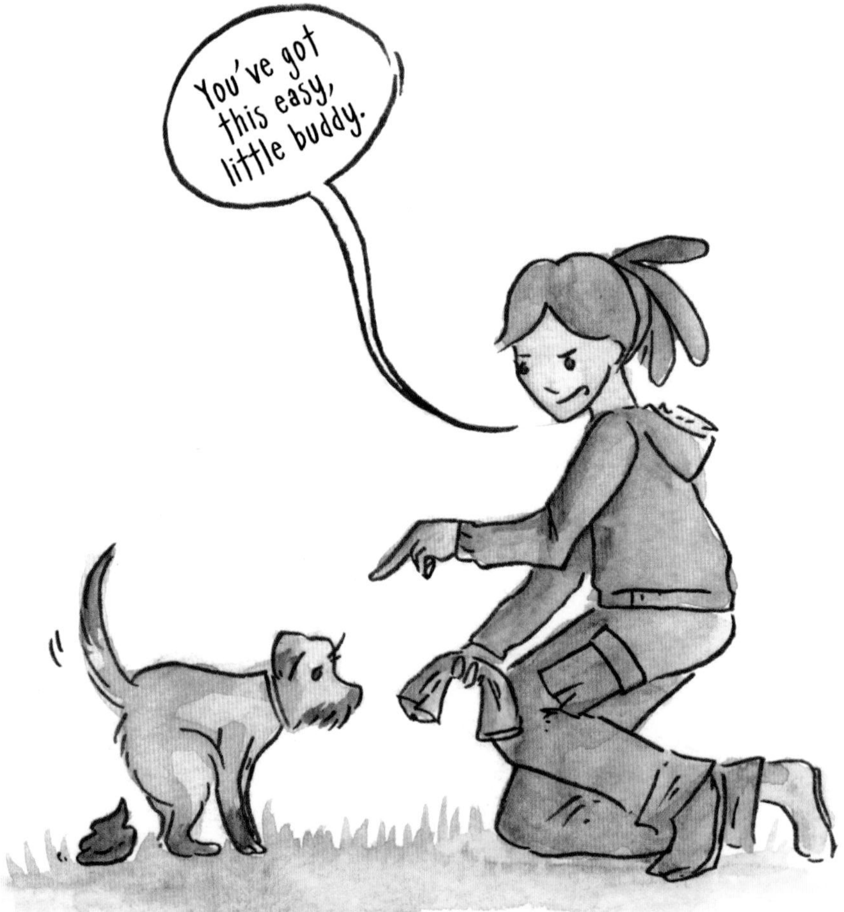
You've got this easy, little buddy.

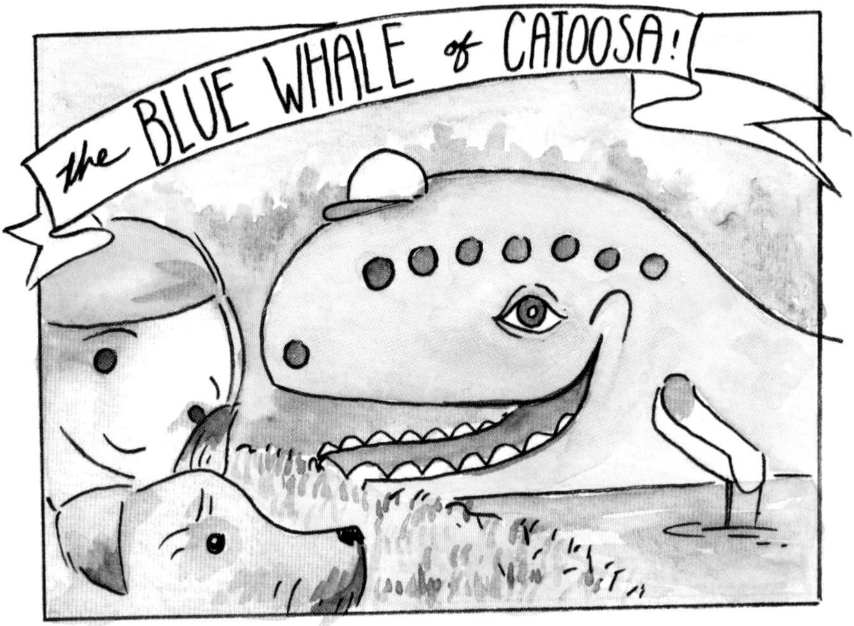
the BLUE WHALE of CATOOSA!

Catoosa, OK

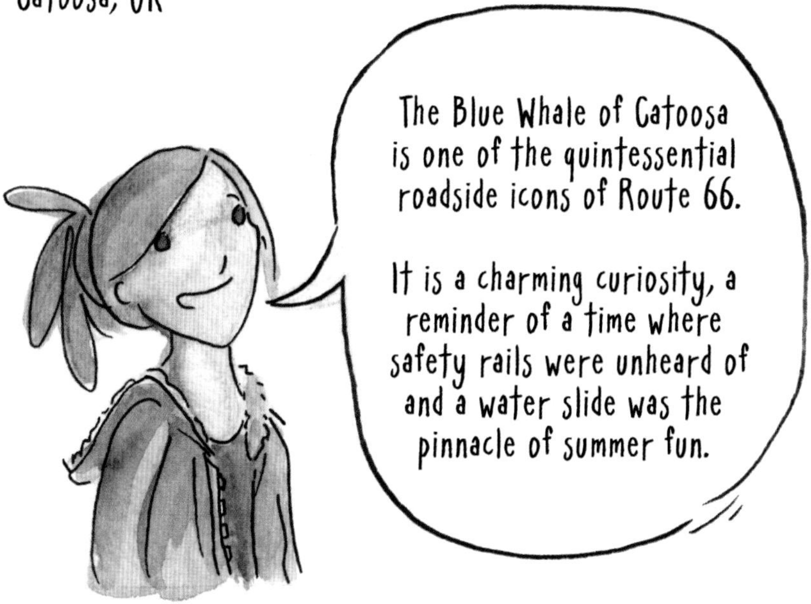
The Blue Whale of Catoosa is one of the quintessential roadside icons of Route 66.
It is a charming curiosity, a reminder of a time where safety rails were unheard of and a water slide was the pinnacle of summer fun.

You can climb into the Blue Whale's head, which is marked by graffiti by families and lovers.

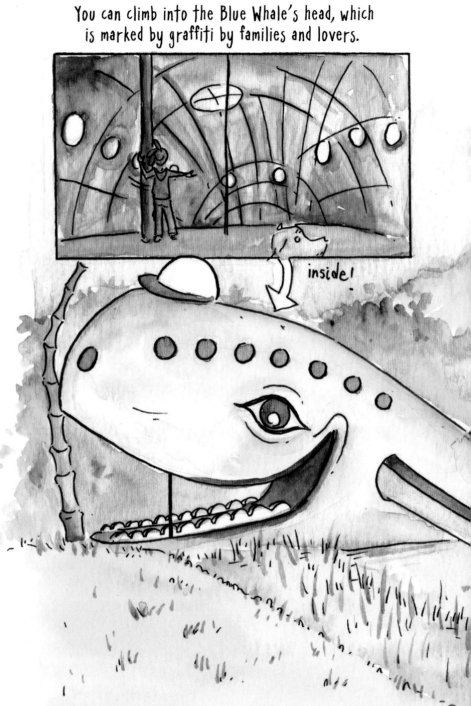

inside!

It's not road trip season in Oklahoma,
and the gift shop and food stand are closed.

It is an unassuming park, and right now
it's completely empty and slightly damp.

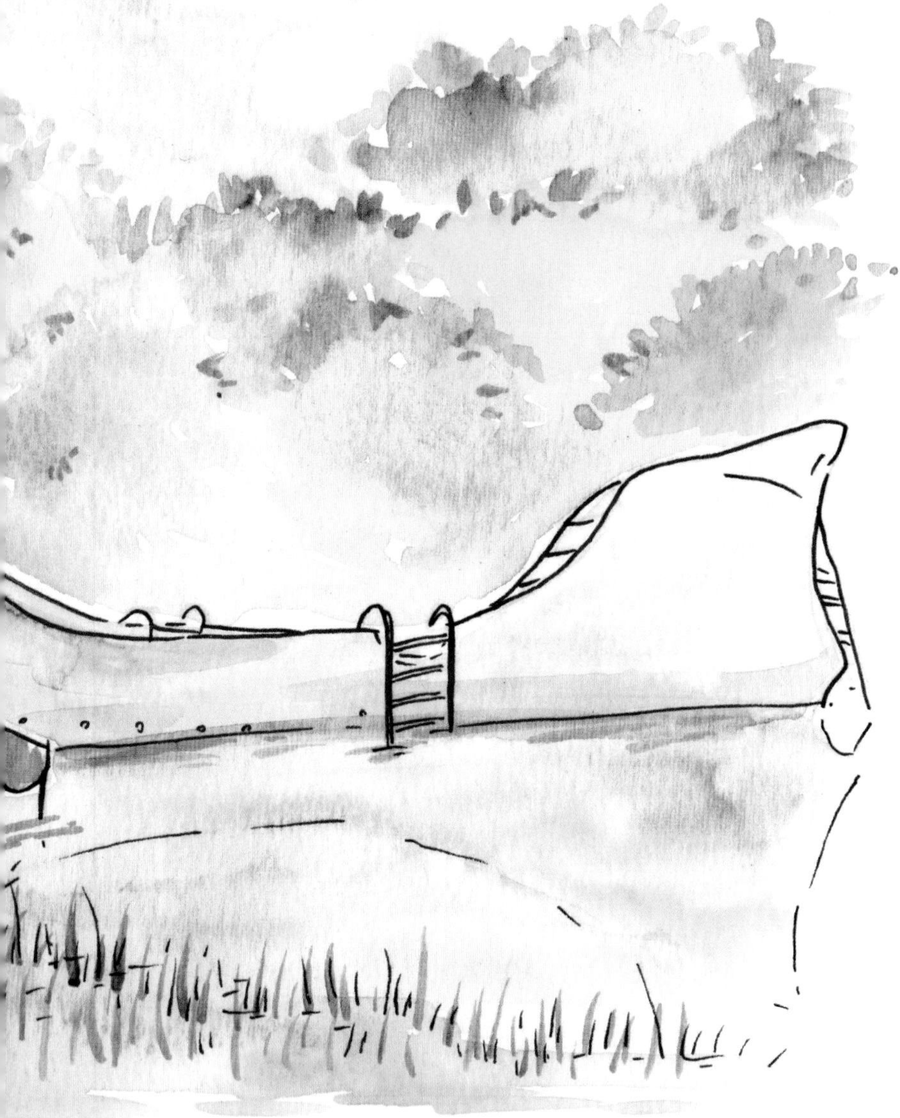

Right now, in the early spring, it's a place for quiet thoughts for a girl and her dog.

In a sense, this deserted park encapsulates how I feel about the American Dream at the moment. I am both exhausted and eternally hopeful, skeptical that the American Dream still exists, and awed at the potential it still holds.

It's a treat to come across a store advertising Route 66 cookies.

The store's proprietors, Charles Duboise and his mother, are pretty enthusiastic about both the cookies and the history of Commerce, OK.

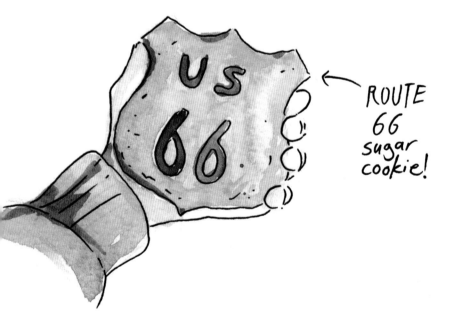

← ROUTE 66 sugar cookie!

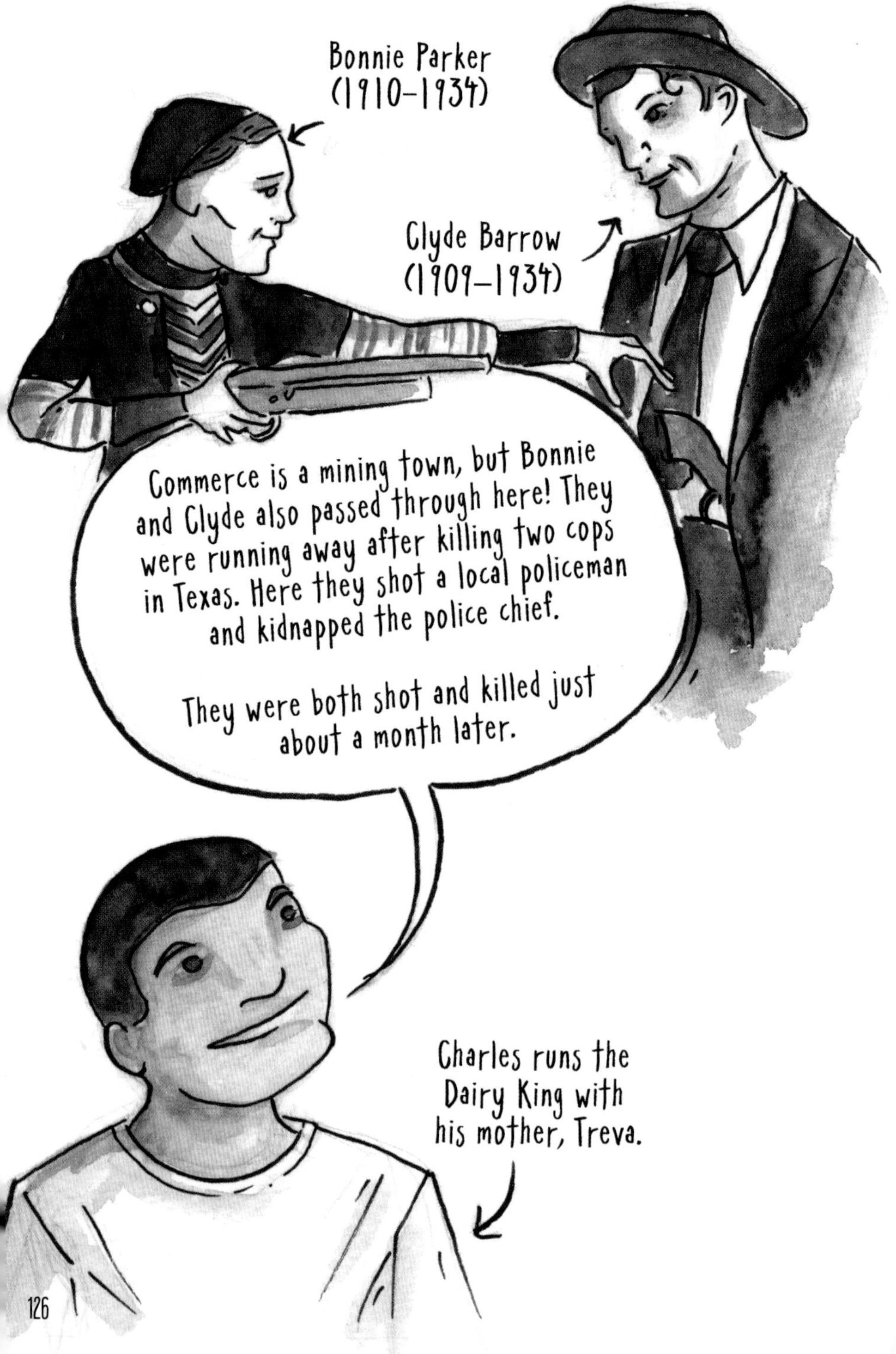
Bonnie Parker
(1910–1934)
Clyde Barrow
(1909–1934)
Commerce is a mining town, but Bonnie and Clyde also passed through here! They were running away after killing two cops in Texas. Here they shot a local policeman and kidnapped the police chief.
They were both shot and killed just about a month later.
Charles runs the Dairy King with his mother, Treva.

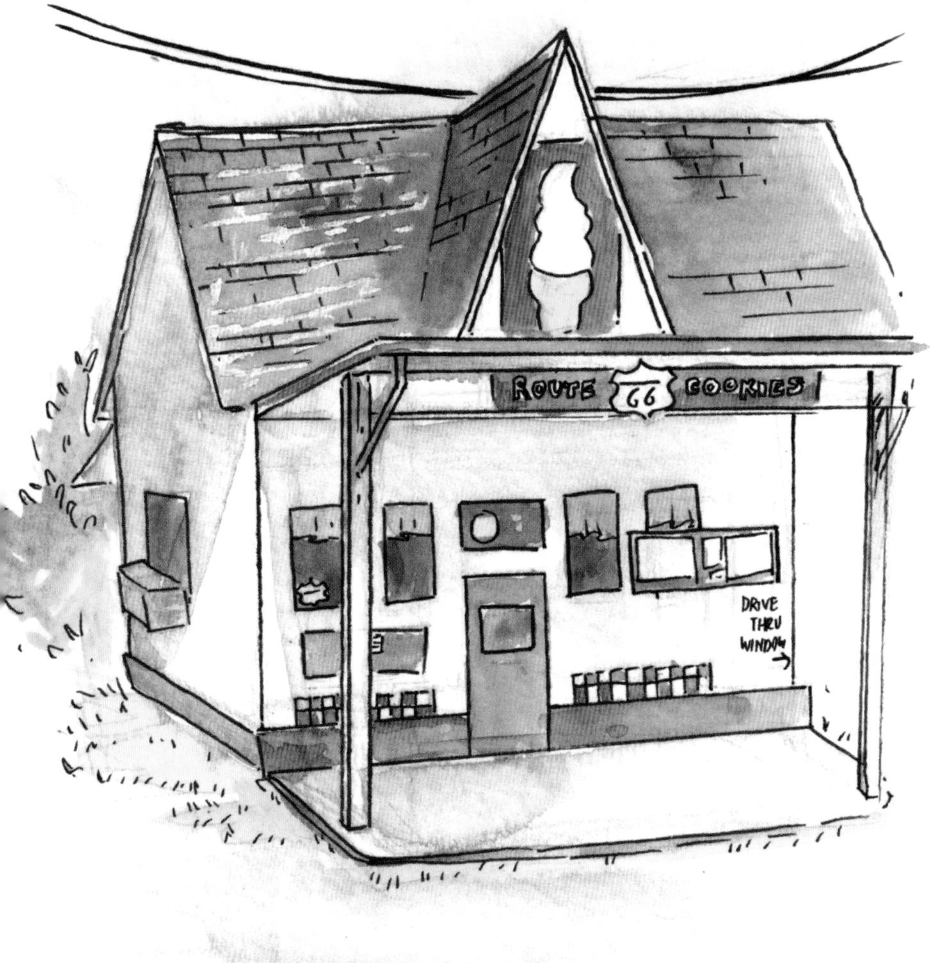
ROUTE 66 COOKIES
DRIVE THRU WINDOW

The Dairy King in Commerce used to be a Marathon Gas Station in the Route 66 days. Now it serves ice cream, burgers, and pretty good sugar cookies.

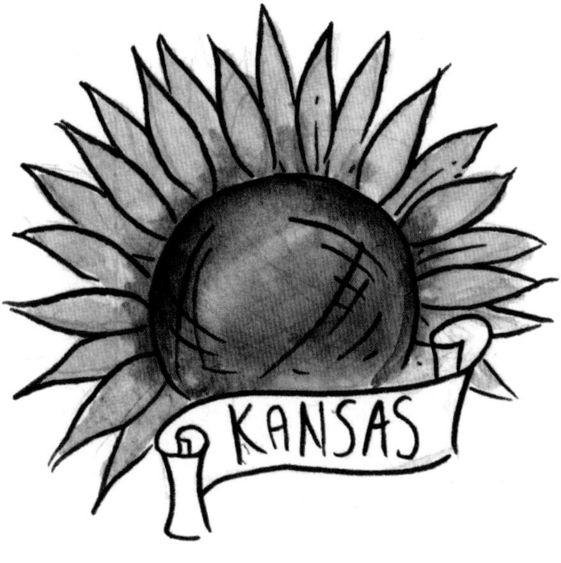
KANSAS

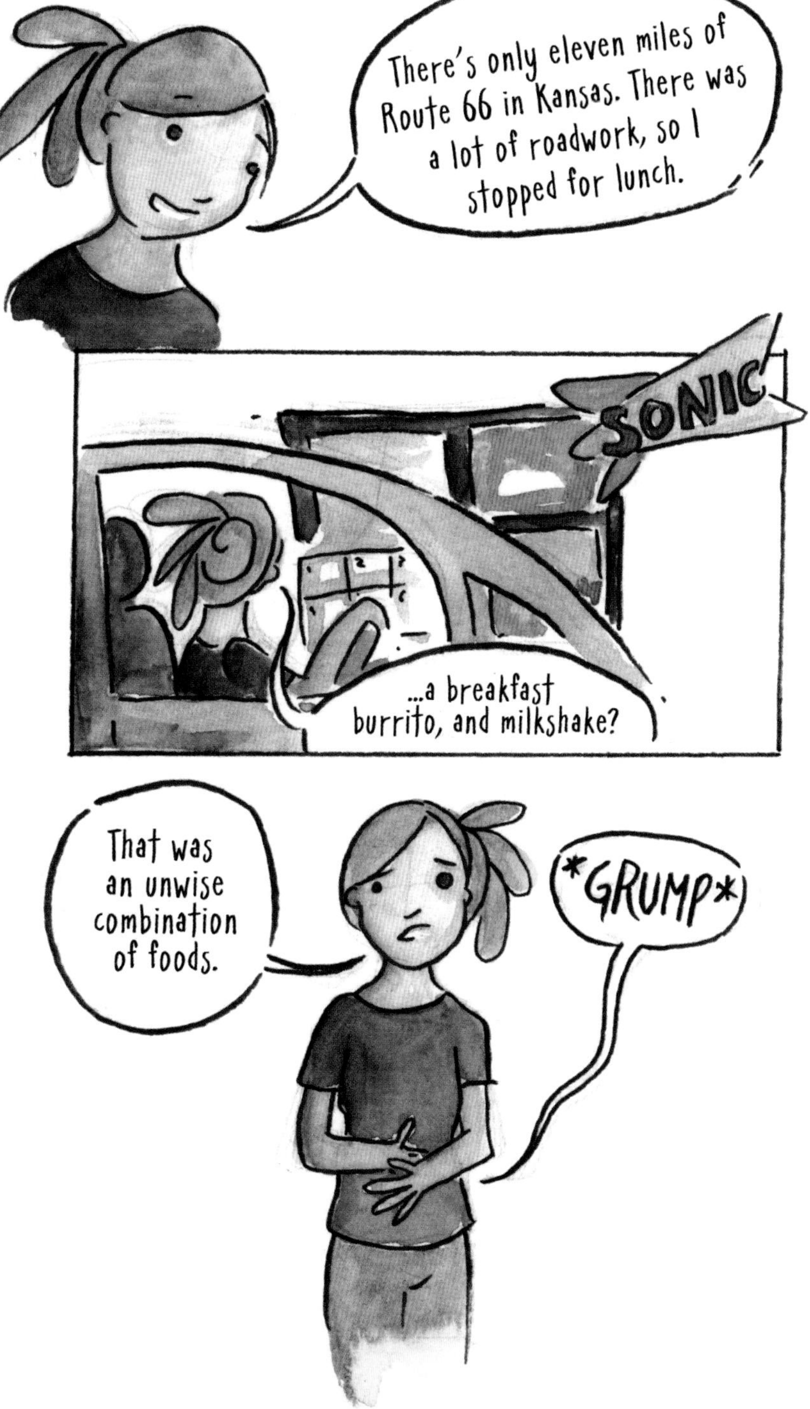
There's only eleven miles of Route 66 in Kansas. There was a lot of roadwork, so I stopped for lunch.
SONIC
...a breakfast burrito, and milkshake?
That was an unwise combination of foods.
*GRUMP*

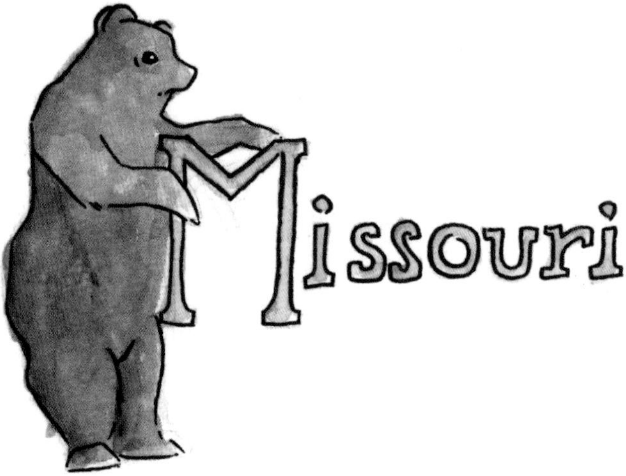
Missouri

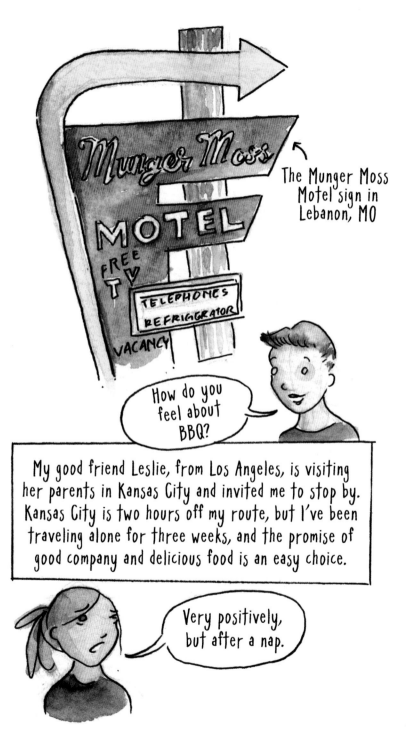

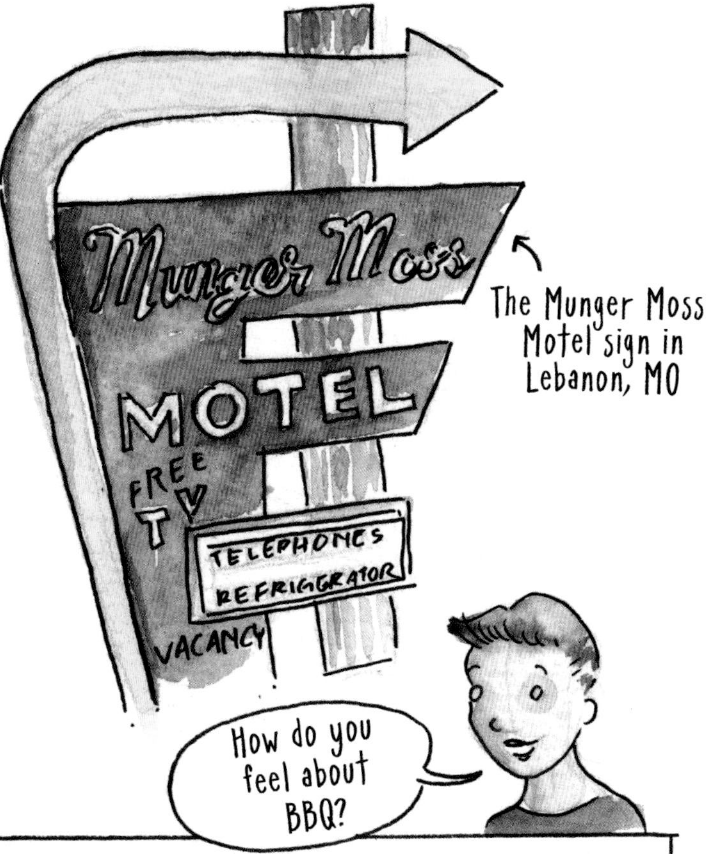
Munger Moss
MOTEL
FREE TV
TELEPHONES
REFRIGGRATOR
VACANCY
The Munger Moss Motel sign in Lebanon, MO
How do you feel about BBQ?

My good friend Leslie, from Los Angeles, is visiting her parents in Kansas City and invited me to stop by. Kansas City is two hours off my route, but I've been traveling alone for three weeks, and the promise of good company and delicious food is an easy choice.

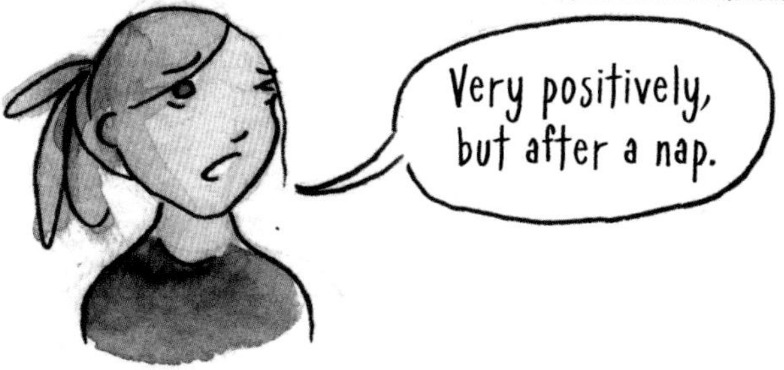
Very positively, but after a nap.

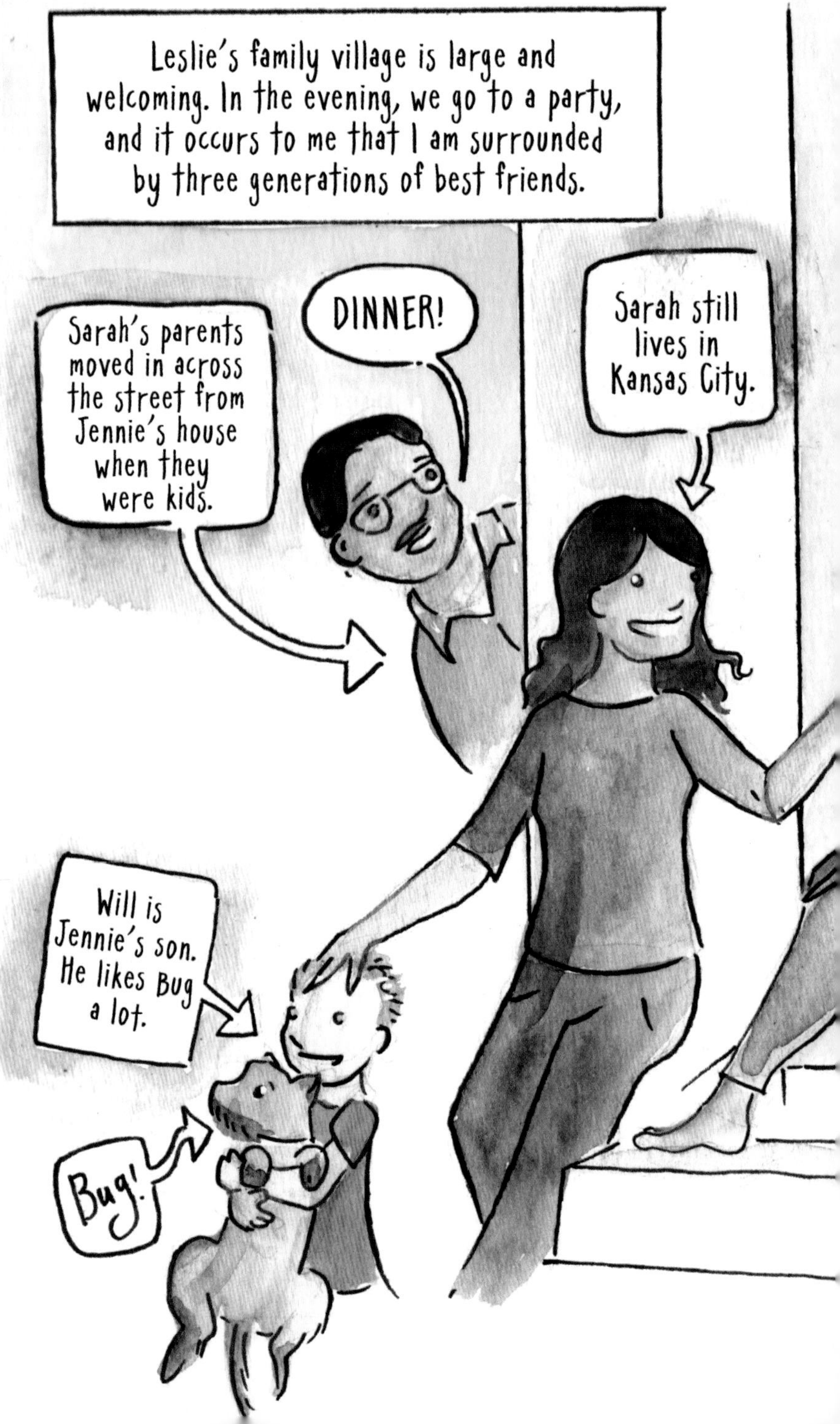
Leslie's family village is large and welcoming. In the evening, we go to a party, and it occurs to me that I am surrounded by three generations of best friends.
Sarah's parents moved in across the street from Jennie's house when they were kids.
DINNER!
Sarah still lives in Kansas City.
Will is Jennie's son. He likes Bug a lot.
Bug!

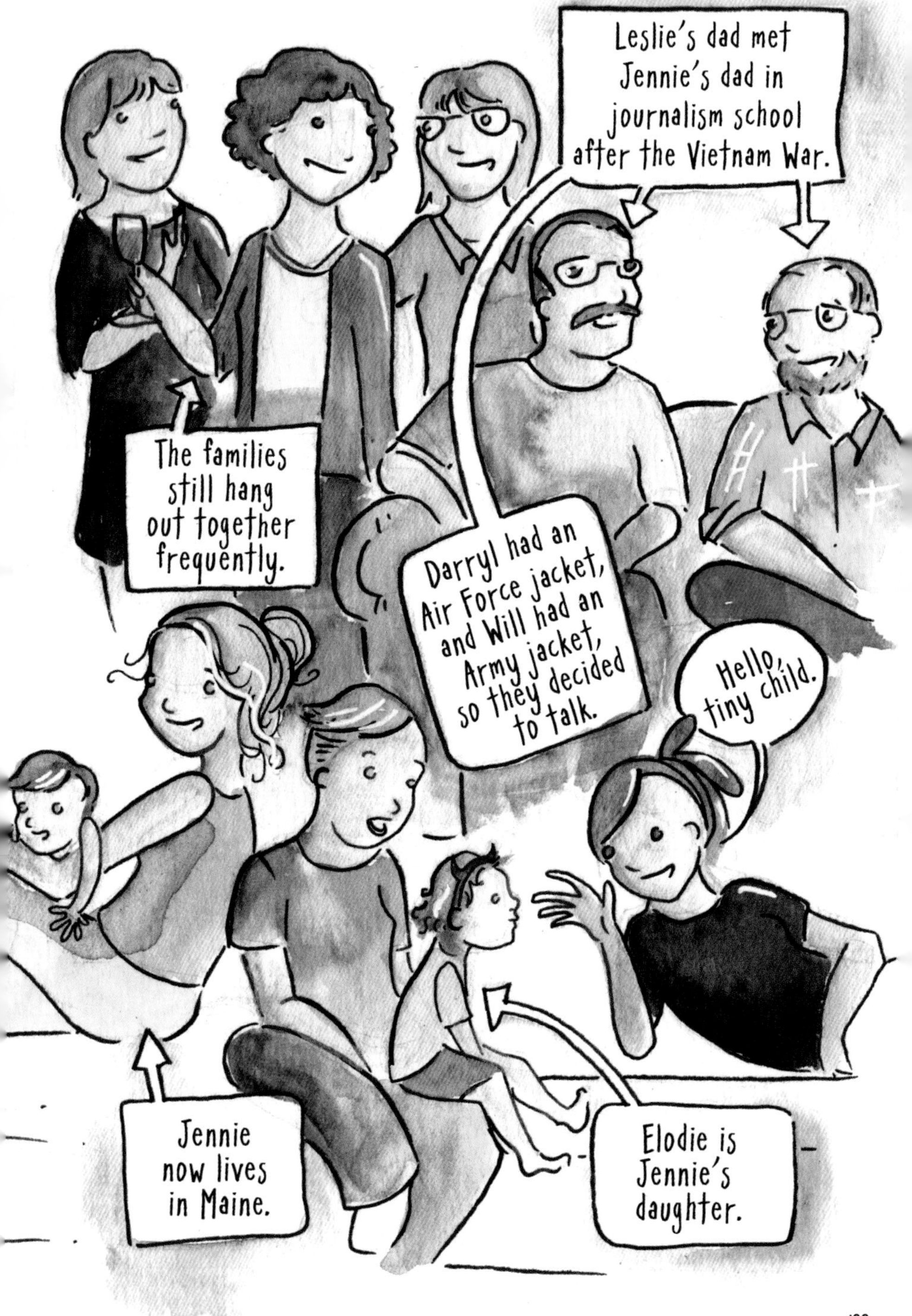
Leslie's dad met Jennie's dad in journalism school after the Vietnam War.
The families still hang out together frequently.
Darryl had an Air Force jacket, and Will had an Army jacket, so they decided to talk.
Hello, tiny child.
Jennie now lives in Maine.
Elodie is Jennie's daughter.

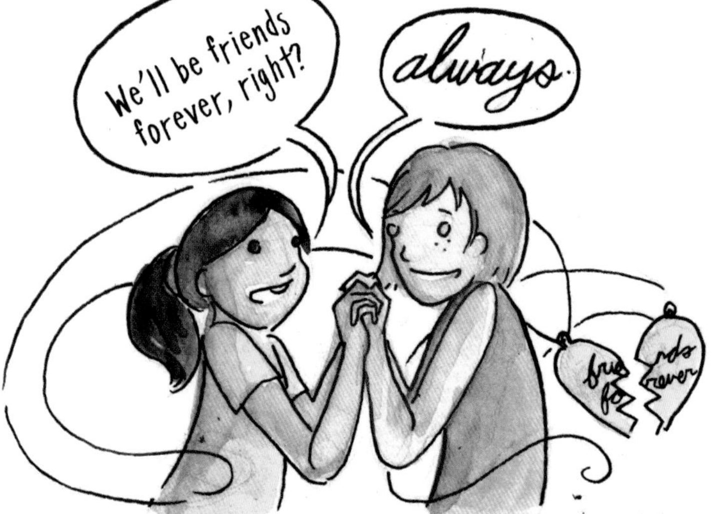
We'll be friends forever, right?
always

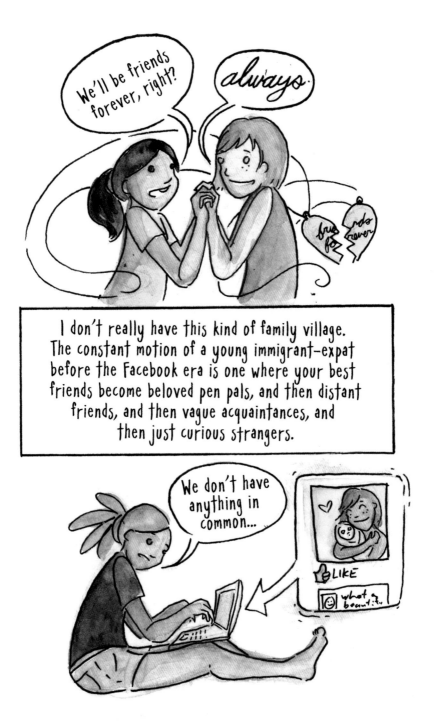

I don't really have this kind of family village. The constant motion of a young immigrant-expat before the Facebook era is one where your best friends become beloved pen pals, and then distant friends, and then vague acquaintances, and then just curious strangers.

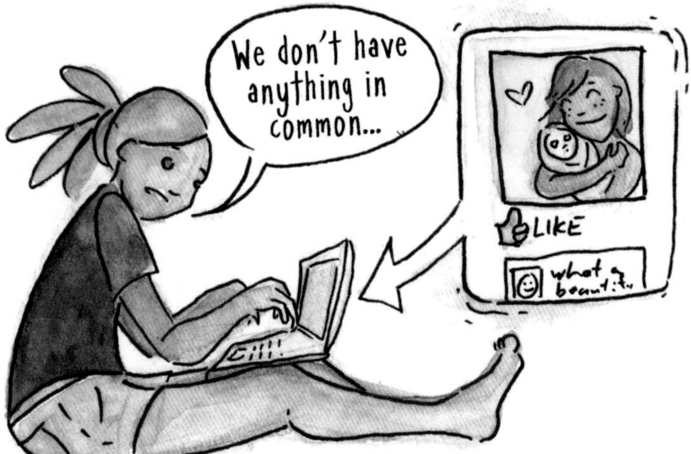
We don't have anything in common...
LIKE

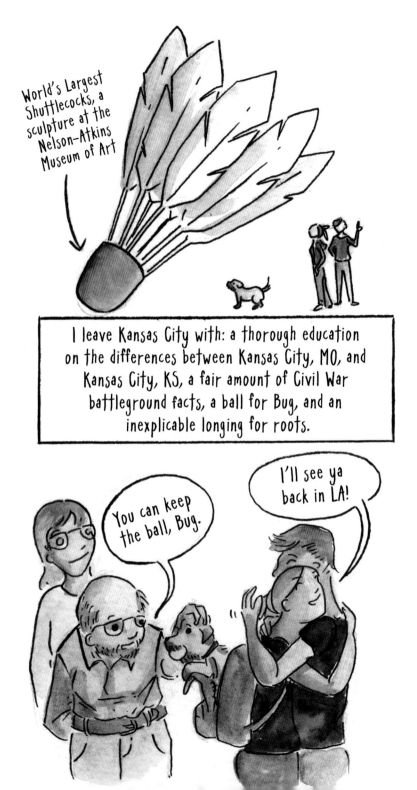

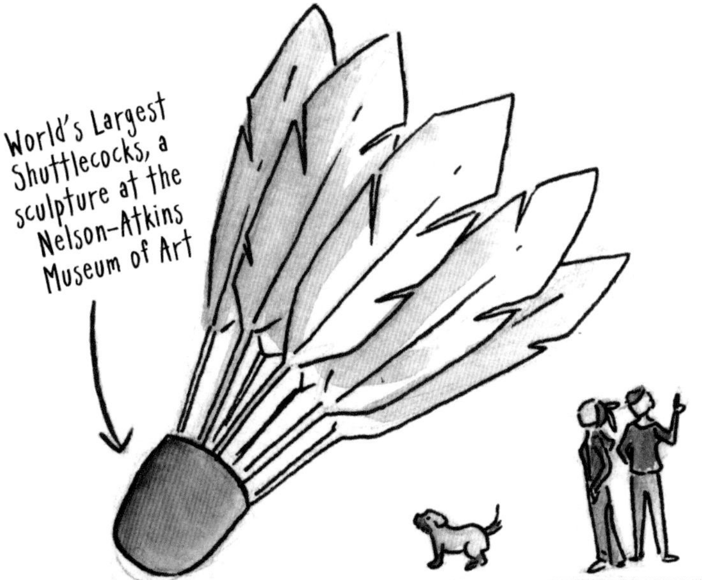
World's Largest Shuttlecocks, a sculpture at the Nelson-Atkins Museum of Art

I leave Kansas City with: a thorough education on the differences between Kansas City, MO, and Kansas City, KS, a fair amount of Civil War battleground facts, a ball for Bug, and an inexplicable longing for roots.

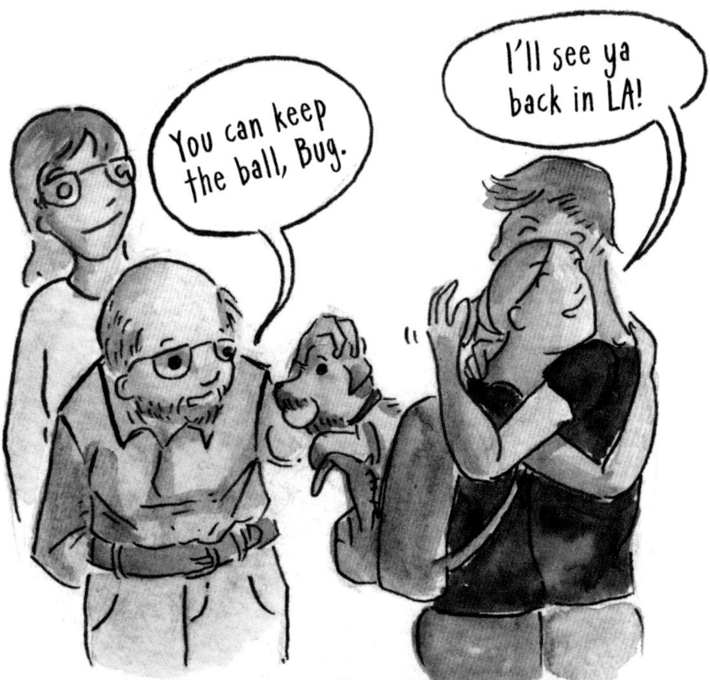
You can keep the ball, Bug.
I'll see ya back in LA!

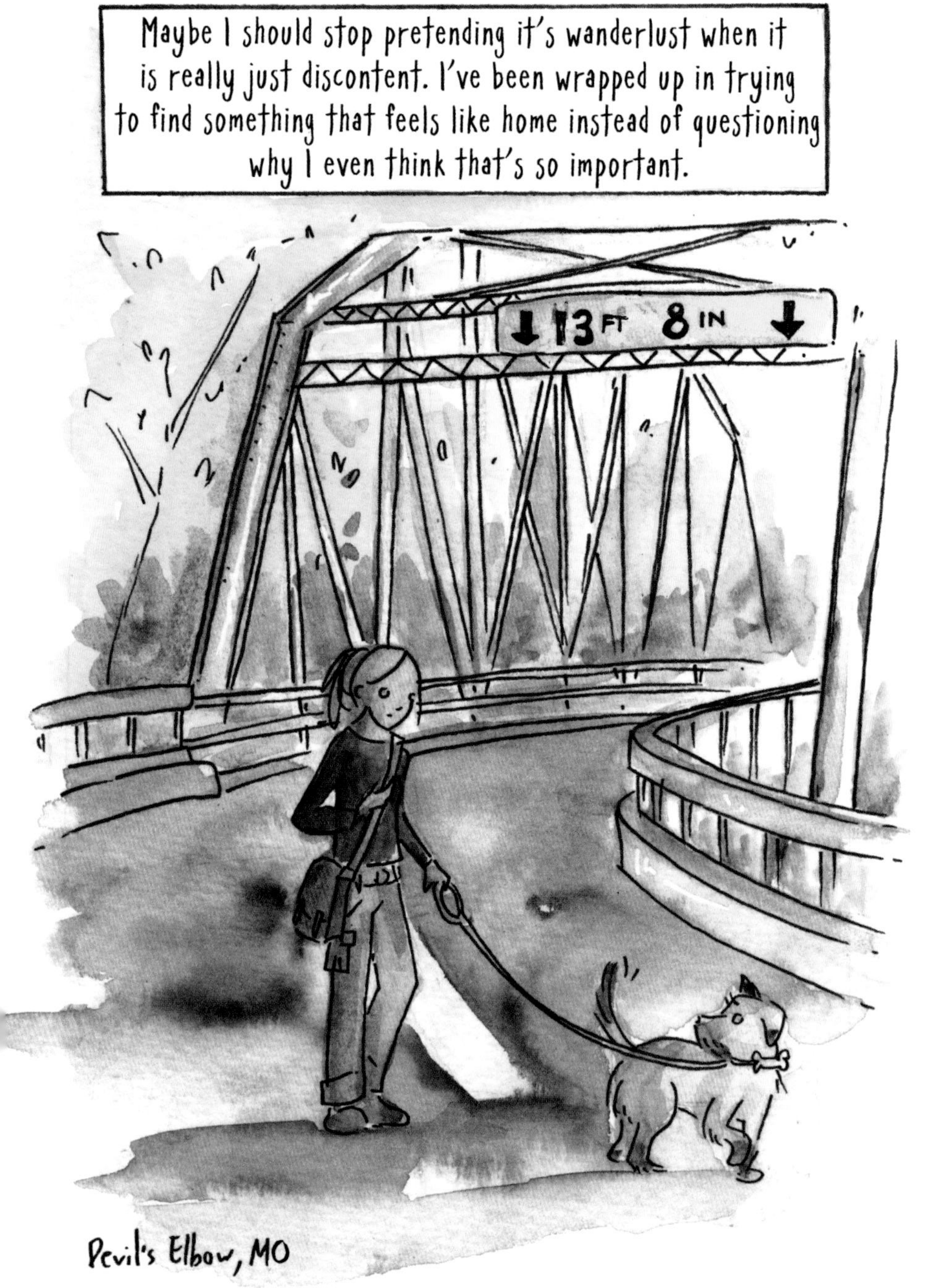
Maybe I should stop pretending it's wanderlust when it is really just discontent. I've been wrapped up in trying to find something that feels like home instead of questioning why I even think that's so important.
↓13 FT 8 IN↓
Devil's Elbow, MO

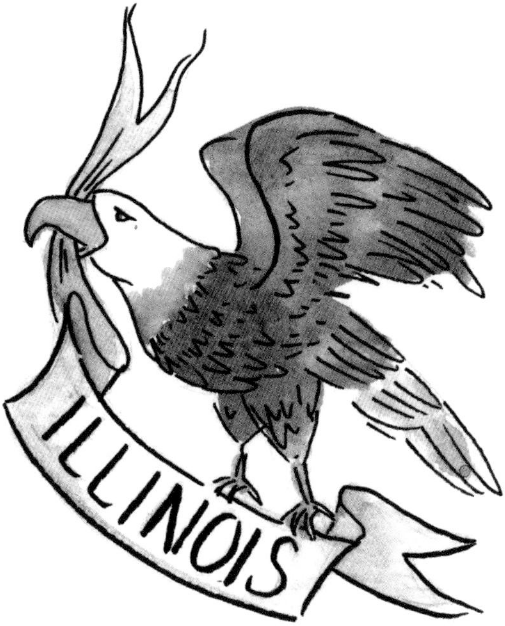
ILLINOIS

By the time I enter Illinois, I've been sleeping in my car in the rain for several days.

Bug is in a great mood. I am not.

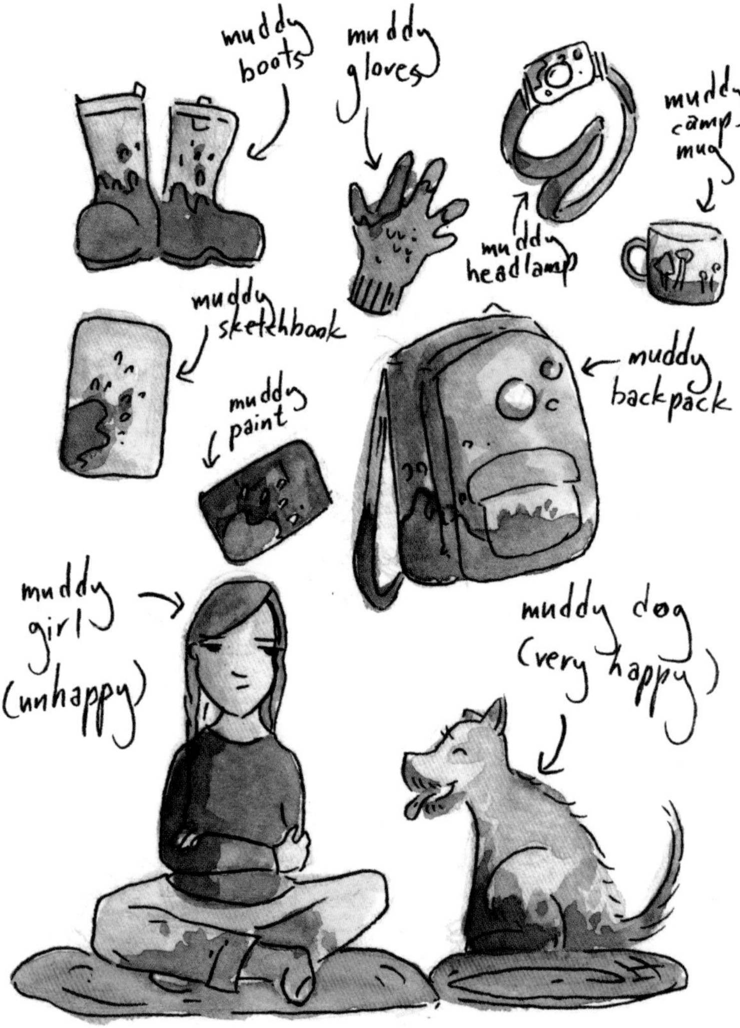
muddy boots
muddy gloves
muddy headlamp
muddy camp mug
muddy sketchbook
muddy paint
muddy backpack
muddy girl (unhappy)
muddy dog (very happy)

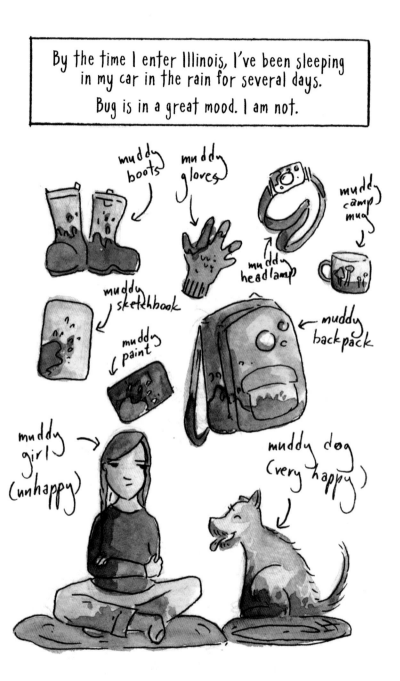

I try to be positive, but I'm craving the city. Chicago is calling to me as a beacon of hope, and by hope, I just mean the ability to order takeout from my phone.

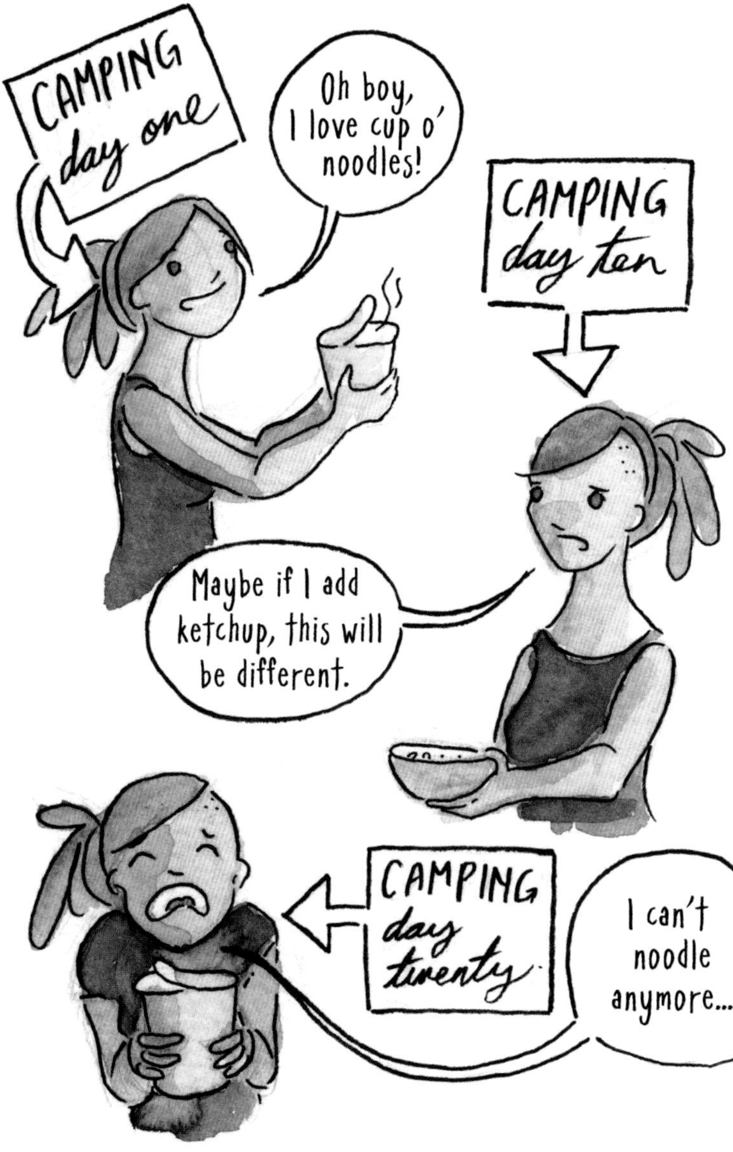
CAMPING day one
Oh boy, I love cup o' noodles!
CAMPING day ten
Maybe if I add ketchup, this will be different.
CAMPING day twenty
I can't noodle anymore...

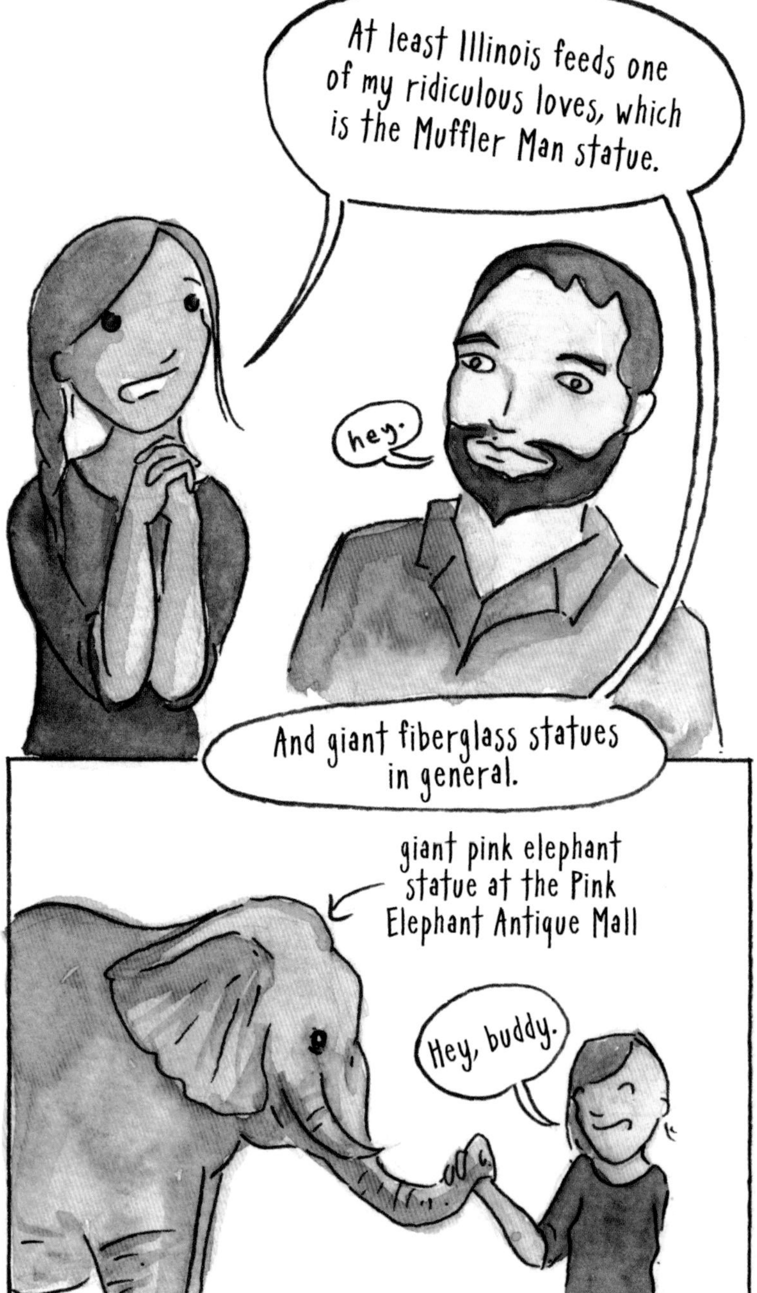
At least Illinois feeds one of my ridiculous loves, which is the Muffler Man statue.
hey.
And giant fiberglass statues in general.
giant pink elephant statue at the Pink Elephant Antique Mall
Hey, buddy.

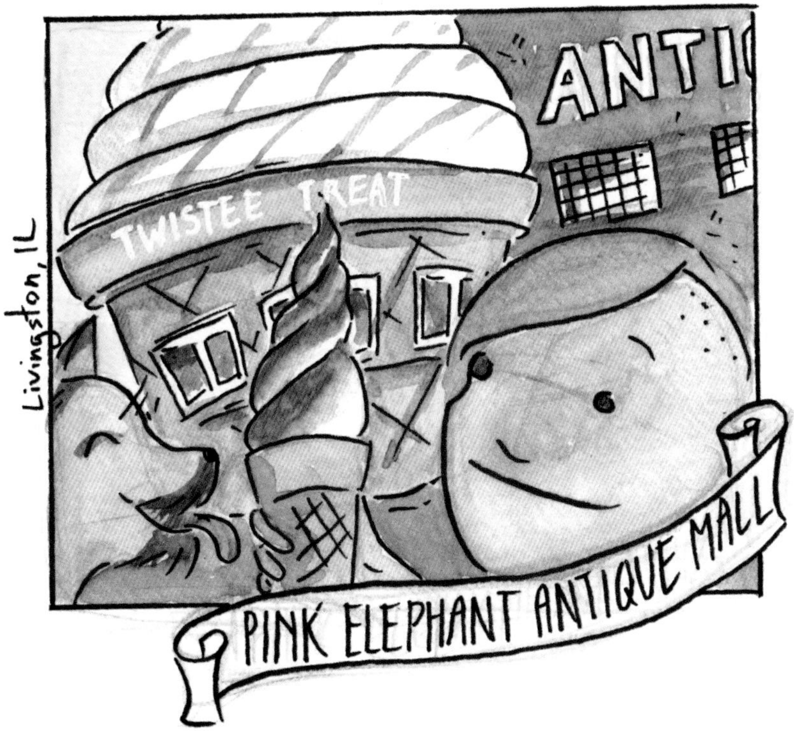
Livingston, IL
ANTI
TWISTEE TREAT
PINK ELEPHANT ANTIQUE MALL

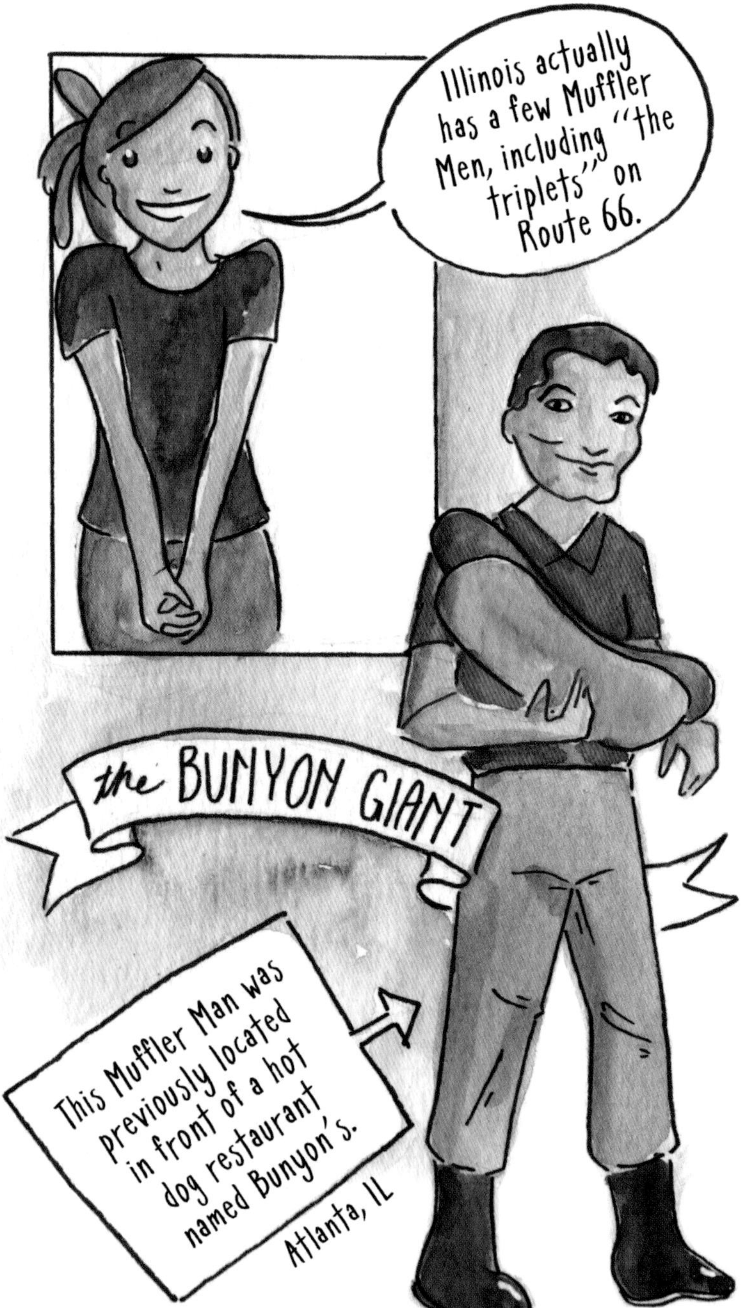
Illinois actually has a few Muffler Men, including "the triplets" on Route 66.
the BUNYON GIANT
This Muffler Man was previously located in front of a hot dog restaurant named Bunyon's.
Atlanta, IL

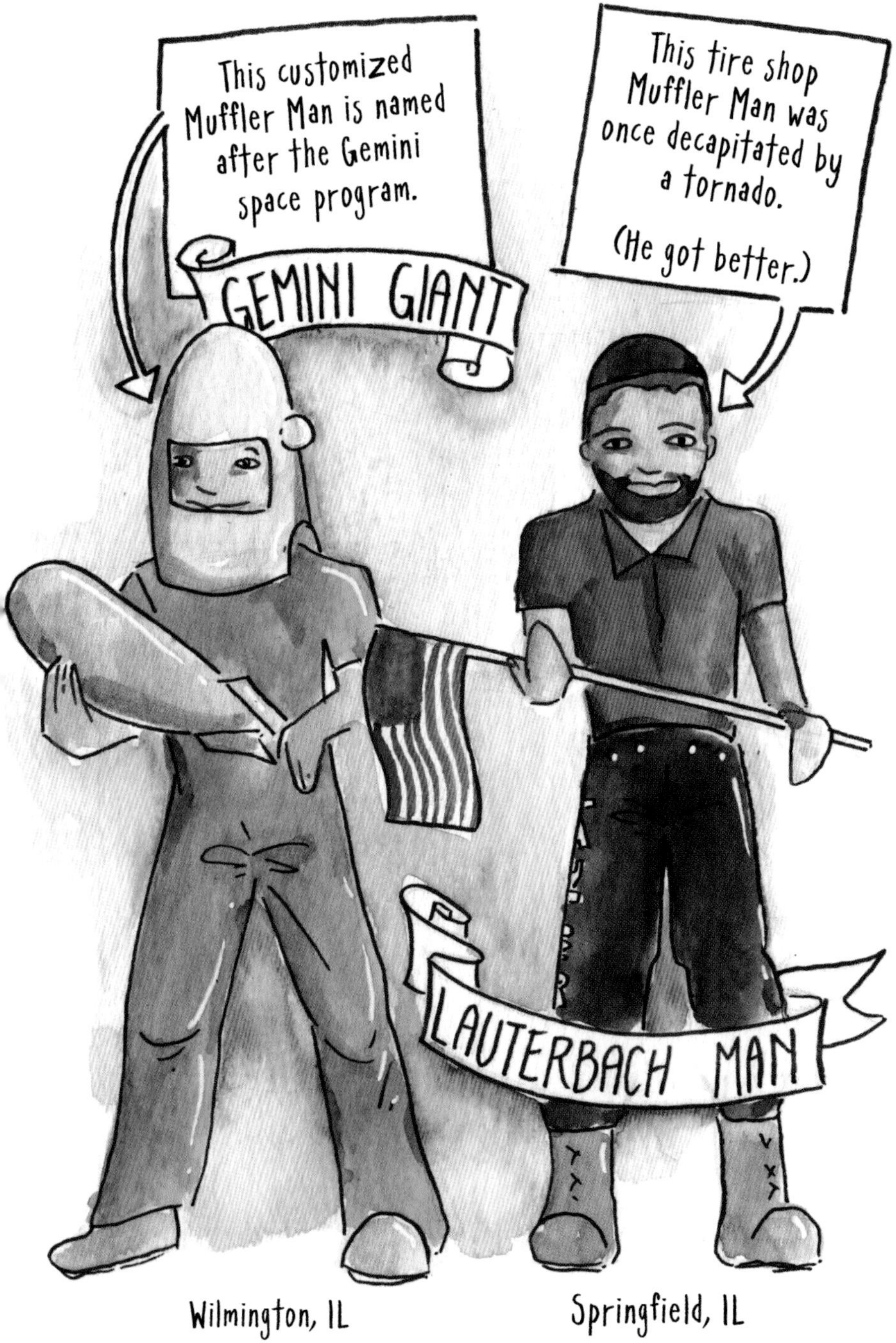

This customized Muffler Man is named after the Gemini space program.
GEMINI GIANT
This tire shop Muffler Man was once decapitated by a tornado.
(He got better.)
LAUTERBACH MAN
Wilmington, IL
Springfield, IL

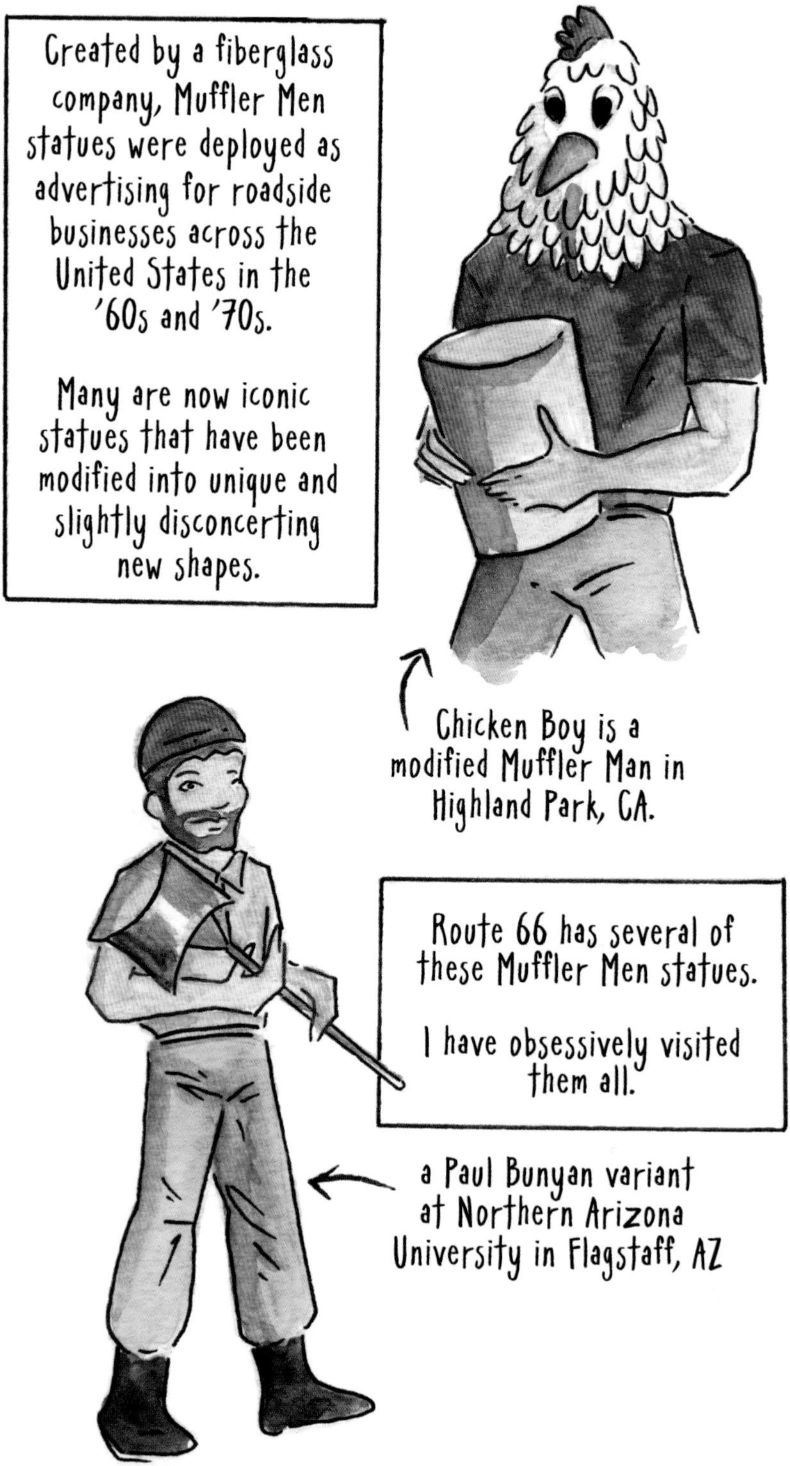
Created by a fiberglass company, Muffler Men statues were deployed as advertising for roadside businesses across the United States in the '60s and '70s.
Many are now iconic statues that have been modified into unique and slightly disconcerting new shapes.
Chicken Boy is a modified Muffler Man in Highland Park, CA.
Route 66 has several of these Muffler Men statues.
I have obsessively visited them all.
a Paul Bunyan variant at Northern Arizona University in Flagstaff, AZ

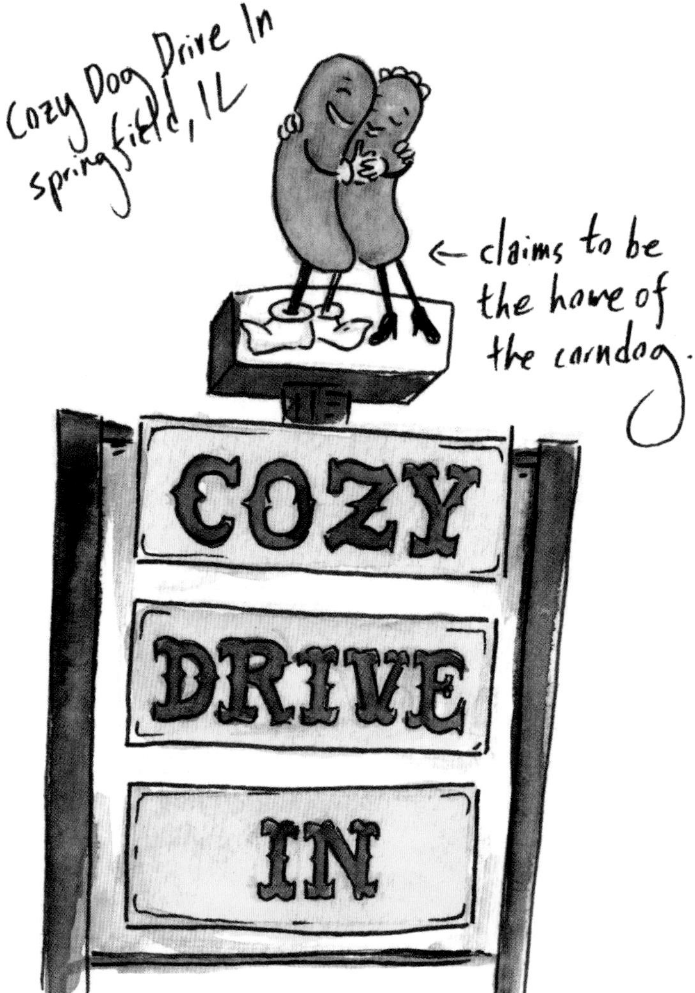
Cozy Dog Drive In
springfield, IL
← claims to be the home of the corndog.
COZY
DRIVE
IN

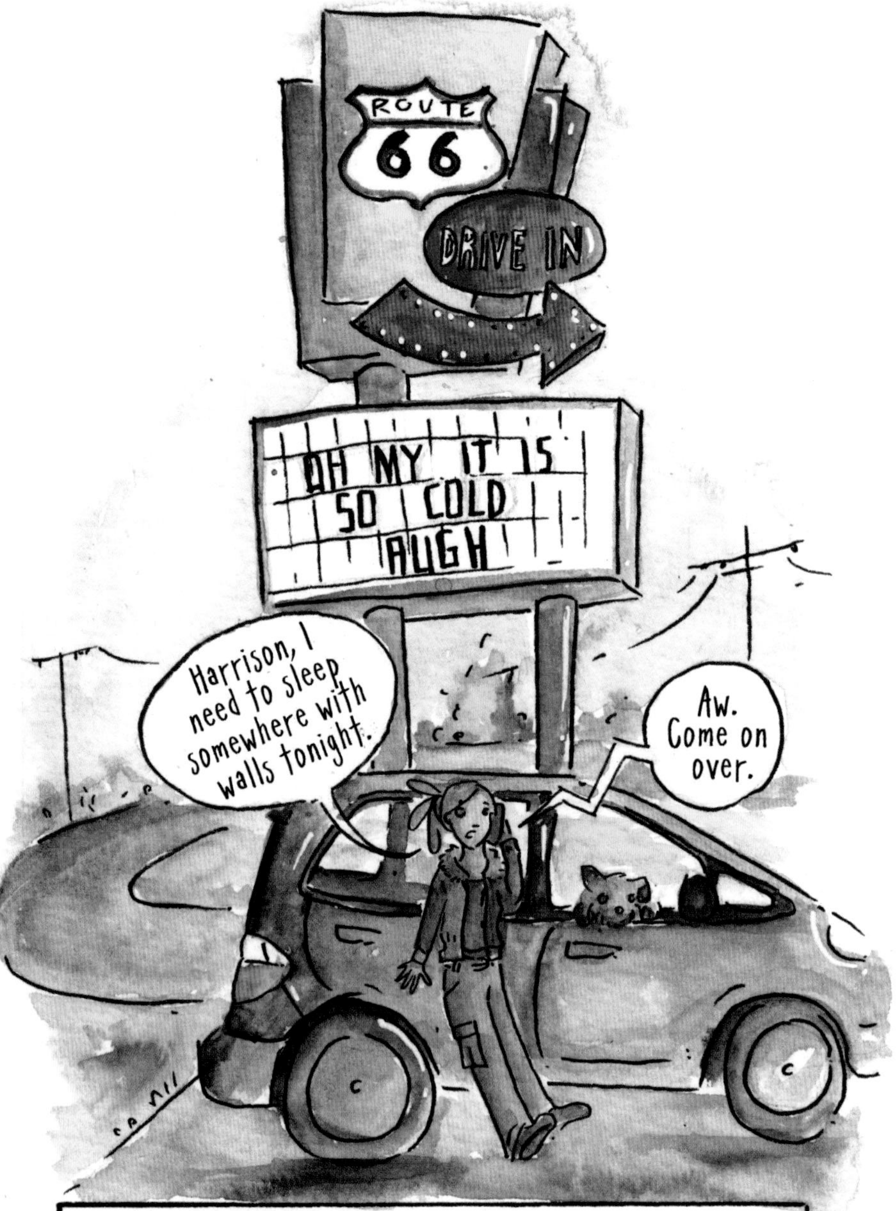
ROUTE 66
DRIVE IN
OH MY IT IS SO COLD AUGH
Harrison, I need to sleep somewhere with walls tonight.
Aw. Come on over.
I finally give up somewhere in Springfield, IL.

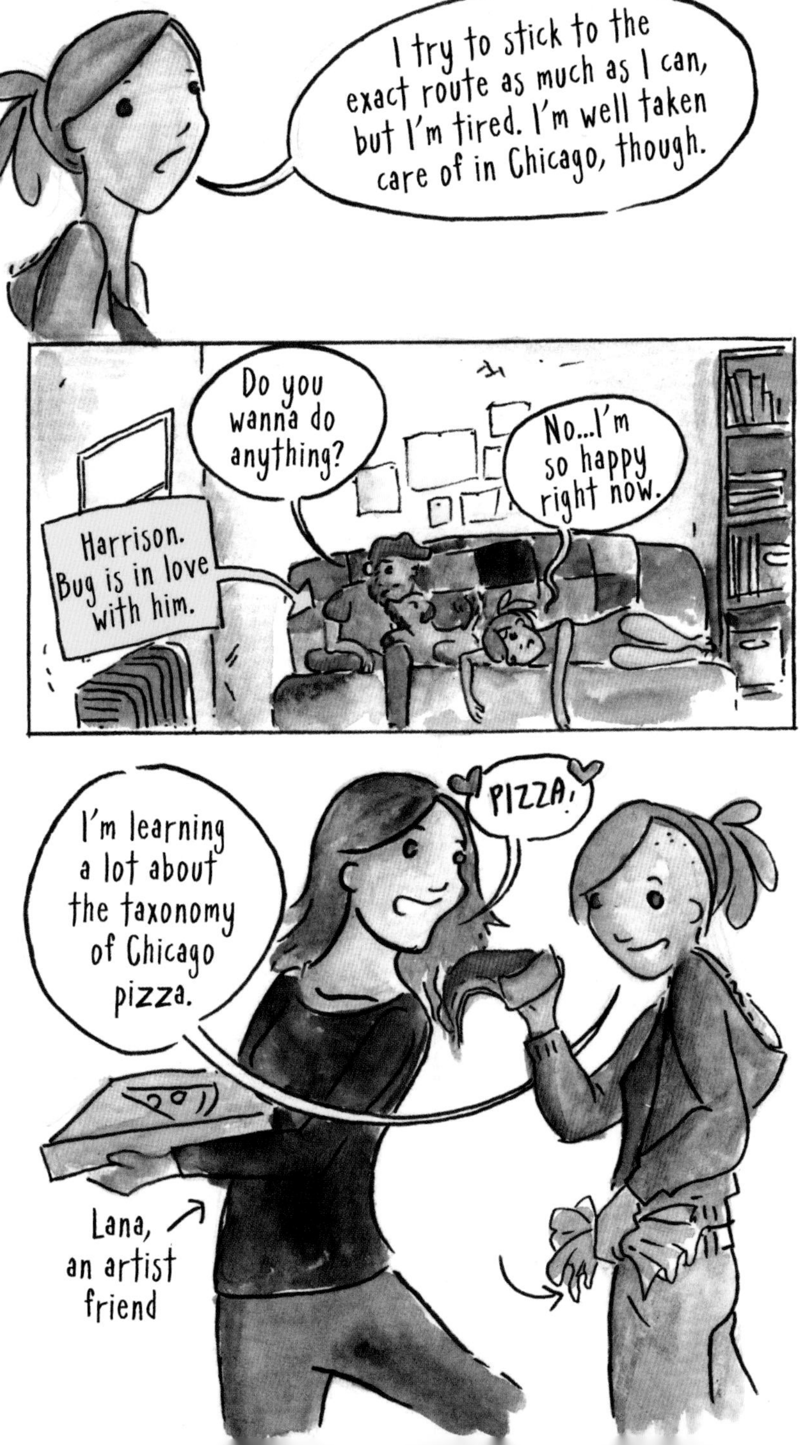
I try to stick to the exact route as much as I can, but I'm tired. I'm well taken care of in Chicago, though.
Do you wanna do anything?
No...I'm so happy right now.
Harrison. Bug is in love with him.
I'm learning a lot about the taxonomy of Chicago pizza.
PIZZA!
Lana, an artist friend

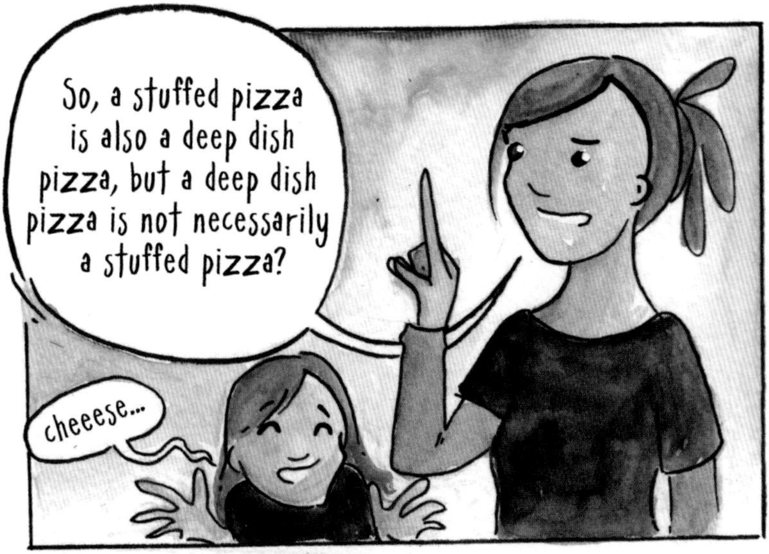
So, a stuffed pizza is also a deep dish pizza, but a deep dish pizza is not necessarily a stuffed pizza?
cheeese...

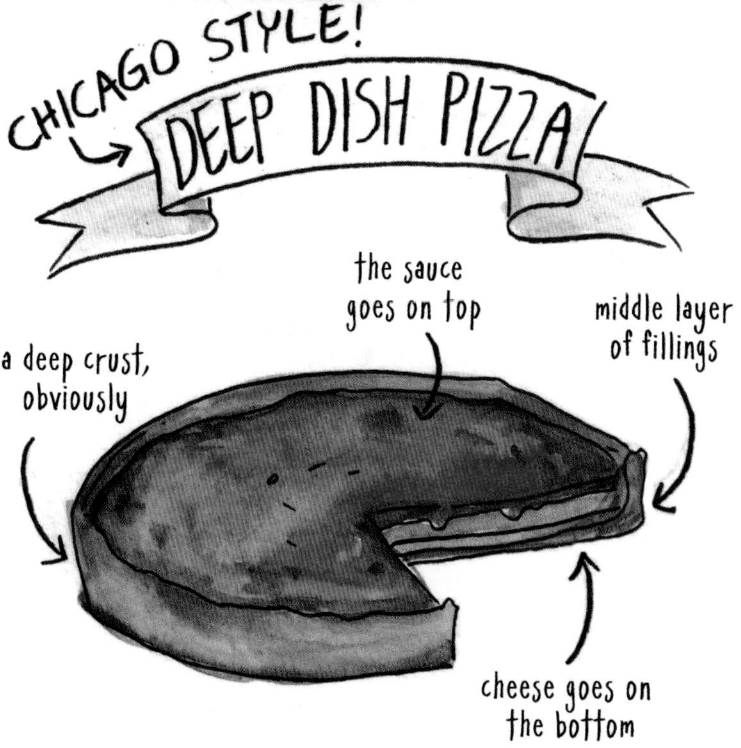
CHICAGO STYLE!
DEEP DISH PIZZA
the sauce goes on top
middle layer of fillings
a deep crust, obviously
cheese goes on the bottom

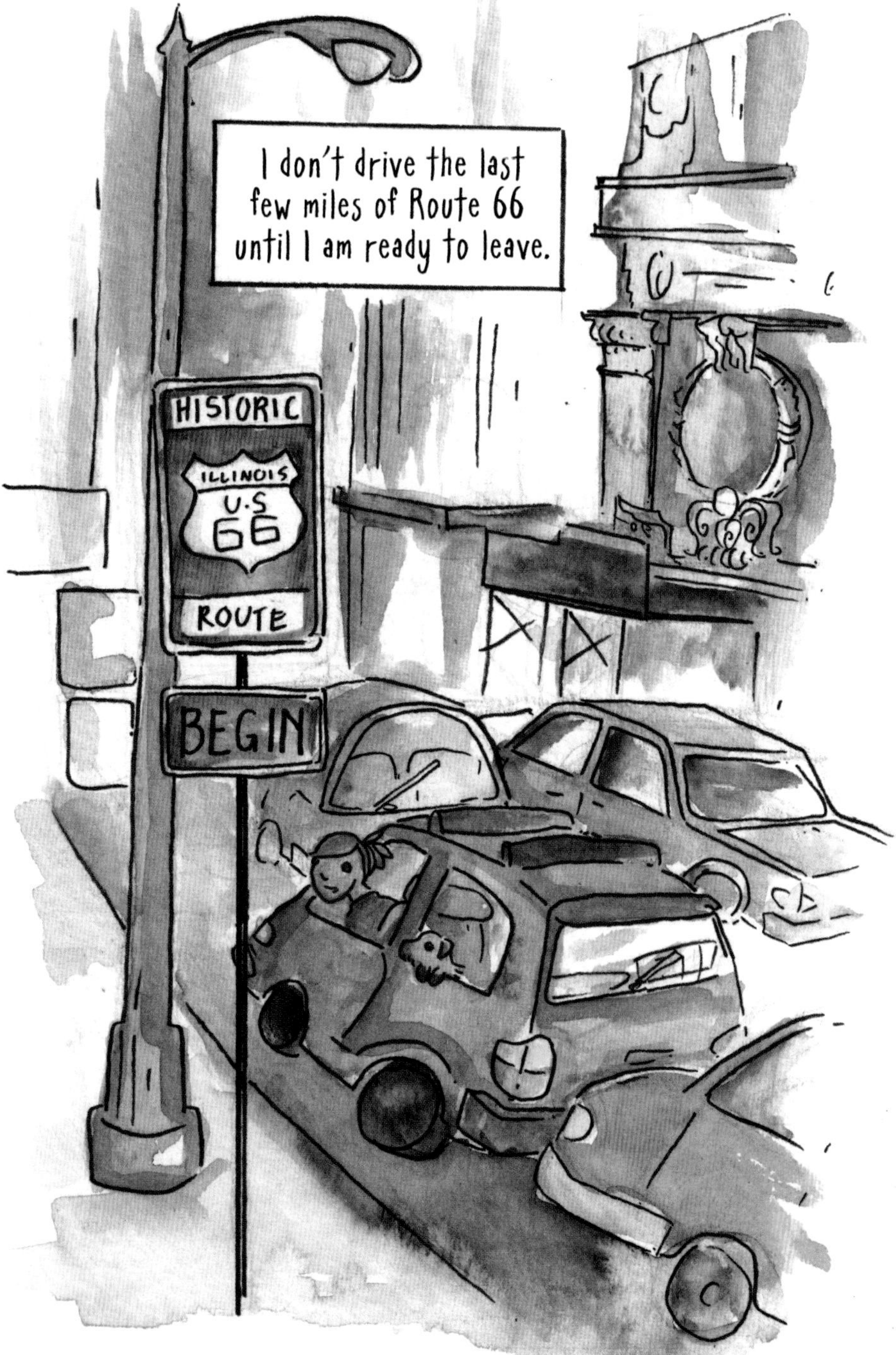
I don't drive the last few miles of Route 66 until I am ready to leave.
HISTORIC
ILLINOIS
U.S
66
ROUTE
BEGIN

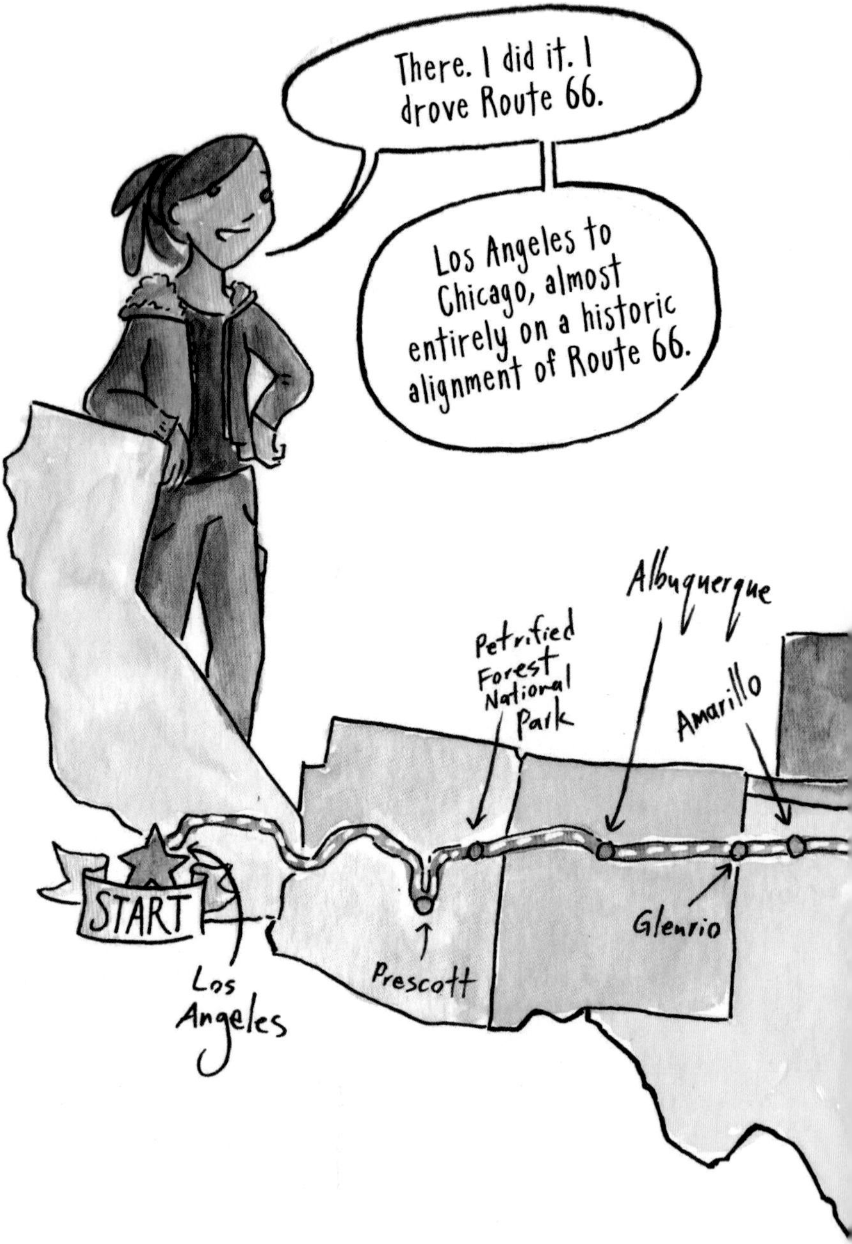
There. I did it. I drove Route 66.
Los Angeles to Chicago, almost entirely on a historic alignment of Route 66.
Albuquerque
Petrified Forest National Park
Amarillo
START
Los Angeles
Prescott
Glenrio

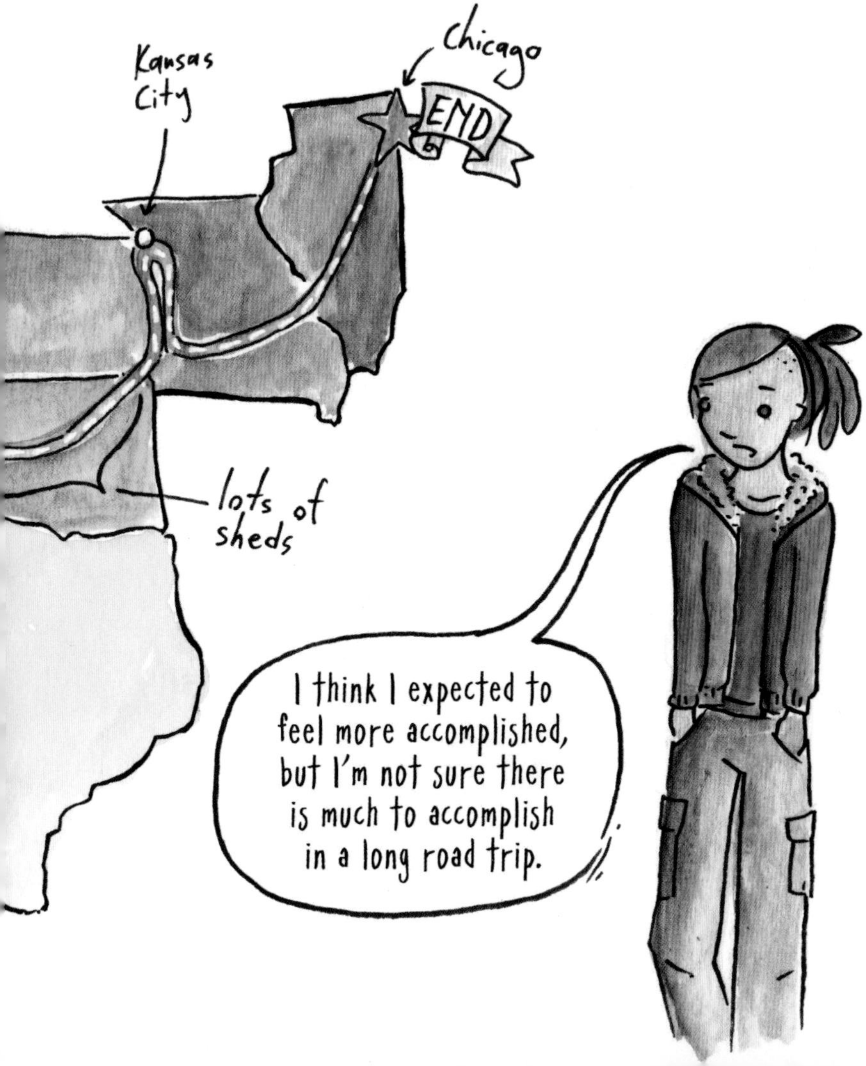
Chicago
Kansas City
END
lots of sheds
I think I expected to feel more accomplished, but I'm not sure there is much to accomplish in a long road trip.

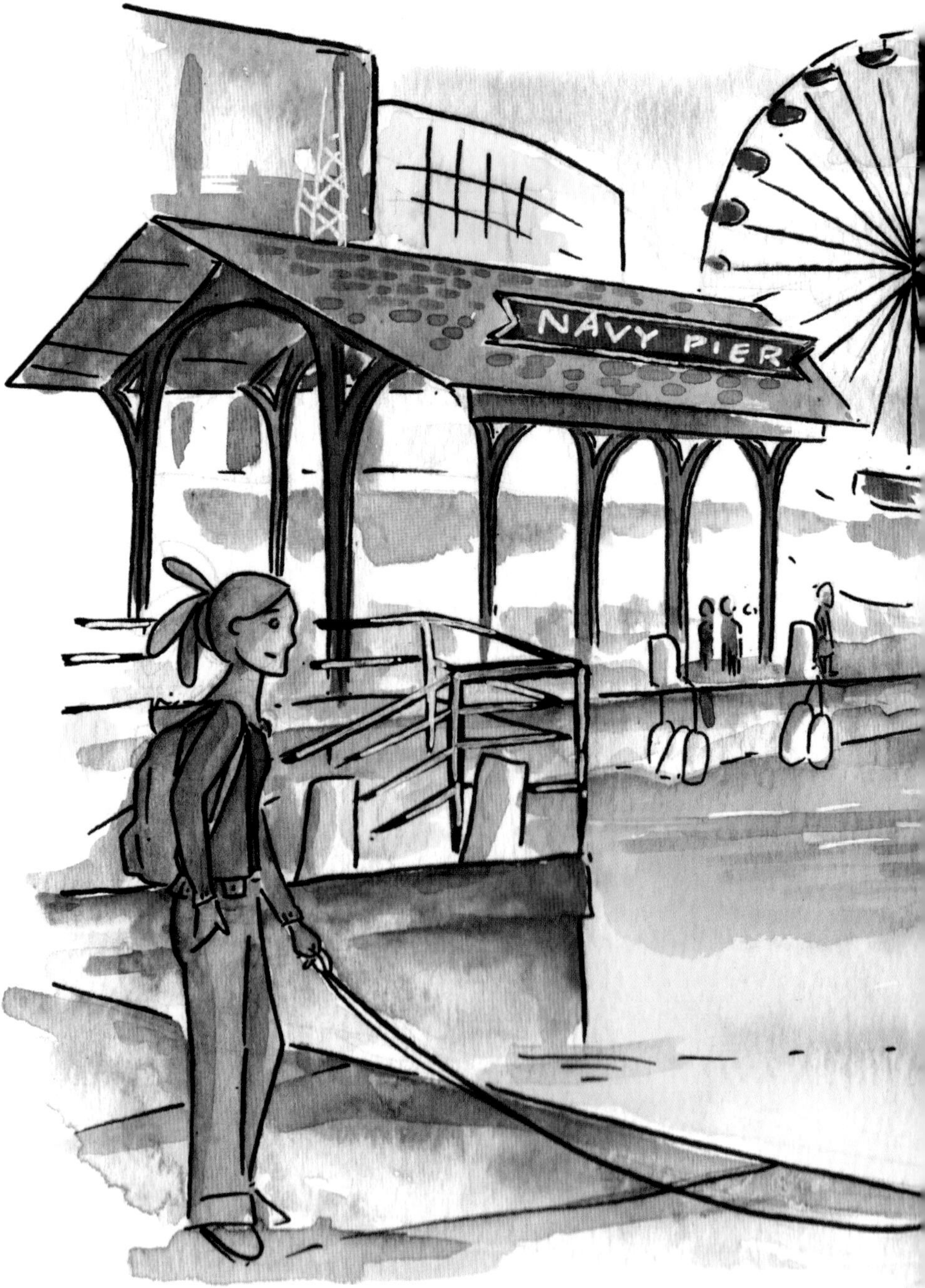
NAVY PIER

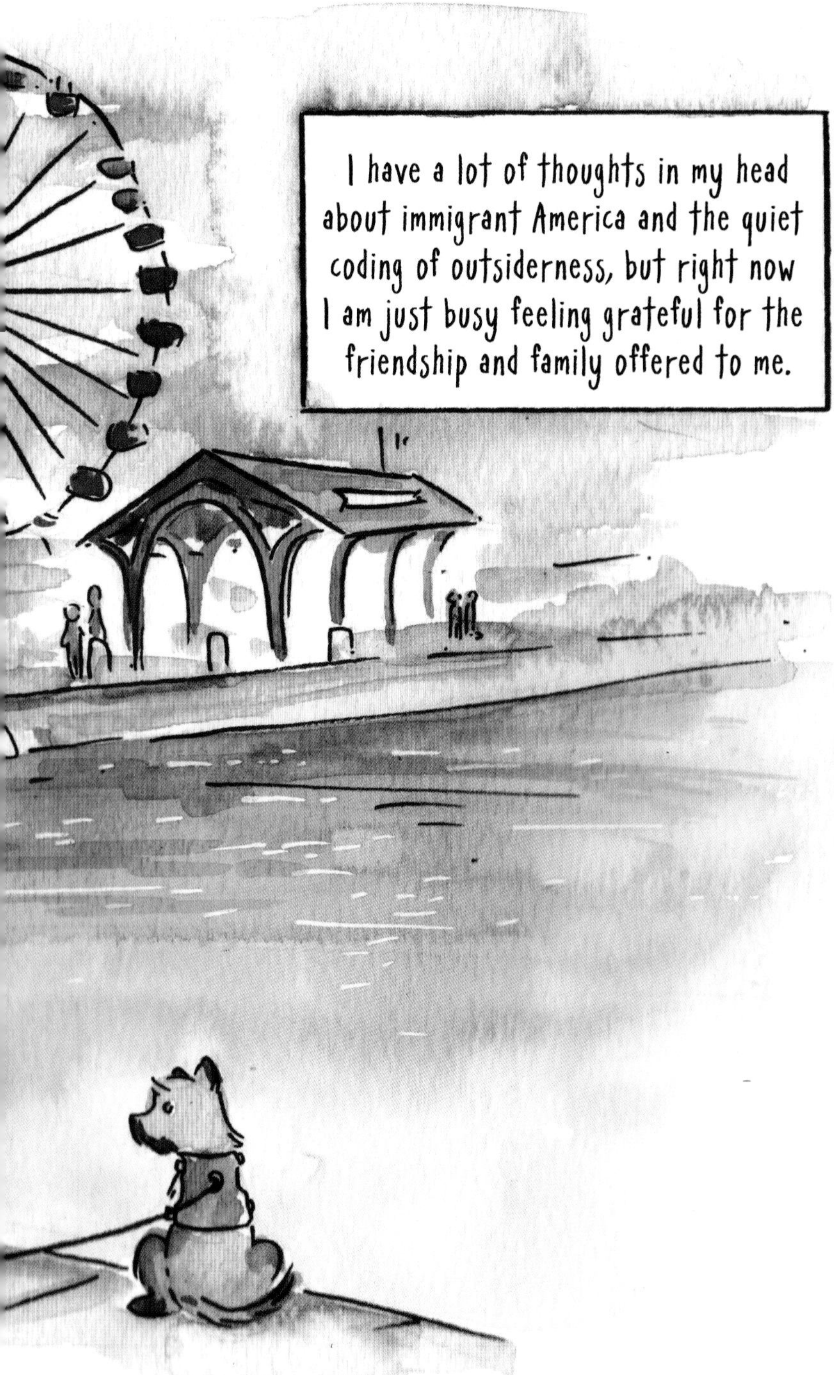
I have a lot of thoughts in my head about immigrant America and the quiet coding of outsiderness, but right now I am just busy feeling grateful for the friendship and family offered to me.

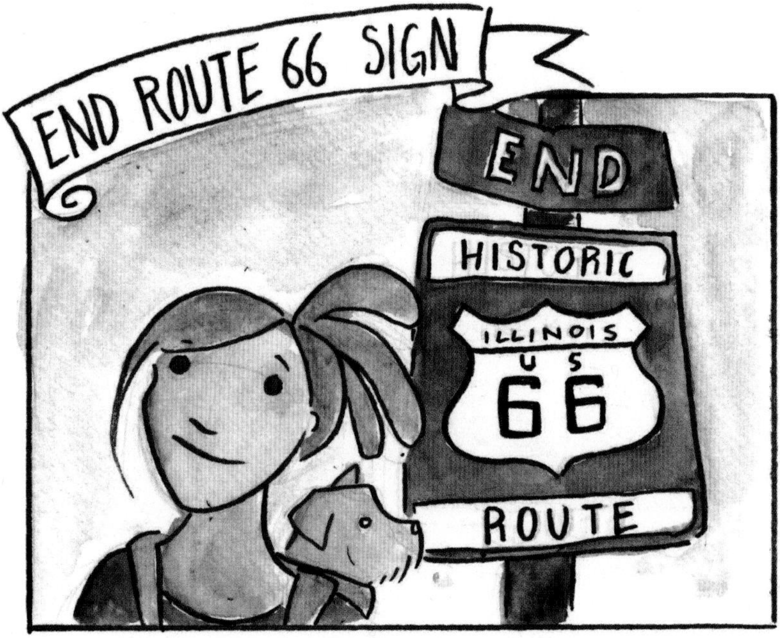
END ROUTE 66 SIGN
END
HISTORIC
ILLINOIS
U S
66
ROUTE

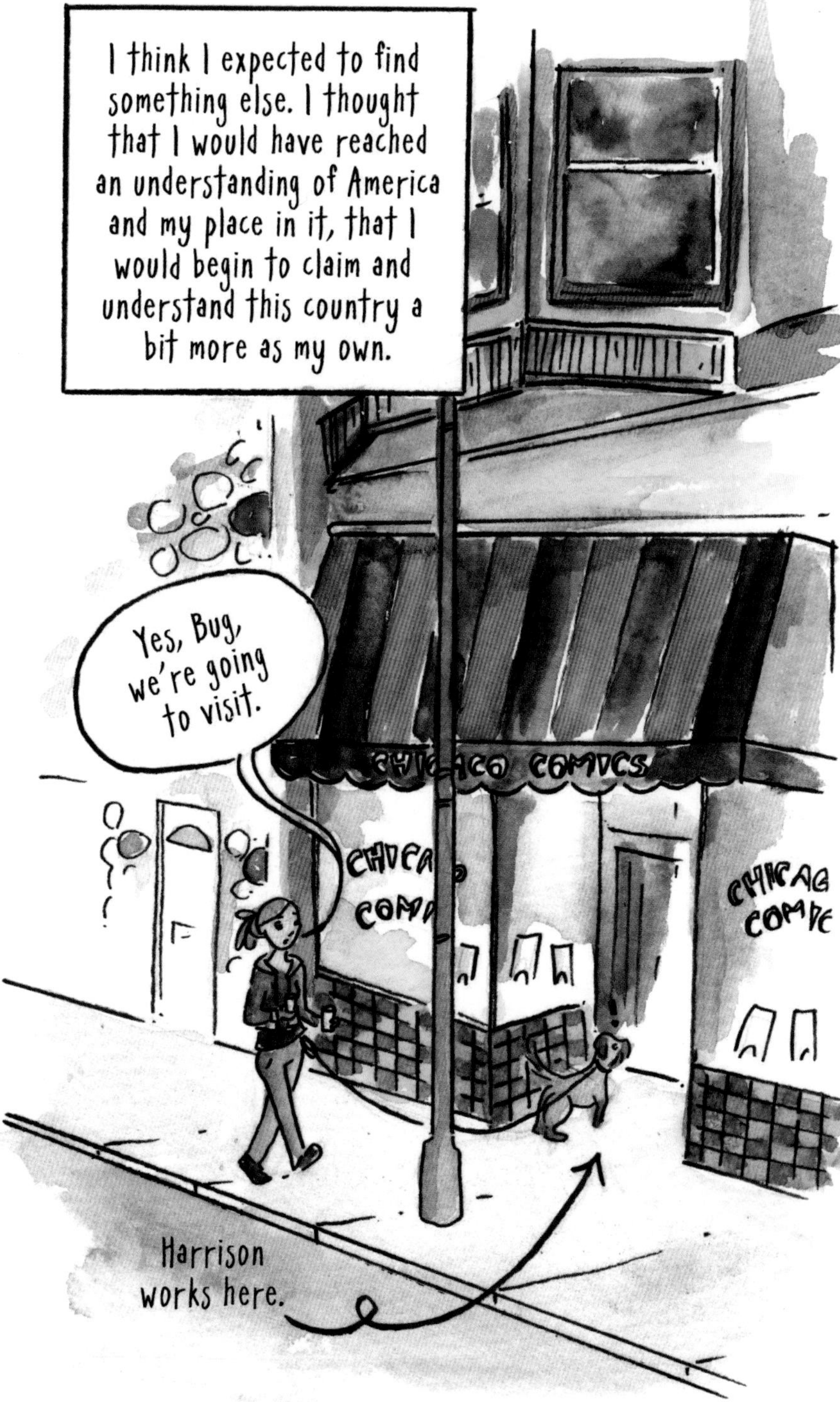
I think I expected to find something else. I thought that I would have reached an understanding of America and my place in it, that I would begin to claim and understand this country a bit more as my own.
Yes, Bug, we're going to visit.
CHICAGO COMICS
Harrison works here.

Instead, I've come to feel more comfortable in motion. There is a calm in the unpredictability of road trip travel, of expecting long, empty roads and intentionally seeking out misadventures and beautiful strange detours.

Excited to head home?

Yeah, I think so.

Perhaps I've been overly preoccupied with the idea of home, of trying to force myself to be comfortable in a skin I've been trying to ease into for years—a skin finally labeled as both immigrant and American.

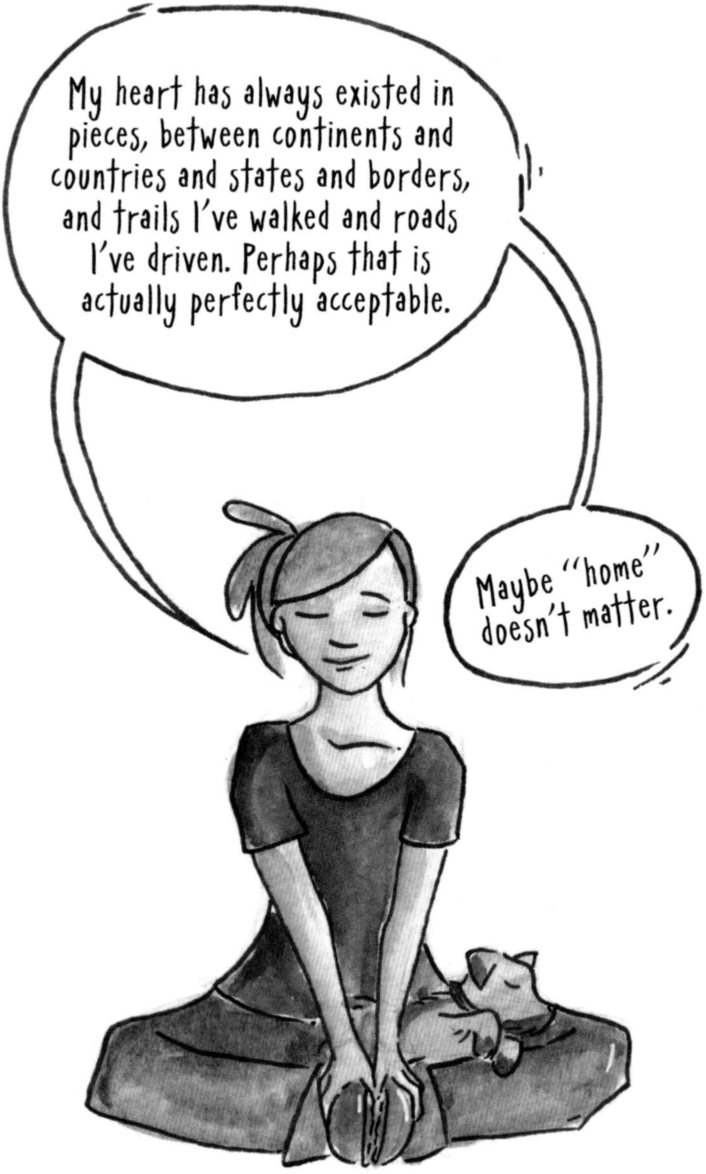
My heart has always existed in pieces, between continents and countries and states and borders, and trails I've walked and roads I've driven. Perhaps that is actually perfectly acceptable.
Maybe "home" doesn't matter.

The traditional way to drive Route 66 is from east to west, mirroring the westward trail of people seeking a better life. In two more weeks, I'll be back in Los Angeles. It may not be home, but it is where I have a house, a partner, and friends. And I will stay and pause for a bit.

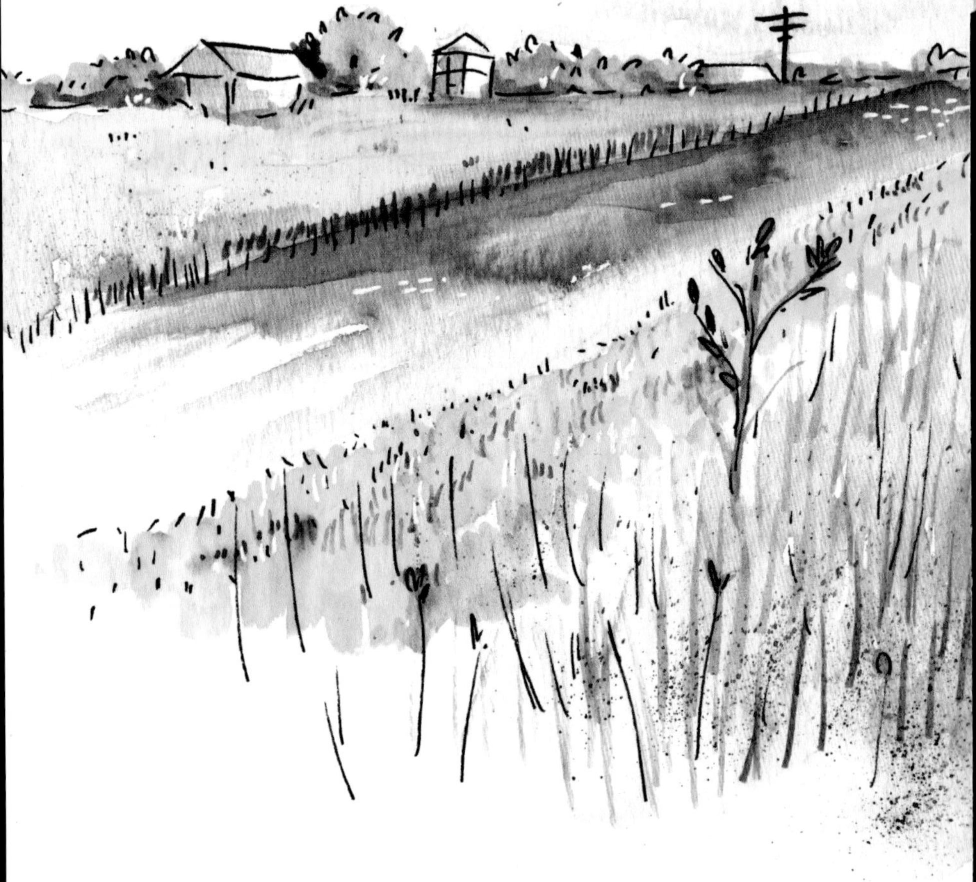

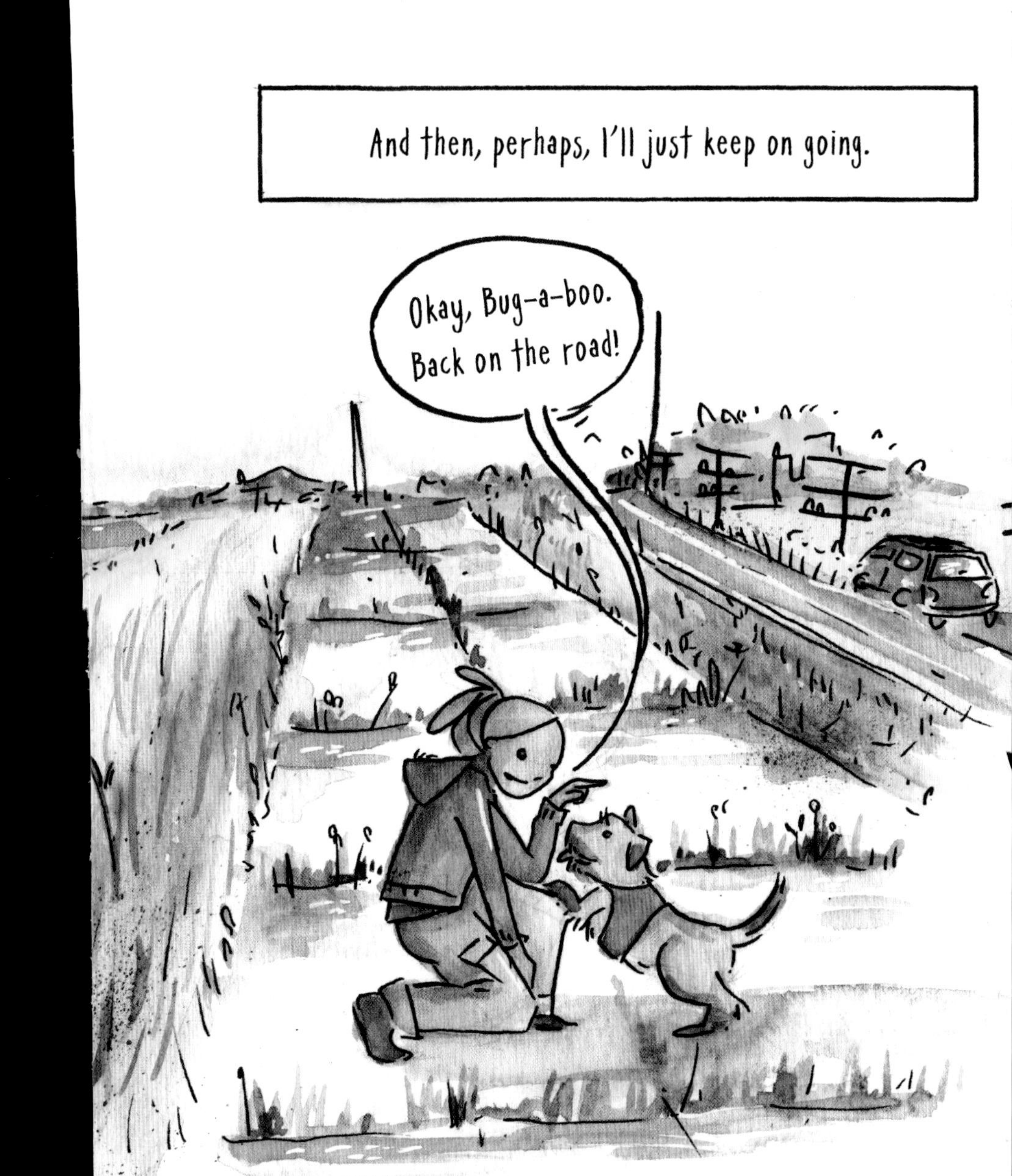
And then, perhaps, I'll just keep on going.
Okay, Bug-a-boo. Back on the road!

# AN EPILOGUE

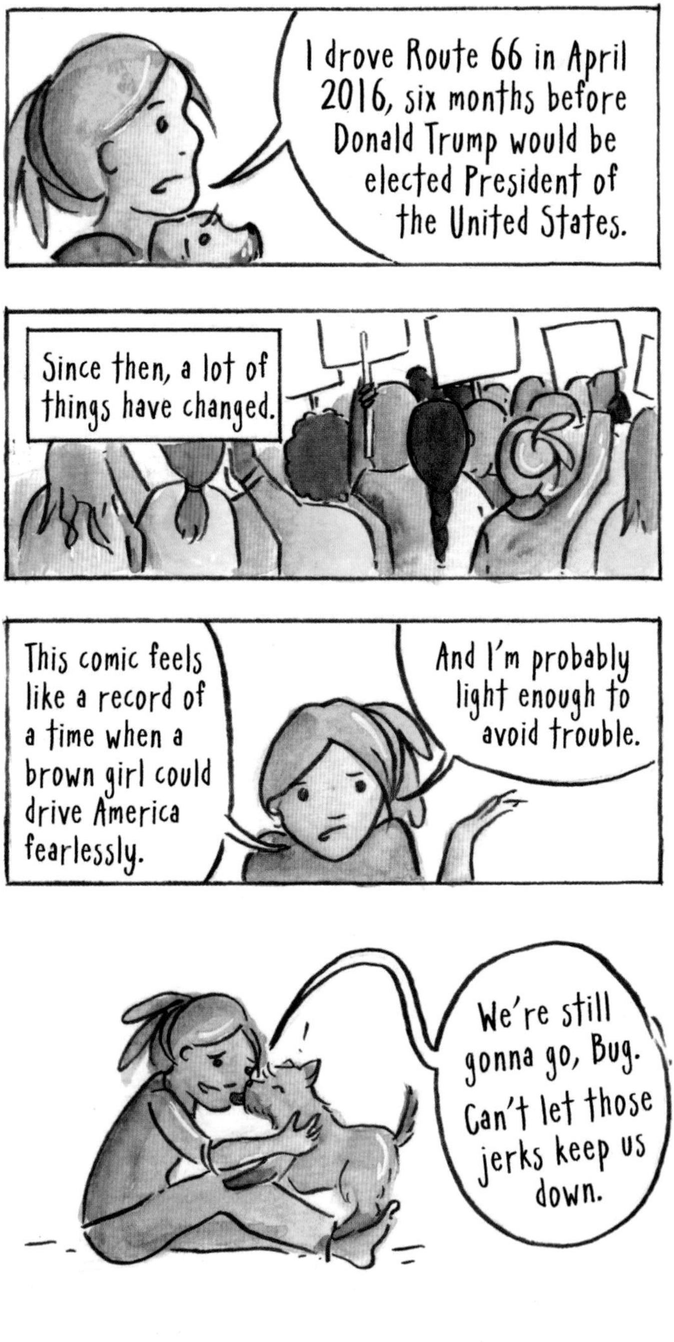

I drove Route 66 in April 2016, six months before Donald Trump would be elected President of the United States.
Since then, a lot of things have changed.
This comic feels like a record of a time when a brown girl could drive America fearlessly.
And I'm probably light enough to avoid trouble.
We're still gonna go, Bug. Can't let those jerks keep us down.